Manuel Castells

Manuel Castells

The Theory of the Network Society

Felix Stalder

polity

First published in 2006 by Polity Press

Reprinted in 2008

Polity Press
65 Bridge Street
Cambridge CB2 1UR, UK

Polity Press
350 Main Street
Malden, MA 02148, USA

ISBN: 978-0-7456-3276-6
ISBN: 978-0-7456-3277-3 (pb)

A catalogue record for this book is available from the British Library.

Typeset in $10\frac{1}{2}$ on 12 pt Palatino
by SNP Best-set Typesetter Ltd, Hong Kong
Printed and bound in the United States by Odyssey Press Inc.,
Gonic, New Hampshire

The publisher has used its best endeavours to ensure that the URLs for external websites referred to in this book are correct and active at the time of going to press. However, the publisher has no responsibility for the websites and can make no guarantee that a site will remain live or that the content is or will remain appropriate.

For further information on Polity, visit our website: www.polity.co.uk

Key Contemporary Thinkers

Published

Jeremy Ahearne, *Michel de Certeau: Interpretation and its Other*

Peter Burke, *The French Historical Revolution: The Annales School, 1929–1989*

Michael Caesar, *Umberto Eco: Philosophy, Semiotics and the Work of Fiction*

M. J. Cain, *Fodor: Language, Mind and Philosophy*

Rosemary Cowan, *Cornel West: The Politics of Redemption*

Colin Davis, *Levinas: An Introduction*

Maximilian de Gaynesford, *John McDowell*

Matthew Elton, *Daniel Dennett: Reconciling Science and our Self-Conception*

Simon Evnine, *Donald Davidson*

Chris Fleming, *René Girard: Violence and Mimesis*

Edward Fullbrook and Kate Fullbrook, *Simone de Beauvoir: A Critical Introduction*

Andrew Gamble, *Hayek: The Iron Cage of Liberty*

Nigel Gibson, *Fanon: The Postcolonial Imagination*

Graeme Gilloch, *Walter Benjamin: Critical Constellations*

Karen Green, *Dummett: Philosophy of Language*

Espen Hammer, *Stanley Cavell: Skepticism, Subjectivity, and the Ordinary*

Phillip Hansen, *Hannah Arendt: Politics, History and Citizenship*

Sean Homer, *Fredric Jameson: Marxism, Hermeneutics, Postmodernism*

Christopher Hookway, *Quine: Language, Experience and Reality*

Christina Howells, *Derrida: Deconstruction from Phenomenology to Ethics*

Fred Inglis, *Clifford Geertz: Culture, Custom and Ethics*

Simon Jarvis, *Adorno: A Critical Introduction*

Sarah Kay, *Žižek: A Critical Introduction*

Douglas Kellner, *Jean Baudrillard: From Marxism to Post-Modernism and Beyond*

Valerie Kennedy, *Edward Said: A Critical Introduction*

Chandran Kukathas and Philip Pettit, *Rawls: A Theory of Justice and its Critics*

James McGilvray, *Chomsky: Language, Mind, and Politics*

Lois McNay, *Foucault: A Critical Introduction*

Philip Manning, *Erving Goffman and Modern Sociology*

Michael Moriarty, *Roland Barthes*
Harold W. Noonan, *Frege: A Critical Introduction*
William Outhwaite, *Habermas: A Critical Introduction*
Kari Palonen, *Quentin Skinner: History, Politics, Rhetoric*
John Preston, *Feyerabend: Philosophy, Science and Society*
Chris Rojek, *Stuart Hall*
Susan Sellers, *Hélène Cixous: Authorship, Autobiography and Love*
Wes Sharrock and Rupert Read, *Kuhn: Philosopher of Scientific Revolutions*
David Silverman, *Harvey Sacks: Social Science and Conversation Analysis*
Dennis Smith, *Zygmunt Bauman: Prophet of Postmodernity*
Nicholas H. Smith, *Charles Taylor: Meaning, Morals and Modernity*
Felix Stalder, *Manuel Castells: The Theory of the Network Society*
Geoffrey Stokes, *Popper: Philosophy, Politics and Scientific Method*
Georgia Warnke, *Gadamer: Hermeneutics, Tradition and Reason*
James Williams, *Lyotard: Towards a Postmodern Philosophy*
Jonathan Wolff, *Robert Nozick: Property, Justice and the Minimal State*

Forthcoming

Maria Baghramian, *Hilary Putnam*
Sara Beardsworth, *Kristeva*
James Carey, *Innis and McLuhan*
George Crowder, *Isaiah Berlin*
Thomas D'Andrea, *Alasdair MacIntyre*
Reidar Andreas Due, *Deleuze*
Eric Dunning, *Norbert Elias*
Neil Gascoigne, *Richard Rorty*
Paul Kelly, *Ronald Dworkin*
Carl Levy, *Antonio Gramsci*
Moya Lloyd, *Judith Butler*
Nigel Mapp, *Paul de Man*
Dermot Moran, *Edmund Husserl*
Stephen Morton, *Gayatri Spivak*
James O'Shea, *Wilfrid Sellars*
Nicholas Walker, *Heidegger*

Contents

Acknowledgments

At the beginning of the process that has now taken the form of this book stands Arthur Kroker and a short essay that I sent to him, without solicitation, in mid 1997 for *CTheory*. He rejected it, but was kind enough to invite me to write a review of the Information Age trilogy, which I had mentioned in this essay. Having just begun my graduate studies, I was happy to oblige. By the time the review of the first two volumes appeared in 1998, the final volume had been published as well, so it was logical to revise and expand it into a review essay covering all three volumes. This appeared in the *Information Society* journal later that year. It was my first academic paper to be published. As happens with such publications, reactions were slow to come in. In fact, it took four years. By then I was doing a post-doc at David Lyon's Surveillance Program at Queen's University (Kingston, Ontario), and Manuel Castells received an honorary doctorate there, his first in North America. This provided a chance to meet in person for the first time. Another year later, the post-doc finished, the invitation of Polity Press to write this book came as another happy surprise.

Writing this book has been a rewarding challenge, particularly because I could draw on the generous support of people who offered encouragement, material, and criticism at the appropriate times. Important were David Lyon, Patrice Riemens (with Diiino), Regine Buschauer, Peter Marcuse, Bob Jessop, Andrew Clement, Ana Viseu, Martin Ince, and Raimund Minichbauer.

The staff at Polity Press, my commissioning editor John Thompson, Ellen McKinlay, his assistant, and the copy-editor Ann

Bone guided this project with patience and professionalism. It has been a pleasure to work with them.

Three people deserve to be mentioned separately. First, Manuel Castells. He supported this project generously, devoting time and attention to interviews and email exchanges, and providing me with new material before it appeared in print without seeking any controlling influence on the development of the manuscript. Indeed, as I add the finishing touches, he has still not seen it. Thus the book was written under conditions of complete independence from its "object." Second, Keith Hart. He followed the whole process from beginning to end and read the entire manuscript more than once. Without his care and advice, offered in many emails, my analysis would have been considerably weaker than it is now. Of course, the remaining problems are entirely my responsibility. Lastly, Andrea Mayr. She made sure that writing this book would not remain the most significant project of the last two years. For this, I am very grateful to her.

Introduction

Manuel Castells's theory of the network society has a unique place
among the many attempts by social scientists to come to terms with
the contemporary dynamics transforming the fabric of everyday life
around the globe. It provides the single most comprehensive
framework through which to connect, in an integrated analysis,
very diverse phenomena, ranging from demonstrations of gay
activists in Taipei to money laundering in the financial networks,
from the globalization of production to the renewal of democracy
at the local level. This makes it the lone contender as the grand narrative of the present, signaling the return of sociological macrotheory after years of postmodern pessimism about the possibility,
or even desirability, of such a project. It brings to a close three
decades of research on the "postindustrial" or "information
society," two concepts which, as Castells convincingly argues, are
inadequate to frame the present. In their place, the theory of the
network society opens up new perspectives on a world reconstituting itself around a series of networks strung around the globe on
the basis of advanced communication technologies. Indeed, networks, as the name indicates, are what the theory is all about. Its
central claim is that in all sectors of society we are witnessing a
transformation in how their constitutive processes are organized,
a shift from hierarchies to networks. This transformation is as
much an organizational as a cultural question. There is a deep
relationship between how social processes are organized and the
values they embody. An uneasy adaptation of the structural and
cultural logic embedded in a myriad of projects, each reflecting

imperfectly the particular agendas of its members, is what drives the evolution of the network society.

The breadth and interdisciplinarity of Castells's analysis is without parallel today and puts it in the same league as Max Weber's classic, *Economy and Society*. In Castells's case, its enormous scope is the consequence of two assumptions shaping his entire perspective: holism and multiculturalism. A holistic approach contends that society cannot be reduced to any of its parts, no matter how important that part might be. Rather, there are multiple sources of change which need to be understood on their own terms as well as in their relation to each other. There is no privileged vantage point from which to understand society as a whole by analyzing a supposed key aspect, be it the economy, politics, culture, or technology. In order to understand one aspect we have to understand the whole, yet the whole emerges from a myriad of interdependent events. Multiculturalism, on the other hand, stresses that contemporary social developments cannot be understood in terms of less and more advanced societies all striving to emulate, with varying degrees of success, the single most advanced model, whether it is Silicon Valley, America, the West, or the East. Rather, the particular character of the present period stems from the interaction of multiple models, each shaped by the historically determined resources that people can draw on in dealing with the challenges and opportunities of a world integrated and fractured as never before. Thus it makes no sense to argue that, say, the United States is a network society and Colombia is not. Both societies contain nodes that are deeply integrated into the global flows of information, goods, and people, while others are excluded from them. The cocaine cartels of Medellin and Cali, for example, are very sophisticated organizations, fully capable of using the most advanced networking to their own ends, and they are distinctly Colombian. Depending on the networks under consideration, the geography and culture of the network society looks very different. Yet, despite this multiculturalism, the network society is more than the sum of its parts; it is not a huge patchwork quilt. Through deep flows of information and people along networks that span the globe, innovation (or tradition) travels from its place of origin to where it appeals to people and their agendas. In the process, it is transformed, adapted, and becomes an essential part in the constitution of the very networks along which it flows. This applies as much to production methods as to social movements, to efforts to save the planet as to attempts to destroy it.

Yet, for all its integrative capacity, the theory of the network society is open to the extreme. For Castells, there is no such thing as historical necessity, and there are no social laws to be uncovered. Progress, as he puts it, "is an ideology." While social transformations are far from random and exert strong pressures, they are not assumed to have a preconfigured directionality. Whether society is improving or decaying is a matter of whose values are taken to be relevant to answering this question. Reflecting this commitment to openness, Castells identifies the beginning of the historical transformation as an "accidental coincidence" of three independent trends, interacting "serendipitously": microelectronics and the IT revolution, starting with the creation of the microprocessor in 1971; the crisis of industrialism, in Western capitalism and in statism (Soviet-style socialism), that became apparent in both systems in the early 1970s; and the profound cultural challenge mounted by diverse "freedom-oriented" social movements in the late 1960s. None of these developments was caused by, or was even a direct reaction to, the other trends. Yet in their subsequent path they deeply intertwined to constitute a new historical period. The rise of the network society is thus not seen as a social or technological necessity, nor stemming from a single cause or driver. Rather, it resulted from surprising, unpredictable effects of multiple and changing sets of social actors, struggling with the cultural and material circumstances in which they found themselves, each pursuing their own agenda, following their own, limited understanding of the situation they faced. Taking this openness to heart, the theory of the network society is explicitly not "a venture in social forecasting," as Daniel Bell saw his own work on postindustrialism,[1] even though the two share significant ground (which I will discuss in detail later on). Castells restricts himself to analyzing the present, on the basis of available empirical evidence, taking into consideration that the network society, perhaps more than any other, has the ability to deliberately alter its own path of development, for better or worse.

This analytical commitment to holism, multiculturalism and openness provides the core character of Castells's theory. Immediately striking is the fact that the enormous scope of the theory is matched by the equally broad range of empirical studies through which it is developed. *The Information Age* trilogy, containing the argumentative core of the theory, is some 1,500 pages long and has already been substantially revised for its second edition. Castells draws freely on more than three decades of his own prior research, that of a very wide range of other scholars, and on the work of the many doctoral students he supervised during his career. Quite fittingly, the trilogy has been called "encyclopedic" more than once. Yet, the theory of a network society is not simply a long list of items strung one after the other, but a complex, integrated analytical framework. Furthermore, it represents both the culmination of a major research effort and the start of a new one. Castells has since continued the development of the theory in numerous additional books, scholarly articles, and major research reports.

To the reader, Castells's work as a whole poses three general challenges. Two are related to coming to terms with the work itself, and the third arises from the particular focus of the theory of the network society, bringing into view some of its limitations. First, in an argument as large as that, it is easy to lose sight of the wood for the trees, and it is hard to assess the internal coherence of the analysis. This goes not just for the reader but also for Castells himself, who allows more than one internal contradiction, strange gap, and imprecision of vocabulary. So, if *grand* is indisputable, what, precisely, is the *narrative*? To bring into the foreground the core argument of why we are supposed to have entered a new historical epoch is the first aim of this book. On this level, it provides a critical introduction to, and overview of, the theory of the network society. This is the basis for the book's second aim: to assess the theory as *a work in progress*. To call it a work in progress is, in itself, not a critique, but reflects another aspect of its openness. Castells's theory, by necessity of its particular construction, is under constant development. Thus, the theory of the network society is both a major analytical achievement in its own right, and a highly flexible framework able to be adapted to reflect new empirical findings. Indeed, empirical findings are what this theory is all about.

It is from this that the second challenge to understanding Castells arises. For him, the value of theory lies primarily in its ability to provoke and structure empirical studies. In this sense, theory is an intermediate step rather than the ultimate goal of research. Thus Castells shows significant reluctance to provide anything more than rough definitions of the terms used or to participate in an explicit way in major theoretical debates. Yet to assess the theory, in both its ground-breaking audacity and its real limitations, it is necessary to make some of the connections to major debates more visible. The contextualization offered here is not intended as an intellectual history, tracing the long flows of ideas among scholars. It will be limited to providing the foundation of the constructive critique necessary for a continuation of the collective processes of theory-building. This is particularly crucial for two reasons. First, Castells has adopted a strategy of "communicating theory by analyzing practice." The theory provides the scaffolding that gives shape to the empirical research, but it is removed from sight once that research is deemed to be able to stand on its own. Second, Castells constructs his narrative to be as "autonomous" as possible. Contemporary theory from the social and natural sciences is copiously integrated (and duly referenced), but rarely discussed. This particular communication strategy makes the accounts of the network society highly textured and accessible, but obscures the main argument. Like a tree in summer when leaves make it hard to see the branches, the empirical richness makes the analytical argument fuzzy and thus hard to deal with. It will be necessary to reconstruct this scaffolding by removing much of the detail provided by the case studies. Thus I will shake off many leaves, trying to reverse the trade-off between clarity and richness of argument.

This will bring into view the third, and most substantive, challenge arising from Castells's particular strategy in integrating the enormous breadth of cases: shifting the focus of his analysis from conflict to forms. This has culminated in declaring a form, the network, to be the signature of the new, well, network society. This shift has turned out to be tremendously fruitful, not just because Marxist theory – particularly the structuralist paradigm under which Castells had worked – had driven itself into a dead end during the 1970s. More importantly, this shift enabled Castells to expand the scope of the analysis to the point where it can justifiably be called holistic and multicultural on a global scale. Yet this reorientation came at a price. Conflicts had to be relegated from being the main engine of social transformation to being subsumed under the heading of identity. Its main driver is no longer structural contradictions, but reflexive social movements. Thus actors regain a central place, but the conflicts in which they engage appear skewed in the analysis. Collective actors on one side, processes on the other. This might be an adequate rendering of the inner view of most social movements, according to which people fight against systems. But as a result of this perspective, Castells's theory of power, particularly in the analysis of the economy and of politics, has been hollowed out. It will be one of the main challenges to the further development of the theory of the network society as a critical project to reintegrate conflicts and power more prominently into the analysis without reverting to Marxist reductionism.

This is not just an issue of abstract theory-building. Rather, it is an urgent matter of empirical analysis. Each period has its defining conflicts. Under industrialism, the struggle between labor and capital provided the main political dynamic within industrialized countries as well as in global politics (cold war). In the "information age," a new set of social conflicts is likely to become defining. A possible candidate: the fight over access to information and knowledge. Struggles are already arising in areas as diverse as agriculture (patents on plants), health care (access to medicine), cultural industries (copyright), and global institutions (international treaties). These conflicts point to the emergence of a new global power structure, with social movements playing an important role in articulating a countervision. Yet, if we want to understand both sides of the struggle, these conflicts cannot be subsumed under the heading of identity. Here an analysis focusing on forms reaches its limits.

This book is structured as follows. The first chapter focuses on the transformation of baselines that have shaped Castells's work over close to four decades now. Every narrative is based on a set of assumptions and concepts along which the formulation of the actual work proceeds. The theory of the network society is shaped by the evolution of these baselines, in the sense that it evolved out of series of continuations from and breaks with Castells's own earlier analytical ventures. In particular, the success and failure of the early Marxist urban sociology provide the background against which many of the core arguments of the theory of the network society are developed. Central, as mentioned above, is the shift from conflicts to forms. Another building block whose particular character can only be understood in reference to his early work is "informationalism" as the technological paradigm of the network society. Finally, his early Marxist experience has also deeply affected the epistemology shaping the particular character of the theory as a flexible set of interrelated propositions.

The second chapter deals with Castells's analysis of informational capitalism, focusing on the globalization of economies, the transformation of the structure of firms ("network enterprise"), and the changing realities of labor. It will highlight two problematic aspects of his treatment of contemporary capitalism. There is the lack of attention to the construction of new forms of property at the core of the most advanced processes of global capitalism. And somewhat more implicit, but equally problematic, is the claim that the economy is, for practical purposes, beyond the control of anyone. What do we win, and what do we lose, when we call the financial markets an "automaton"?

The third chapter discusses Castells's analysis of social movements as the subjects of contemporary social change. Through a detailed analysis of his treatment of feminism and of religious fundamentalism, the argument that these movements are at the same time autonomous sources of new values, and a distinct reflection of the character of the network society, will be assessed. The fourth chapter deals with Castells's analysis of politics and governance, focusing on the crisis of liberal democracy and the transformation of governance ("network state"). I will examine Castells's theory of power, and question how adequate it is for analyzing the new realities of dominance through networks.

Chapters 2, 3, and 4 cover the main pillars – production, experience and power – on which the theory and its empirical argument rest. The fifth chapter deals with what I consider to be Castells's most far-reaching theoretical innovations: the concepts of the "space of flows" and, somewhat less developed but equally consequential, "timeless time." Space and time are the foundations of all aspects of social life, and the analysis of their transformations goes a long way toward unifying the theoretical framework. Despite the structural dominance of flows, places do not become obsolete as long as people have bodies as we know them. Rather, the space of flows and the space of places interact, transforming cities and creating entirely new urban agglomerations, the metropolitan regions. This interaction is at the core of the new, nonlinear character of (urban) geography and the fragmented character of contemporary societies held together less by physical contiguity than by informational networks.

But what exactly are informational networks, and why does this transformation from hierarchies to networks as the dominant form of social organization matter so much? This will be the focus of the sixth chapter, which discusses in depth the particular conception of the network that emerges from Castells's wide-ranging analysis. If the transformation of social morphology from hierarchies to networks is, indeed, a process of historical significance, then there must be something particular about networks independent of the various projects that are realized through them. Castells calls this the "network logic," but remains guarded about what this is. By way of complexity and organizational theory, the content of this logic and the way it shapes the theory of the network society will be analyzed.

The conclusion assesses the theory as a whole in order to point out its key strengths as well as areas that need significant further development.

Castells's theory, because of its unique combination of integration and openness, can be read almost like a hypertext. It can be entered at many different places, thus providing insights to people with various interests, while offering to all links that connect their field with what is argued to be the general dynamics of the network society. This present book should be understood as a personal engagement with, rather than as the authoritative interpretation of, the theory of the network society. It is therefore not a shorthand for dealing with Castells himself. It is also not an intellectual biography, and nor does it chronicle the extensive debates inspired by Castells's work over more than three decades.[2] Rather, I present a direct, personal engagement with Castells's arguments, hoping to preserve the engaging quality of the work itself and entice each reader to find his or her own individual ways through the conceptual matrix that is the theory of the network society.

1

Transformation of Baselines

Seen as a whole, Castells's body of work exhibits both striking continuities and substantial transformations. The continuities are provided by a number of themes which he pursued through his entire career. One is the changing spatial configuration of advanced industries as a key indicator of the restructuring of the economy in general. In his doctoral thesis he examined the locational patterns of the high-tech industry around Paris in the mid 1960s.[1] The same subject provides the bedrock of the argument in the *The Informational City* (1989a), this time in the North American context. It still plays a significant role in his analysis of the Finnish information society in 2002.[2] The role of the state as a source of – and a mediator in – conflictive social dynamics is the second of his continuing research interests. The expansion of the welfare state in the 1960s significantly expanded the field of the political and the role of the state in society. Tracing the transformation of this role has been a major axis along which Castells's works have unfolded ever since. Social movements as self-conscious actors in contemporary social transformations provide the third long-term focus in Castells's work. They are a central element in his first book, *The Urban Question*, written in the early 1970s, and the main focus of *The City and the Grassroots* a decade later. Social movements provide one of the two pillars on which the central argument of *The Information Age* trilogy rests – the tension between the net and the self. Thus the transformation of space, as the most structural expression of human culture, people's attempts to (re)define social values and create meaning, and the state's intervention in both processes are concerns present throughout his work.

At the same time, Castells's approach today is very different from the one that characterized his work during the 1970s. The main difference can be found in the transformation of the basic theoretical orientations along which he (re)formulated the treatment of these major research areas. His early work focused on places and was developed within a neo-Marxist framework. He was particularly influenced by the attempt of Louis Althusser (1918–1990) to renew Marxism by putting it on a "scientific" basis. For Althusser, this meant focusing on structural determinants. At the same time, the events of May 1968 and the work of his thesis advisor, Alain Touraine, suggested the importance of deliberate collective action. Trying to integrate social movements into structuralist Marxism for the analysis of urban change was Castells's main theoretical project of the 1970s. This turned out to be both a tremendous success and a profound failure. Success because it reinvigorated the entire field of urban sociology by raising new questions relating to conflict and power, and proposing new perspectives for research. A failure because, at the end of the 1970s, Castells reached the conclusion that the two perspectives simply could not be combined. He identified the inflexibility and outdatedness of Marxism in general – rather than the particulars of his Althusserian approach – as the chief source of the problem. Consequently, he abandoned Marxism as the dominant theoretical framework. Shortly afterwards, he recognized that many of the most important processes are no longer place-bound but have become increasingly organized around real-time information flows. To simplify things radically, over the course of the 1980s his perspective shifted from place-based conflicts to flow-based forms.

Equally importantly, he radically redefined the role of theory in his work. In Althusser's brand of Marxism, theory dominated empirical research to the extreme. Castells, on the other hand, has always been an empirical researcher. This is the second reason why, for all his initial fervor and hard line, he was a rather untypical Althusserian. After dropping the grand theoretical ambitions for good, his approach became firmly grounded in empirical research. Since then, theory has served as a way of organizing and interpreting empirical material, rather than as a goal in itself. In fact, for someone who has produced the single most comprehensive analysis of contemporary societies, Castells today has a surprisingly ambiguous relationship to social theory.

In the following, I will concentrate on how some of the baselines of Castells's work shifted over the years, shaping the formulation of his own, distinct argument. I will do so from today's point of view. Revisiting all the early meanderings and tangents would be pedantic and tedious, not least because Castells has pointed out many of them himself.[3] Rather, I will concentrate on those elements that are still relevant in terms of shaping the theory of the network society.

However, before dealing with the work, a brief biographical sketch will help to provide some necessary personal background. While Castells acknowledges the importance of his personal experience to his work, he also downplays it. He argues that it should be irrelevant to the reader, who should judge the work independent of the author. While I generally agree with this view, some of the themes that characterize Castells's work are directly connected to his uncanny ability to put himself in the middle of revolutionary changes, even if the definition of "revolution" has changed over time, and thus the man and the work should not be totally separated.

Castells was born in 1942 in Hellin, a small town in La Mancha, Spain, the region known as the home of Don Quixote. Spain was ruled by a Fascist dictatorship and Castells's parents were strongly conservative, to the degree that his father's career as a civil servant seems to have been hampered by what the political authorities considered to be insufficient enthusiasm for the party line. The family moved several times, and Castells grew up mainly in Barcelona, a city that has remained close to his heart, and inspiring to his work, ever since. Under the repressive regime of Franco, he was politicized early. On entering the university at the age of 16, he joined the Catalan Socialist Party, which was, like all oppositional parties, working underground and subject to severe persecution. By the age of 20, he had had to flee the country in order to escape prison and torture, a fate suffered by many of his comrades. A political refugee, he went to Paris where he completed his master's degree in law and economics.

Activism remained important, and as a way to combine his political and intellectual interests, he changed to sociology, studying for a doctorate under Alain Touraine at the Sorbonne. By 1968, he was Assistant Professor in Sociology at Nanterre, a new campus of the University of Paris. At the time, the faculty was chaired by Touraine and included Fernando Henrique Cardozo (who went on to be president of Brazil, 1995–2003), Henri Lefebvre, Michel Crozier, and, as one of the other assistants, Jean Baudrillard. Perhaps not incidentally, the Nanterre campus became the epicenter of the 1968 student

protest. Daniel Cohn-Bendit, the prominent leader of the movement, was among their students. Castells deeply immersed himself
in the political struggles, to the degree that, in June 1968, he was
expelled from France and found himself exiled for a second time.

First he went to Chile, where Cardozo was already doing
research, and he was then appointed Assistant Professor at the University of Montreal, one of the centers of the Quebecois cultural
nationalism that was stirring up the placid Canadian political
system. While he never deeply connected to Quebecois nationalism,
the experience sharpened his view on the difference between nation
and state, an issue he had already encountered in Catalonia. He
regularly returned to Chile until Pinochet's putsch against the
left-wing Allende government made this impossible.

In the meantime, in 1970, he was reappointed to be Associate Professor at the École des Hautes Études en Sciences Sociales in Paris,
thanks to lobbying by Alain Touraine. There, together with Henri
Lefebvre (and, to a lesser degree, Michel Foucault and some of his
students), he became the leading figure of the new Marxist Urban
Sociology. It had an impact far beyond France, not least because of
Castells's already extensive international reputation. His involvement in the opposition in Spain, particularly in Madrid and
Barcelona, remained strong, and when Franco died in 1975 he
returned to Spain as an active participant in, and researcher of, the
urban social movement which carried the transformation toward
democracy. This reached a high point between 1977 and 1979, when
a series of electoral victories by the left marked the break with the
past and swept many of his comrades to power.

In 1979, after brief stints at the University of Wisconsin at
Madison, he left Paris for good to be appointed Professor of
Sociology and of City and Regional Planning at the University of
California at Berkeley. The post brought him up close to a very different revolution taking place in Silicon Valley during the 1980s
and 1990s. He kept this position for almost a quarter of a century,
until he resigned in 2003. Since then, his main academic appoint-
ments have been as Research Professor at the Open University of
Catalonia in Barcelona, and Professor of Communication Technology and Society at the Annenberg School of Communication,
University of Southern California.

Throughout his career, Castells has travelled incessantly, holding
more than 25 visiting professorships in the Americas, Europe,
Russia and Asia, and has become an advisor to governments and
international organizations. During all that time, and despite his

many political advisory positions, Castells has remained first and foremost an empirical social researcher. He has not joined a political party since fleeing Spain, nor associated himself strongly with a particular political leader – in contrast to, say, Anthony Giddens's support of Tony Blair's "third way" in the UK.[4] The exception to this rule has been his long friendship and collaboration with Jordi Borja, a leader of the Catalan nationalist movement. Indeed, the Catalan experience of cultural nationalism, oriented toward autonomy rather than independence, constitutes for Castells one of the most positive examples for the reconstitution of local identity outside the confines of the nation-state.

Castells's commitment to scholarly work has manifested itself in a steady stream of books, articles, and research monographs, only interrupted in the late 1990s during a hard but ultimately successful struggle against cancer (see the full bibliography below).

The changing political and geographic contexts of Castells's life should be kept in mind when considering the evolution of his work. Yet, for better or worse, once published, ideas cannot, and should not, be controlled by their author. To be of use to others, they need to take on a life of their own, quite independent of the circumstances from which they originated. And for Castells's ideas, this life began in the context of a renewal of sociology through Marxism in the 1960s.

Neo-Marxism and the Renewal of Urban Sociology

In 1968, Castells published his first major paper, asking "Is There an Urban Sociology?"[5] Today's textbooks answer this question as follows: In the first half of the twentieth century urban sociology was a dynamic field. In work pioneered by Georg Simmel (1858–1918) and developed by the Chicago School, important features of modern life in major cities were systematically analyzed, leading to substantial innovation in theory and in research methodologies. Yet in the 1960s this approach was already well past its prime. Its main concepts, such as the integration of immigrants into city life ("urban culture"), or the distribution of land-use patterns within cities ("human ecology"), were poorly suited to dealing with the most pressing problems of the time, particularly the urban unrest culminating around 1968. At that time, the main paradigms of urban sociology had been exhausted and the field as a whole was lacking direction.[6]

Castells, however, delivered a much more severe verdict. He proclaimed that there had never been an urban sociology. The underlying argument through which this counterfactual statement was developed showed the strong influence of Althusser. For Althusser "science" was characterized by an "epistemological rupture" from "ideology." The defining feature of science was the existence of a "theoretical object" that enabled an analysis of the determining, that is structural, features of social dynamics. Ideology, on the other hand, failed to define such an object and hence it lacked the solid foundation from which to overcome its own nonscientific preconceptions (ideology) and reach the structural heart of the matter. Althusser's profoundly antiempirical conception of science is too complex, counterintuitive, and ultimately untenable to be expanded here.[7] What is important in the present context is that it led Castells to ask the following question: has anyone ever been able to identify what is specifically urban as a way to understand the city's structural features and their transformation? In a wide-ranging review of the existing literature Castells came up empty-handed. He found the preceding literature lacking a real, scientific object around which to establish a scientific discipline. The focus of the preceding studies had been either too vague (ecology) or not specifically urban (culture). Thus, he concluded flatly, "urban sociology is an ideology."[8]

Castells set out to develop such an object on which to base a real, "scientific" approach to the study of cities.[9] His goal was to develop "a general theory of the city from the perspective of the process of social change."[10] For this, Castells had to define what was specific to the city that enabled the observation of fundamental structural processes of advanced capitalism. This was imperative, because "the urban system is not external to the social structure; it specifies that structure, it forms part of it."[11] He viewed the urban as a specific instance of broader structures. The question was: which aspects of the general social structure instantiated in the city were specific to the city as a spatial form? As he had observed in his early studies on the locational patterns of high-tech industry, the most advanced forms of production were organized on a scale larger than the city. Not just in the general sense of an economy being a large, interdependent process. More specifically, individual productive units were no longer contained on an urban scale because "the transmission of information by telegraph, radio and telex . . . made possible . . . the concentration of company head offices and the hierarchized decentralization of the centers of production and distribution."[12]

This was to become a major theme in his later research. For now, it disqualified production as the focal point of urban sociology, because its spatial forms did not coincide with those of the city. Yet Castells did not discount the economy altogether. Rather, his proposal for a new urban sociology centered around a particular and highly original reformulation of the theory of consumption. Marx had distinguished between three types of consumption: "productive consumption" (what is reinvested in the productive process itself), "individual consumption" (what is required to reproduce labor power), and "individual luxury consumption" (what goes beyond satisfying bare needs). Such a way of thinking about consumption, Castells argued, had a number of problems. The first category was not really consumption, but actually belonged to the process of production. Furthermore, it was impossible to differentiate reliably between reproductive and luxury consumption, particularly in the context of the welfare state.[13] Yet consumption was important to understanding the city. Indeed, it was consumption, rather than production, that was specific to the city.[14] From the city, workers drew all the resources for their survival. Thus the city was the framework for "the reproduction of labor power." As Castells concluded, "the urban units thus seem to be to the process of reproduction what the companies are to the production process."[15] In other words, reproduction of labor power was taking place within the city, in the same way as production was taking place within the company.

What was particular about cities in advanced capitalism, he continued, was that many of the resources necessary to accomplish this reproduction were not provided by the market and not consumed individually. Rather, during the 1960s a new field of social relations had assumed central importance, which Castells termed "collective consumption." This field created a new and distinct "urban question," by which he meant the social conflicts arising from "the organization of the means of collective consumption at the basis of the daily lives of all social groups: housing, education, health, culture, commerce, transport, etc."[16] Focusing on housing and transportation, Castells found that the changing logic of capitalist development had created new demands on the city as a spatial system. Yet capitalist firms did not satisfy these demands, mainly because supplying the required goods and services was not sufficiently profitable. Somewhat simplified, capital was interested in cheap labor, but not in providing affordable housing. To alleviate this contradiction, the state began to provide more and more of these services itself. Governments built public transportation infrastructures to serve the new industrial and commercial spaces, financed large public housing complexes, created new parks, expanded hospitals, etc. Yet the problems which these interventions into the spatial layout of the city tried to address were structural and intrinsic to advanced capitalism. Hence all they really achieved was to displace the contradictions from the field of the economy, where they originated, to the field of politics, where they were now articulated.

After World War II the scope of the state intervention grew continuously to satisfy rising demands from workers and capitalists. On the one hand, the "the historical definition of need" kept changing. Workers demanded better housing and more extensive health care than they had a generation earlier. On the other hand, changes in the economy increased the demand for highly skilled labor, putting pressure on the state to expand public education and to finance the cultural services demanded by the rising class of professionals. Yet there was a limit to the growth of state intervention, and this limit was set by the increasing unwillingness of capital to accept the rising taxes necessary to finance collective consumption. After all, the very purpose of state intervention, Castells argued, was to unburden capital from having to provide necessary but unprofitable services. The goal was to counteract what Marx had identified as an inherent tendency of capitalism, "the falling rate of profit." To depress profits through ever increasing taxation would have defeated the entire rationale for intervening in the first place and was politically not acceptable to the dominant classes. In Castells's view, this contradiction triggered the economic and political crisis of the 1970s.[17]

The theory of collective consumption went deeper than just the state building new subway lines and housing complexes and therefore remaking the city in support of advanced capitalism. The state's intervention had turned city itself into a political category, and hence conflicts over spatial dynamics were essential to the new political struggles that emerged in the 1960s. This enabled Castells, at least initially, to combine a structural analysis – state intervention to alleviate the contradictions of capitalism – with the analysis of urban social movements – collective actors reacting to the new condition of state intervention into domains of everyday life. The analysis unfolded, somewhat uneasily, in line with what Althusser had identified as the three main levels of society: the economy, politics and ideology.[18] Each of these levels had a "relative autonomy," that is, was characterized by its own contradictions and dynamics, but in the "last instance" they were nevertheless tied to the structures of the economy.[19] The somewhat contradictory formulation of "relative autonomy" was intended to soften, or even overcome, the economic determinism of Marxism without breaking with the fundamentals of historical materialism.

Empirically, Castells examined the politicization of space in the resistance of workers to their displacement in the process of urban renewal;[20] in "the rise and fall of the grand ensembles," the major new housing development projects on the outskirts of Paris;[21] in new industrial policies for the development of regions;[22] the transition of Spain from Fascism to democracy driven by urban social movements;[23] and also in the emergence of environmentalism. The latter proposed most fundamentally a new definition of space around issues such as quality of water, land, and air, which Castells also integrated into his theory of collective consumption.[24]

As part of a broader, in fact quite heterogeneous, neo-Marxist movement,[25] Castells's theory of collective consumption reinvigorated urban theory in the early 1970s. With great success, neo-Marxists established issues such as power and conflict, and economy and politics as the heart of urban dynamics. Their critical perspective "became the predominant, if not exclusive, orientation in the 1980s and continue[s] to guide current work."[26]

For Chris Pickvance, who as translator and editor played a major role in introducing Castells to English-speaking audiences, the appeal of the approach could be attributed to

> on the one hand, his attempt to integrate the study of sociological, economic and political aspects of the city which had until then been fragmented. On the other hand, it was part of a broader theoretical framework which appeared to grasp how society was evolving and which identified a place for action (urban movements) to affect its evolution.[27]

This retrospective assessment is echoed by the generally more critical Peter Saunders, for whom

> Castells's early writings succeed in pinpointing many of the core issues and problems in urban studies at the time and . . . they generated intense interest and argument mainly because they challenged existing orthodoxies and assumptions while pointing the way forward to new research agendas.[28]

Around the mid 1970s, Castells played a preeminent role in the formulation of neo-Marxist urban theory.

Yet this tremendous success did not satisfy Castells for long. He soon began to feel constrained by the dominance of theory characteristic of structuralist Marxism. This was particularly so after he experienced serious difficulties in trying to follow this approach in his first major empirical study, on the development of the Dunkirk region.[29] Furthermore, the basic contradiction characteristic of his approach at the time, namely insisting on structural determination at the level of the economy while examining social movements as autonomous collective actors, could not be overcome. Rather, it became more pronounced as he expanded the range of the social movements shaping urban dynamics.[30] The new social movements focused predominantly on issues *outside* the productive process. The concept of collective consumption allowed at least a tenuous, indirect connection with the productive process and thus seemed to conform to the key orthodoxy of historical materialism: the dominance of the economy over other areas of everyday life. However, many progressive social movements did not even relate to the economic process indirectly. They dealt primarily with cultural, social, or even biological questions, for example regional nationalism (Quebec, Catalonia), feminism, or environmentalism. In Marxist terms, all these issues should have been subsumed under the dominance of contradictions within the sphere of production.

Clearly, given the observable developments, Castells's project of an integrative theoretical framework was not an easy task to accomplish. The most serious problem arose from expanding the sources of conflict fueling social transformation by including noneconomic struggles, yet still insisting that, ultimately, social relations could be reduced to class struggle. In the *The Urban Question*, written shortly after the experience of May 1968, Castells attempted to reconcile these conflicting demands in a highly formalized way. The formalization was necessary because there was a notable gap between the basic theoretical assumptions and the findings of these detailed and open-minded case studies. He would admit, for example in the case of the squatter movement in Chile, "the connection between [this] movement and the workers' struggles is generally weak or nonexistent."[31] Yet, on a very abstract level, he still claimed to be able to reconcile this observation with the fundamental demands of Marxist theory.

With the benefit of hindsight, one can find many indicators that Castells himself was less than convinced about the prospects of his project. He soon bemoaned "a certain process of fetishization [of my argument] that has crystallized into theoretical principles what were merely stammerings emerging from a phase of work centered above all on the critique of the ideologies of the urban and recognition of the historical terrain."[32] At the end of the 1970s, Castells could simply not integrate the two themes in a way that, in his eyes, would do justice to both. A few years later he described the problem in the following way: "the logic of the analysis never allows them to interact in a meaningful structure. As a result, we are left with urban systems separated from personal experiences; with structures without actors, and actors without structures; with cities without citizens and citizens without cities."[33] For the next decade, the two themes, the agency of social movements and the structural transformation of the economy, would be treated more or less separately. One remained centered around places, the other began to integrate the new realities of translocal information flows. In *The City and the Grassroots* (1983a) there is comparatively little economic structure, and in *The Informational City* (1989a) there are no social movements. It would take Castells another decade before being able to present a new synthesis in *The Information Age*, dealing with structural change in the economy and with self-conscious social movements within a unifying framework incorporating electronic information flows into its core.

Castells's personal experience and his empirical research clearly showed the importance of understanding social movements on their own terms, which were fundamentally different from those presented by theories of structural determination. For him, it became evident that the social movements in Spain, and elsewhere, were driven by the hopes, dreams, and desires of self-conscious participants/actors. Of course, they were rooted in particular places and cultures, and had to deal with the circumstances in which they found themselves, yet they did so creatively and unpredictably, rather than simply being a logical expression of underlying economic dynamics.

Characteristically, Castells followed the lead of his empirical research; yet this meant adopting a different theoretical perspective and leaving the Marxist tradition. This might have been facilitated by the establishment of democracy in Spain. Shedding the common language of political struggle was no longer a betrayal of comrades under siege; rather, it could be seen as a necessary reorientation after a rather successful turn of events. This sense of accomplishment and closure might help to explain the remarkable ease with which Castells dropped the Marxist framework, yet retained some of the key concepts from the earlier period. For example, in the triad of production, power, and experience – conceptualized as dynamics which are interacting with one another as well as following their own internal logic – there is still an echo of Althusser's three levels of economy, state, and ideology, each developing with "relative autonomy." The formalism of Althusser may have also eased the shift in perspective from transformative conflicts to the transformation of forms. The early project of developing a scientific basis for social theory may have made him more receptive to new attempts to develop a general theory of networks mounted by physicists and complexity theorists. I will return to this point in detail in the final chapter of this book.

More urgent right now is another continuity that can be observed: his conception of the role of technology in social change. It remained essentially unchanged until well into the 1990s. Only very recently did he abandon the last remnants of structuralist Marxism and develop a notion of the role of technology in the constitution of society much closer to that of McLuhan. A very unusual intellectual trajectory.

Technology and Social Change

Technology has always played a role in Castells's analysis, if only because it led him to discount production as the key to understanding the city during the 1970s. However, since the early 1980s technology has continuously grown more prominent in Castells's work, as it became oriented toward flows. In this reassessment of technology as a part of social dynamics, he has not been alone. Over the last two decades, the relationship between technological development and social dynamics has emerged as a key theme in the social sciences. This is not a coincidence. It has become impossible not to notice an ever increasing "technicization" of all aspects of life, including – due to medical technologies and genetic engineering – life itself. It is not just that there is more technology. It is also of a different kind. Compared with industrial technology, new technologies tend to be more open, flexible, amenable to being configured and transformed. They also penetrate more deeply into the user's experience, into the very structure of how people relate to one another and to the world. Technology is becoming personal and intimate. There is a distinct difference between how we use a train and how we use a personal computer or a mobile phone. As anyone who has ever configured, or just worked with, a complex machine has experienced firsthand, it is becoming increasingly difficult to distinguish clearly the boundaries between the social and the technical.

Addressing this blurring of the boundaries, entire new domains of inquiry – the sociology of technology and the social studies of science – have been established.[34] Their aim is to reconceptualize, to use Bruno Latour's terms, the relationship between "humans" and "non-humans," their fusion into "hybrids," exploring the "socio-technical worlds" created in the process.[35] At stake is nothing less than the definition of a new ontology for the (social) sciences. Bitter battles, the "science wars," are being fought over how to think about the relationship between the social, technical, and natural.[36] Undoubtedly, this is a problem central to any attempt to come to grips with the particular character of contemporary, technology-intensive societies.

For a long time, none of this touched Castells. His conception of the relationship between technological innovation and social transformation remained remarkably unchanged throughout most of his career. Only very recently has this begun to change, under the weight of empirical evidence. In his conceptualization of the relationship between technological development and social development, Castells stuck – as in no other aspect of his theory – to an argument developed by structural Marxists. Attempting to come to terms with the dynamism *within* capitalism, they expanded a distinction, already introduced by Marx, in the analysis of the economy between the "mode of production" and the "mode of development."

Put simply, the mode of production is the social relationships that make up the economy. The mode of production is characterized by the general goal according to which economic activity is organized. In the capitalist mode of production, the overriding principle is the accumulation of profit by the owners of capital, based on private ownership of property, market principles, and competition between participants. This goal defines how the social relationships between capital and labor are organized and what kind of economic investments are undertaken. Expectation of profit is the key determinant for where investment takes place, and the realization of profits determines what remains available in a capitalist economy. In what Castells calls the "statist mode of production" (characteristic of the former Soviet Union and its satellites), the central principle determining the organization of the economy is not profit maximizing, as under capitalism, but maximizing the power of the state/party bureaucracy. No economic development was allowed that could undermine the bureaucrats' control.

The mode of development, on the other hand, is characterized by "the technological arrangements through which labour acts upon matter to generate a product, ultimately determining the level of surplus,"[37] or, to use more contemporary terminology, it determines productivity. Each mode of development is defined by the element that is fundamental to increasing the output of the production process. Put very simply, in the agrarian mode of development, characteristic of "preindustrial" societies, output is increased linearly with the increase of labor input. To raise the production of food, more people have to till the soil; to increase manufacturing, more people have to work as artisans. In the industrial mode of development, the output is increased by introducing new sources of energy (the steam engine, the nuclear power plant), and finding qualitatively new ways (the factory, mass production) of using the energy to transform raw material into products. And now, Castells claims, a new, informational mode of development has emerged.

Before we turn to what this new mode of development is, it is necessary to stress that this structuralist perspective does not assume that the two modes change in parallel or have a fixed relationship. The mode of production is defined politically, the mode of development technologically. Capitalism and statism were, until the early 1970s, both based on the industrial mode of production, even though they were very different, even antagonistic, political regimes. Technologically speaking, factories were the same on either side of the iron curtain. Pol Pot and his Khmer Rouge disastrously tried to create communism in Cambodia in the 1970s based on an agrarian mode of development, depopulating the cities and sending people to the countryside to work on primitive farms, a strategy derided as "stone age communism."

The two modes do not determine one another. Characteristically, Castells assumes a "relative autonomy" of technological development in relation to other social dynamics. As he puts it, "modes of development evolve according to their own logic; they do not respond mechanically to the demands of modes of production."[38] This assumption of a certain distance between technological and economic development, which lies at the heart of Castells's conceptualization of the technology, has repeatedly been criticized as technological determinism. Frank Webster, for example, argues that "this division [between the two modes] is far too clear cut, that it drifts too easily into technological determinism, and that it too readily presumes that the rise of a new technological paradigm occurs without being designed or propelled by social – or even capitalist – values."[39]

It is certainly the case that the division between the two modes is too clear-cut. They can be hard to distinguish empirically, for example in the case of commercial research and development (R&D). Yet this can be said about most theoretical abstractions. More substantive is the critique that this separation into two modes places technological development outside society. Webster elaborates that

> above all . . . it is an approach which misconceives social change because it desocialises key elements of social change, persistently separating technology/technique from the social world (where values and beliefs are found), only to reassert it by asserting that this autonomous force is the privileged mechanism for bringing about change.[40]

This critique misreads Castells. Webster implies that stating that technological development is not necessarily determined by the economic process would be equal to arguing that it takes place outside society. But there are also social contexts within a capitalist society that are not determined by a strictly economic logic. Most important in this respect is science, which does not respond directly to market signals and is not driven primarily by the profit motive (the commercialization of academic research might change that, though). Yet, of course, it is also an eminently social activity. There are also other contexts in which people develop technology for largely noncommercial reasons, for example hobbyists, or social activists. Like scientists, they do not work under the direct command of capitalist actors. There are many motivations and social values – ranging from academic ethos, to curiosity, individual inventiveness, idiosyncratic needs and desires, political utopias, and, among all of these, also the profit motive – that contribute to technological development. How much each of these different sets of values contributes to technical innovation depends on the specific innovation under consideration.

Castells undertook only one sustained analysis of the development of a technological system, the internet. He identifies four major social groups, or "cultures" as he calls them, each with partially overlapping, partially conflicting values and agendas, that contributed to shaping the technologies.[41] At the beginning, there was the "techno-elite," composed of parts of the advanced research branch in the military and academia. The values of their "techno-meritocratic culture" – technological excellence, contribution to a field as a whole, peer review and peer esteem – have profoundly shaped the technology they developed. "Hackers" and their culture of individuality, creativity, access, and sharing are also an essential part of the history of the internet and they left their traces from the earliest days in the technologies created. Somewhat later, in the 1980s, came the "virtual communitarians," with their drive to establish new places of social experimentation and communal experience, partly reacting to the failure of the communitarian movement of the 1970s. Historically the last culture (so far) to put a decisive stamp on the internet's development is the (global) business culture, whose supreme value is profit, based on private (intellectual) property. Each of these groups developed their own technologies, often adapting elements developed by others or finding novel uses for technologies that the original developers did not even imagine. The tension between these groups, and the different values they seek to promote through the internet, still shapes its technological development.[42]

With such an analysis, Castells is not very far from a moderate "social construction of technology" approach, which argues that different "relevant social groups," each pursuing their distinct agendas and values, shape technology, rather than any qualities inherent in the artifacts themselves. Consequently, there is no necessary path of development. Yet he makes no reference to such theories.

So far, so good: technologies reflect the values and goals of those who make, and remake, them. However, from the point of view of Castells's social macroanalysis, this is only half of the equation. The mode of development is not simply the state of the art of the technology. Technology, as long as it remains only in the hands of those who develop it, has limited social relevance. For Castells – and this is the crucial and problematic point related to the structural legacy of this conceptualization – technology only becomes relevant by being integrated into the economy, thus spreading to society at large. As he puts it, "modes of development emerge from the interaction between scientific and technological discovery and the organizational integration of such discoveries in the process of production and management."[43]

Here the economic bias of this perspective becomes visible. Technological development can be triggered from outside the economy, but gains its social relevance primarily from its integration into the economy. From there, it diffuses throughout society. Technology, then, acquires its influence primarily by being employed by economic actors. Importantly, this integration of new technologies into the process of production is not straightforward. Not all technologies become integrated, and they are not always integrated in the ways the original developers thought about them. Rather, the integration is selective, following the patterns set out in the social relations of production, that is, today, capitalism.

For Castells, this is not prescribed by technological development per se, but a historical process that began to take shape in the 1970s. In other words, a number of politically indeterminate technologies – the microprocessor, networking technology, gene splicing– were all developed roughly at the same time, the first half of the 1970s. Yet technologies do not remain indeterminate for long. Either they disappear again, or they are appropriated by social actors, pursuing their goals, making bets that these technologies will help them to eke out a competitive advantage. And in the 1970s and 1980s, the economic crisis had created significant pressure on capitalist enterprises to search for better ways to pursue their goals (profit making). They also had the necessary resources to invest in new and expensive technologies. For Castells, the simultaneity of fundamental innovations and capitalist restructuring was a "coincidence," as these technological breakthroughs were not made as a part of a focused capitalist strategy. However, "regardless of what could have happened with new information technologies in a different historical context, the fact that they blossomed in their potential applications at the moment when capital was transforming itself to enter a new stage of development is of fundamental significance."[44]

Initially, these technologies were used to do the same things more efficiently (automation of tasks); afterwards, they began to be used to do things differently (reconfiguring the processes of production and consumption). It is because of this second step that a new mode of development really took root (rather than just the old one being upgraded). Castells calls this new mode of development the informational mode of development, in which the main source of productivity is no longer new sources of energy, but "the action of knowledge upon knowledge itself."[45]

This economistic view characterizes Castells's framing of the relationship between technology and social transformation during most of his career. Technological change is mainly relevant as a question of economic transformation and it is primarily through this that the rest of society is affected. In the analysis of other forces transforming society, for example social movements, the role of technology has been treated as negligible. In his 1983 survey of urban social movements, *The City and the Grassroots*, technology only appears as transforming the economic background against which the social struggles are carried out. It plays no direct role in the struggles themselves.[46] In *The Informational City* (1989a), technology plays an important role, not surprisingly as the study is focused almost entirely on the economy (and its effects on spatial patterns).

The trilogy of *The Information Age* receives its basic structure from this conceptualization. Technology plays a fundamental role in shaping the structural forces of the economy, but plays a very small one in shaping the social values as expressed by social movements. Hence only the first volume, which deals with the economy, rather than the entire trilogy has the *Network Society* in its title, because the networks Castells focuses on are all dependent on information technology. Emerging as a central theme of the entire trilogy is the tension between "the Net and the Self," set up as structural opposites, one side being shaped by dynamic technologies under the relentless drive of capitalism, the other by (reconstituted, or even entirely fabricated) "a-historical," stable values.[47] While Castells understood early on social movements as creatively responding to technology-dependent socioeconomic changes, he was late in considering how technology shapes their own practices.

Recently, this split between economic structure affected by technology and social movement unaffected by technology has become impossible to maintain. Again, "everyday experience" has been posing new problems too significant to ignore. This time, the iconic city was not Paris, but Seattle, and the year was 1999 (World Trade Organization protests). There it became plain to see that social movements were using new technologies in creative and powerful ways. Characteristically, the force of empirical events led Castells to adapt the theory. Since then, he has reconsidered the role of technology not only in social movements but in society at large. The resulting reconceptualization is on the surface subtle, but in substance significant.

Castells's new way of thinking about the role of technology is based on a different interpretation of the split between the mode of development and the mode of production. Reflecting on his own reorientation, he writes:

In principle, [technology] could be assigned primarily to the process of production ... as proposed in the Marxian model, and as I had proposed in my own work. I now think this is questionable. Because technology is as decisive in the realm of power (military technology, for instance) as in the realm of production. Similarly, technology plays an essential role in framing the relationships of experience: for instance, human reproductive technology frames family relationships and sexuality. Therefore, we must integrate technology, on its own ground, as a specific layer of the social structure.[48]

Now the mode of development is basically a way of doing things efficiently, a kind of "best practice," that is not restricted to the economy, but applies to a much wider range of social processes. And today this "best practice" (almost) always involves information technology. This might look like an insignificant difference, but it entirely changes the frame of reference in terms of conceptualizing the role of technology. We have just left the last remnants of structural Marxism and entered into the field of "media studies" as pioneered by Harold Innis (1894–1952), Marshall McLuhan and, often forgotten, Jacques Ellul (1912–1994).

Ellul used the term "technique," by which he meant not a particular technology, but something much more pervasive, "a method of action."[49] Technique, the whole complex of technological systems and social conventions engendered by and through them, progressively shapes the entire society, remaking it according to its internal logic, efficiency, the search for the "one best way." The very quest for efficiency is technique. There is much that is dated in Ellul, who remained firmly rooted in the industrial logic of automation and central command. What is important right now is that he conceptualized technology as a realm whose logic permeates society as a whole.

Similarly, McLuhan saw (communication) technology as an all-encompassing environment which shapes, in particular ways, all aspects of culture. McLuhan argued that the influence of communication technologies as such is different from, and independent of, the influence of the particular content they carry at any one time. He condensed his focus on the former into the slogan that became his trademark: "the medium is the message."[50] By this he meant that the most profound impact of communication technologies is not in what they communicate, but how they structure all communication that happens through them. McLuhan based his analysis on Harold Innis's radical thesis, developed in the late 1940s and early 1950s, that the state of technology, particularly communication technology, affects even a culture's sense of time and space.[51]

This does not suggest that Castells has formulated this new approach in explicit reference to these ideas. There is not a single reference to Ellul. This is not surprising, because Ellul, as a deeply religious thinker, occupied a peripheral position in the French intellectual universe of the 1960s dominated by Marxism. Castells with customary frankness notes that his account of the transformation of time and space is not in agreement with Innis.[52] Even McLuhan's influence is more indirect than systematic. In the only direct reference in the whole of *The Internet Galaxy*, despite the obvious homage to McLuhan's *The Gutenberg Galaxy* (1962), Castells misspells his name![53]

Rather, it was the weight of empirical evidence, particularly the very visible integration of information technologies into social struggles, that forced Castells to quietly abandon the concept of the informational mode of development, which so clearly belongs to an economic analysis. It is replaced with a much more general concept, informationalism, which can be applied to all domains of society and is thus much closer to media studies than to Marxism.[54] Althusser is out, McLuhan is in.

Informationalism

Informationalism is a technological paradigm. A paradigm "integrates discoveries into a system of relationships characterized by its synergies – that is, by the added value of the system vis-à-vis its individual components. A technological paradigm organizes the available range of technologies around a nucleus that enhances all of them."[55] In other words, a technological paradigm is a particular way of organizing the material base of society across (potentially) the full range of social contexts, not just the economy. A technological paradigm is characterized by the most advanced technologies and methods (the "nucleus"), but in the long term it alters the organization of the entire base of society. Under industrialism, agriculture did not really lose its importance. After all, food continued to be the basis of human life. Rather, its production was reorganized by applying new sources of energy (fertilizer), new technologies (tractors and other machinery), and new management methods. This increase in productivity was such that the number of people necessary to supply food to the entire society dropped lower and lower. Therefore, it is no contradiction to speak of *industrial agriculture*. Similarly, it is easy to imagine how an *informational agriculture* will be characterized by machinery incorporating real-time information feeds from satellites in the cultivation of genetically modified organisms. This is already happening.

Informationalism is "based on the augmentation of the human capacity in information processing around the twin revolutions in microelectronics and genetic engineering."[56] Both information technology and genetic engineering, Castells argues, have three major, distinctive features:

- self-expansion
- recombination
- distributional flexibility.

Self-expansion refers to the fact that computers are the basis for constructing new computers, and the more powerful computers become, the more complex the technologies that can be built using them. Whereas the printing press was used to disseminate information about itself and hence advanced the development of better printing presses, this relationship was indirect. One could not use printing presses to make printing presses in the same way that one can use software to make software, or that advanced genetic research relies on advanced computing technology.[57] Hence the development of printing technology was at best linear, whereas the direct feedback loop creates exponential development. This self-accelerating cycle of development is best captured by the famous "Moore's Law."[58]

Recombination has two elements. One is the fact that the information technologies are extremely modular. Existing elements can be used to construct entirely new technologies, further accelerating the development cycle. Recombination in this sense is the key to genetic engineering as well. But it is not just the modularity that characterizes the recombination. The other element is the ability of the technology to combine all kinds of information into something new and meaningful. The world wide web is paradigmatic for this. It is characterized by the ability to connect anything with everything and the potential to create new values from these connections that are no longer disciplined by boundaries of professional or academic segregation. The recombination of genetic information, even across the once absolute boundaries separating species, is already commonplace.

The last point, distributional flexibility, refers to the fact that information, once it is digitized, can be processed anywhere, and it can easily shift from one state of aggregation to another, say, from a sound file on a CD to a stream on a cellphone, or a graph on a screen. This facilitates the endless reorganization of information flows and the social organizations built around them.

These three features – self-expansion, recombination and distributional flexibility – provide the distinct character of informationalism, based on the application of computing and genetic engineering. Informationalism, then, is a set of features that comes to characterize the social organizations which rely in their practice on information technology and, with increasing importance, on genetic engineering. Castells is adamant that it makes no sense to speak of the essential role of knowledge and technology per se, as is implied by terms such as "information society" or "knowledge economy." For information and knowledge have always been important. The Roman Empire, for example, cannot be understood without taking into account its engineering and public works, or systems of codified knowledge, such as Roman law. Something similar could be said about other periods of the European history, indeed, about all civilizations.[59] What is specific about the network society, then, is not its reliance on information and knowledge, but the specific characteristics introduced into the material basis of society by these twin technological revolutions.

Castells does not develop this notion of a technological paradigm into a general theory, though it is implicit in his argument. Each paradigm supports a particular type of social organization (or morphology) in becoming dominant over others. Under industrialism, the dominant social form has been the hierarchy; under informationalism, it is the network. McLuhan's "the medium is the message" is rendered by Castells into "the network is the message." Under the paradigm of informationalism, networks are the superior way of organizing social action, *independent of the purpose of action*.

Castells frequently uses qualifiers such as "superior" or "more efficient" to characterize informationalism, though he assures us they are meant to be purely descriptive. He writes:

> historical transitions are shaped by winners. This should imply no value statement. We do not really know if producing more and more efficiently embodies superior value in terms of humanity. The idea of progress is an ideology. How good, or bad, or indifferent a new

paradigm is depends on whose perspective, on whose values, on whose standards. But we know that it's dominant because when implemented, it erases competition by elimination.[60]

Before taking up the claim of presenting a value-free analysis in some more detail, which we will do at the end of this chapter, let us return to the question of technological determinism.

Isn't it techno-determinism to claim that a technological paradigm induces a specific way of organizing that, by virtue of its "superior efficiency," will come to characterize society as a whole? Well, it depends on what we mean by "techno-determinism." In the strong version, often underlying popular accounts of the "technology revolution," technology is for all intents and purposes independent of the social environment.[61] It develops according to an inherent trajectory, and affects all social contexts in the same way. In this view, technology, as a kind of "first mover," provides a privileged vantage point from which to understand social change and predict the future. The focus of the strong claim lies on the social content, on *what* is being done – for example, new technologies will bring about "the end of the nation state."[62] This is, clearly, not what Castells argues.

But what about its weaker form? Here the focus is not on the content, but on the form. Here, analyzing technology will not lead to an understanding of what is being done, but of *how* it is done. How can the two be separated? The content of social development – what is being done – is politically determined. What is being done is a question of social values. It reflects the always precarious balance of conflicting actors and their agendas at a particular historical moment. Whether environmental protection or economic growth is the primary value of social policies cannot be analyzed with reference to the state of technology. Rather, it is shaped by the balance of power and the clash of antagonistic interests that make up the political process.

Yet the form of social organization – how things are being done – is more closely related to the technological paradigm, or perhaps more precisely, to the technologies social actors have access to. Because being able to implement advanced organizational techniques and methods – that is, the most recent technological paradigm – ensures superior efficiency in virtually all aspects of social life. Under the new technological paradigm, informationalism, networks are superior to hierarchies. In other words, the most efficient actors lobbying for environmental protection will likely be

organized as networks. Increasingly, they will "eliminate by competition" those environmental organizations that remain organized
as hierarchies. This says nothing about their strengths relative to,
say, the oil lobby.

Frank Webster summarizes this view pithily: "You may look to a
future without capitalism, but you will still need computer systems
to get by."[63] While he means this disparagingly, in the light of the
emergence of an antiglobalization movement organized over the
internet, this seems like a statement that can be substantiated empirically. Is this determinism? Alain Touraine seems to think so, but
calls it approvingly "technological determinism . . . in an elaborate
sense."[64] An assessment with which Castells has no problem. He
responds to Touraine:

> Is this technological determinism? Yes and no. Fundamentally no,
> because I do not say (and no one in her right mind would say) that
> technology determines society. . . . But yes, if you want, in a particu-
> lar sense, without new information technologies, there could be no
> economic globalization, no network enterprise, no global media, no
> global communication, and no global criminal economy.[65]

For Castells, "society cannot be understood or represented without
its technological tools."[66] Technology is value-free, in the particular
sense that McLuhan maintained that technology is neither good,
nor bad, nor neutral. Strong technological determinism comes in
two flavors, one arguing that technology is necessarily good, the
other that technology is necessarily bad. A technologically sensitive
social analysis, on the other hand, investigates in which sense it is
"not neutral." This is what Castells does by locating the primary
role of technology in transforming the social morphology. Or, as
Greg Calhoun summarizes Castells's current view, "new technologies are transformative . . . even though they do not dictate the
direction of transformation."[67] One might call this "soft determinism" in the sense of Paul Levinson, for whom "media rarely, if ever,
have absolute, unavoidable social consequences. Rather, they make
events possible – events whose shape and impact are the result of
factors other than the information technology at hand."[68] In short,
new technologies are necessary but not sufficient in the analysis of
(contemporary) societies.

Compared to more specialized approaches, Castells's view of the
role of the relationship between technological change and social
transformations is not particularly elaborate. He concentrates

primarily on one aspect, how technology affects the social form of social organization. While this is extremely broad and allows the connection of a great number of phenomena to one another, it is also very general and it sidelines a number of important aspects. For example, economic restructuring, as we will see in the next chapter, is primarily analyzed through the transformation of vertically integrated companies into "network enterprises" operating on a global scale. There is little emphasis on how informationalism is transforming capitalism, for example through changes in the very definition of property or the new social conflicts arising from them. Nor does he analyze how machines can function as "stand-ins" for social actors, and how they may thus enforce very particular social values. In the same sense, as I will detail in the discussion of Castells's theory of power, there is little discussion of how technologies are used to affect the character of power relationships, apart from the transformation of the vertically integrated nation-state into the more flexible and distributed "network state."

Castells does not expand the concept of informationalism into a full-blown theory of sociotechnological change. Rather, he restricts its elaboration to the status of a conceptual tool, custom-made to the immediate, practical task at hand. He leaves it as a theory relatively open to being expanded and transformed to suit future directions of research. This is not a coincidence. Rather, it is a key characteristic of the new epistemology, that is, the theory of knowledge, underlying Castells's work since the 1980s. It is on this level that the "total revision" of his early approach is most radical, most enduring, and most influential for the formulation of his theory of the network society.

Epistemology

As already mentioned, Castells started his career as an empirically oriented Althusserian. This was a rather unusual position, since Althusser's project was theory heavy. In fact, Althusser was a philosopher with rather little interest in empirical research. Theory was to be developed by working upon theory ("generalities"), and the role of empirical research was to confirm theory. Concrete analysis, in so far as it was done at all, served to validate and verify the grand theoretical constructions. The main purpose of theory was to reveal the ultimately determining forces through which visible reality was formed. Grossly simplified, empirical reality was an effect, rather than the cause of invisible structures. These were to be uncovered in the domain of theory, a work for which Althusser coined the term "theoretical practice." However, as Castells experienced early, this was rather unpractical theory. The result was, in Castells's retrospective evaluation, a "fiasco" because of the "abnormal cross-fertilization between our early Althusserian paradigm and the standard procedures of empirical sociology."[69] Trying to reconcile an already overly complex theory with empirical observation could only be done by further increasing the level of complexity, particularly since the theory had significant difficulties in incorporating some of the aspects most visible by "everyday experience," social movements.

Castells was not the only one to experience the problem of unmanageable complexity when attempting to reconcile theory and observation. Around him, he observed that trying to address fast changing realities, Marxist theory was becoming more and more esoteric or dogmatic, or both. As the sophistication of the vocabulary increased, the ability of the theories to communicate to non-initiated audiences decreased. For Castells, the road toward a comprehensive theory appeared more and more as a dead end. This realization may have been sharpened by the suicide of Nicos Poulantzas (1979), the leading structuralist theoretician of the state, who was an important intellectual influence on, and close friend of, Castells.[70]

Doubts about the role of theory as the end point of social research were growing, however, before that. In the mid 1970s, Castells became dissatisfied with what he called the "excessive formalization" of his own work. He came to the conclusion that in the production of theory, "the problem is not so much that of its correctness as it is that of its usefulness."[71] This is a typical formulation for Castells. He slightly redefines the concepts and significantly alters the terms of reference. If we take the "correctness" of the theory to be its central value, then the problem of theory is primarily one of logic, of consistency. Consequently, it can be judged on its own merits and in relation to other theories. Empirical research merely illustrates or "proves" theory. The role of case studies, then, is to serve as an application of the theory. Theory precedes and supersedes empirical research.

However, if we take "usefulness" to be theory's central value, then it can only be evaluated in relation to something else, and this something, for Castells, can only be empirical research. Epistemologically speaking, this is a complete inversion of the relationship between the two. Theory is no longer the goal, but an intermediary step. It becomes a tool for empirical research, without which its value cannot be ascertained. In other words, for Castells, the most interesting kind of theory is that which can be used fruitfully when researching concrete situations. Only there can its value be shown.

This was a very deliberate and explicit reorientation of his approach which was in the making during the second half of the 1970s. It came to the fore in the early 1980s. Now, he argued,

> [my approach] is informed by a methodological perspective that is distrustful of former experiences involving useless construction of abstract grand theories. Therefore we are determined to ground this attempt at theory-building on reliable research, and to avoid hasty formalizations of the proposed conceptual framework. By this cautious strategy, we seek to rectify the excesses of theoretical formalism that have flawed the social sciences in general and some of our own work in particular. . . . On contemplating these failures (a result, we believe, of unnecessary and ill-considered attempts to ape the natural sciences) it seemed to us that our best hope of understanding society lay in a much more patient approach to gathering information and building theories.[72]

The fact that a deep distrust of formalized theories has remained with Castells ever since is testimony to how profound this reassessment of his early approach has been. It is on the level of epistemology that Castells broke most radically with Marxism. He has never regained the old certainties. Hence it was not false understatement when he wrote in 2000, in one of his few texts advancing an exclusively theoretical argument: "I hope the reader will be benevolent enough to use what s/he finds useful in this effort, and discard the rest. I also hope that we all end up adopting the notion of disposable theory."[73]

Of course, Castells did not dispose of theory and revert to a narrow empiricism. He has continued to produce theoretically sophisticated research and to formulate new theoretical concepts. Yet the character of these concepts is distinct. They are primarily "research tools" to be evaluated on the merits of the research they stimulate, and not on their elegance or claims to comprehensiveness. This is what he means by disposable theory. If a concept stimulates research, use it; if it impedes research, drop it. In the face of a contradiction between observed reality and theoretical framework, it is always the latter that should be changed, rather than the former being "reinterpreted" to fit the theory. This, quite fittingly, is not a position that is theoretically particularly sophisticated or controversial – nobody would openly argue that we should force empirical research to conform to preestablished categories. Rather, this position can only be judged based on the actual practice it informs. For Castells, it means primarily continuous "rectification" of concepts. Keeping theories open and flexible has become a central characteristic of his work.

In his theory building, Castells has since adopted an epistemological position usually associated with "grounded theory,"[74] though he makes no mention of it. To put it simply, grounded theory does not test theoretical hypotheses through empirical research, but aims at letting theoretical categories "emerge" from case studies. It is not necessary to discuss here the extensive methodological tool set developed to structure this process, but it is important to point out that it is also not an empiricist, inductive method – where reality is first observed "objectively" and from which an explanatory theory is then distilled. Rather, research proceeds as an iterative process where theoretical propositions are revised in the course of doing empirical research, which in turn shapes the direction of the research. The resulting concepts are to be understood less as formal theoretical propositions and more, in the terminology of grounded theory, as "sensitizing concepts." By this is meant concepts that can help in guiding further empirical research. Such an epistemology has three important consequences characteristic of grounded theory in general and Castells's work in particular. First, the value of a concept, or a theoretical proposition, is primarily established in *comparative* analysis. The central theoretical device for such a comparative study is the "ideal type," as developed by Max Weber. An ideal type, Weber wrote,

> is formed by the one-sided accentuation of one or more points of view and by the synthesis of a great many diffuse, discrete, more or less present and occasionally absent concrete individual phenomena, which are arranged according to those one-sidedly emphasized viewpoints into a unified analytical construct.[75]

In other words, ideal types are constructions that emphasize those aspects of a complex reality that are relevant in terms of the analytical project for which they are developed. They enable a highlighting of the commonalities, and differences, of a range of cases, thus enabling comparative study. This is what Weber did, particularly in his magnum opus, *Economy and Society* (1968), and this is a good deal of what Castells does in his trilogy. Many of Castells's most important concepts making up the theory of the network society are ideal types in the Weberian sense. They emphasize certain aspects, mainly the transformation of the social morphology, over others. Ideal types are created iteratively from case studies and are used for, and adjusted through, further case studies. Concepts such as "the network enterprise," "resistance identity," or "the network state" are, as we will see, quite classic ideal types. There is, for example, no company that is a pure network enterprise. Even the flattest hierarchy still is a hierarchy. The ideal type brings together those of their features that Castells argues are the most relevant in relation to his analytical project.

Whether or not they are indeed the most relevant features is a question that cannot be answered theoretically, but through the application of the concept to empirical research. Theories based on empirical cases and ideal types always have to contend with the problem that each case is unique and that it is unclear how, or whether, it is possible to extrapolate from one case to others. In order to overcome the problem of producing ad hoc explanations, the theoretical construction derived from one case needs to be applied to, and modified by, a whole range of additional cases. The wider the range that can be analyzed fruitfully with a given ideal type, the better, the more useful, it is. This is one of the reasons why Castells's body of work is so voluminous, and why he does not hesitate to revise his own work. There is simply no productive way to abstract the "ideal types" into a comprehensive theory, since any new proposition coming out of such an exercise would need to be validated, again, in a series of case studies. Consequently, Castells views pure theory as either redundant or speculative, at least in the social sciences.

The second reason is that for concepts to be applicable to a wide range of differing cases, they need to be relatively broad and should not be too detailed in their formulation. As Castells puts it, "following the teaching of Gaston Bachelard, we believe that the most useful concepts are those flexible enough to be deformed and rectified in the process of using them as instruments of knowledge."[76]

Rarely does he spend more than a few paragraphs explicating a given concept before plunging into an analysis of numerous cases to substantiate the argument. If one reads only the theoretical section of his work, the argument remains wooden and formulaic. He is fond of definitions that are broad to the point of meaninglessness. For example, it is hard to imagine a statement broader and less specific than "human societies are made from the conflictive interaction between humans organized in and around a given social structure." Adding the definition of social structure as "formed by the interplay between relationships of production/consumption; relationships of experience; and relationships of power" does little to add specificity to the statement. For Castells, the value of such pronunciations lies elsewhere. They provide an entry point to analysis of, say, the crisis of government institutions at a particular historical juncture, and locating it in relation to the dynamics of the economy and of social movements. In such a view, all that theoretical statements really do is establish a particular matrix. This matrix can be thought of as a grid made out of elastic rubber bands. On to this grid, case studies are placed. The weight of evidence stretches and transforms the rubber bands. If they are stretched too far, they tear, that is, the theory is not able to accommodate the cases. New rubber bands need to be strung. If the matrix is constructed well, it holds the evidence and gives it a particular shape. The more material is placed on the matrix, the less the grid will be visible. However, without empirical material the rubber bands are "unnaturally" straight, whereas with the material, they are "deformed." The real value lies not in the matrix as a set of straight lines, but the matrix as a particular landscape created by the pressure of evidence.

The third consequence of Castells's epistemological stance is that the resulting theory can never be comprehensive. This is not a point of practicality, reflecting the fact that the object of study is simply too large, varied and dynamic to be fully accounted for. Rather, it is a direct consequence of the concepts being derived from case studies and, ultimately, only applying to them. If there are many case studies from which the concept is derived, its scope is consequently larger, but still this method, or epistemology, does not allow for extrapolation. It is, therefore, necessarily incomplete.

The Politics of Research

Related to the transformation of his epistemological stance are Castells's changing politics of research. Together with Marxism, he has abandoned the idea that theoretical knowledge could, or should, directly inform political practice. Over the years, the distance between his analytical work and his political engagement has grown, despite being personally politically engaged and a self-proclaimed social democrat.

At the end of *The Information Age* trilogy, he reflects on the practical, political usefulness of social analysis. Referring to Marx's famous line – "philosophers have only interpreted the world in various ways; the point, however, is to change it" – and his own youthful calls for a "theoretico-practical approach,"[77] he writes: "In the twentieth century, philosophers have been trying to change the world. In the twenty-first century, it is time to interpret it differently."[78] The real usefulness of social analysis is now to be found in its distance from the political process, in its independence and methodological rigor. This is the only thing it can offer to those seeking to translate its insights into particular courses of action, specific to their time, locality, and constituency. As he puts it, "I believe that knowledge should precede action, and action is always specific to a given context and a given purpose."[79] This translation, however, cannot be done by the social scientist, partly because she or he doesn't share the context of action with the political activist, partly because there is a fundamental difference between social analysis and political strategy.

If we take the difference between theoretical knowledge and political action to be that action is always specific to social contexts, then there is at least the implication that knowledge is not, or is at least much less, context specific. The problem of the contextuality of knowledge has plagued the social sciences for much of their existence, and contributed a great deal to their inferiority complex as soft sciences compared to the natural sciences and their hard knowledge. The two poles of the discussion are the following. Positivism argues that the rigor of the scientific method (à la Popper) ensures the creation of objective, or at least intersubjective, hence decontextualized, knowledge. This position has been severely criticized for as long as it has existed. On the other hand, there is the postmodern claim that all knowledge is instrumental, or at least context dependent. The consequence of such a position is either what has been called "infinite regress" (the never-ending spiral of contextualizing the context), or profound relativism, accepting that truth claims are, ultimately, incommensurable.

Castells never entered this debate. Rather, his epistemological stance today reflects an influence of Weber that goes far beyond a fondness for ideal types. Rather, he shares certain aspects of Weber's neo-Kantian positivism. By this I mean that Castells, like Weber, starts from an understanding that concepts precede empirical observation. Without such concepts, empirical reality would appear as a chaotic mess. There is no way of accounting for reality in any pure way (this is the Kantian part). Yet the use of these concepts is confined to statements about what is empirically observable, and based on these observations, the concepts can, and have to be, revised (this is the positivist part).

In terms of the resulting objectivity of the research, Castells is guarded. On the one hand, he clearly believes that there is objective, in the sense of intersubjective, knowledge. It is possible to establish reliable knowledge about social phenomena that can stand on its own. Yet, given the historical character of the social sciences, the value of this knowledge needs to be reasserted all the time. Social knowledge has a short life. Entirely absent in Castells's work is a problematization of his own position. He never situates his own work, either in terms of the context of production (elite institutions of academia), or in the context of his own biography. Rather, he argues for the need for a cross-cultural analysis to avoid the biases of ethnocentrism. Yet, when directly asked, he has no problem pointing out how aspects of his biography have had a profound impact on his thinking. Yet, for Castells, this should not be relevant to the reader of his work, as he explains:

> In this, I have always kept a materialist view of the research process. I think you produce knowledge, you produce a pair of shoes, it is material production. How you reach this material production is not a matter for the consumer. If your pair of shoes is uncomfortable for people, they are bad shoes. My point is that the product has to be judged by itself. Certainly, there is a relationship between what I think and who I am and ultimately it goes into a product, but unless the product is yourself and your position, these are different matters.[80]

Elsewhere, he speaks of theory as "an artisan fabrication of analytical tools to make sense of observation. [And] the relevance of theory, in my epistemology, is tested by its ability to yield understanding of what is being studied."[81] Here, again, we have the criterion of usefulness. If your feet hurt, get different shoes, if the theory is impractical, don't use it.

However, since the usefulness of a theory is different for a scientist (in terms of doing research) than for a politician (in terms of governing), the researcher is no more, but also no less, equipped than anyone else to give political advice. This is why Castells regards his political opinions as private and separate from his research publications. Suffice to say, in practice, Castells has not always separated politics and research as clearly as he claims to do. He has been a frequent advisor to heads of state, and served on more than one expert committee. Over the years, he has had close relationships with many politicians. Perhaps the most profound one, in terms of influence on actual policies, has been Castells's long friendship with Jordi Borja, a key figure in the democratic movement for Catalan autonomy. Among other things, they wrote a research report for the United Nations Center for Human Settlements in 1996, later published as a book.[82] In it, they gave detailed political advice on how to make cities competitive in a globalized economy. Here, as elsewhere, Castells proposed moderate social democratic policies, through which the (local) state might play an important role in providing conditions for economic competitiveness, through investment in infrastructure and education. This advice, as we will see, is fully consistent with his general analysis of the network society, reflecting many of its strengths and some of its weaknesses. It is to the concrete arguments that underpin the theory that we will now turn.

2

Production

Of the three pillars on which the theory of the network society rests – production, experience, and power – production, that is the economy, emerges as the central one. This is not in the sense that the economy would determine social or political life, or that it could be analyzed without reference to the other two. Castells's theory is much too sophisticated to allow for such reductionism. Rather, the centrality of the economy stems from the conviction that many of the most pervasive, most powerful dynamics transforming societies around the globe are created in the pursuit of economic goals. Not least, as we have already seen, because for a long time Castells took technology to affect society mainly through its incorporation into the economy. More important for the central position of the economy in the theory is an assumption that "productivity and economic growth still organize societies around their logic, both in the work process and in the distribution of wealth thus generated."[1] It is significant that Castells focuses on "productivity and economic growth." These are the aspects of the economy that determine its dynamism from *within*. In other words, in the absence of radical outside shocks – political revolutions, wars, natural disasters – the transformation of capitalism is driven by attempts to sustain economic growth, simply because capitalism itself has an expansionary logic. Its internal competitive pressures reward those whose productivity is highest.[2] Consequently, Castells maintains that if we are to understand how contemporary society changes, we have to start with analyzing the strategies implemented by economic actors aiming at increasing their efficiency, or, to use Daniel Bell's famous phrase, "to do more with less."

The reference to Bell is not spurious. Rather, Bell's work plays an important role for Castells. The theory of "postindustrialism" has long dominated analyses of contemporary economic changes. Castells's own argument can be understood as an attempt to overcome what he sees as fundamental flaws in this approach while keeping it as a key reference point. Thus this chapter starts with Castells's critique of postindustrialism, before turning to his differing account, starting with what he takes to be the trigger of the epochal restructuring: the economic crisis of the 1970s. I will then review Castells's account of informational capitalism which emerged as a consequence of this restructuring. This will unfold along the four main dimensions of Castells's economic analysis: the internationalization of the economy; the rise of global financial markets; the network enterprise; and the individualization of work. At the end of the chapter, I will point out some of the problematic aspects of this account, both in terms of what is argued and in terms of some notable gaps in the theory.

Postindustrialism

Among the theorists analyzing the economic transformations of the last quarter of the twentieth century, Daniel Bell has long held a pre-eminent position. Since the publication of *The Coming of Postindustrial Society* in 1973, Bell's theory has exerted a profound influence on the discourse on the economy in the information age. His basic argument was greatly popularized by futurists like Alvin Toffler, particularly in the bestseller *The Third Wave* (1980). Both, in somewhat different ways, thought they had detected a historical shift from the creation of goods to the provision of services as the core activity of advanced economies. This transformation, they argued, is roughly equal in importance to the industrial revolution, which shifted the bulk of economic activity from extracting resources from nature, through agriculture and mining, to producing goods for mass markets. Bell declared famously that "industrial societies are goods producing societies. Life is a game against fabricated nature . . . A postindustrial society is based on services. Hence, it is a game between persons."[3] The disappearance of many manufacturing jobs in North America and Europe and the rise of new professional occupations lent strong intuitive credence to such a view.

Castells has used the theory of postindustrialism since the mid 1970s as a foil to argue with and argue against.[4] Despite his dislike of the futurism so characteristic of postindustrialist analysis, Castells's perspective overlaps with Bell's in important areas. In the first place, both locate the crucial changes primarily at the level of the technical relations of production (*mode of development*), and only secondarily at the level of its social relations (*mode of production*). This allows them to speak at the same time about profound change (in the way economic value is created) and about continuity (in the way value is appropriated). This distinction has long been central to Castells's analysis. It can still be found in the conclusion of *The Information Age* trilogy where he speaks of a "new form of capitalism" having emerged in the last quarter of the 20th century. Second, postindustrialism is, at its core, an empirical theory, as is the theory of the network society. Building on the foundational work of Fritz Machlup and Marc Porat,[5] the argument took changes in the composition of the labor force as its bedrock. As has been shown repeatedly, after the late 1960s the majority of the paid labor force in the US was no longer employed by the first sector (agriculture), or the second (goods manufacturing). Rather, they were recorded as working in the third, or service, sector. This profound and indisputable statistical reality provided much of the force that propelled the argument through three decades, and into popular consciousness.

Yet, however persistently the disappearance of manufacturing jobs manifested itself in national employment figures year after year, it makes, Castells argues, a poor foundation for social theory. His critique, and the thrust of his alternative conception of the *informational economy*, is twofold. First, the manufacturing jobs did not disappear. They just moved out of sight of the national statisticians. "While analysts were proclaiming the de-industrialization of America, or of Europe in the 1980s, they simply overlooked what was happening in the rest of the world."[6] Globally, he points out, manufacturing employment rose by 72 percent between 1963 and 1983, and it has continued to grow since then. In other words, despite claims to the contrary, Bell took the US to be the general model which all advanced countries would follow. Developing or underdeveloped countries were deemed of no particular importance to the emerging service economies. They were either ignored (as external to the system and hence irrelevant to the argument) or assumed to be somewhat further behind on the one and only road of development. This ethnocentrism is, in Castells's view, the first of the central analytical weaknesses of postindustrialism.

Castells's second point of critique is that even within advanced economies, the shift from industry to services has been much less clear-cut than Bell and his followers have claimed. For one thing, so far neither sociologists nor statisticians have been able to come up with a precise, or at least workable, definition of "service." Thus it remains a residual category which simply lumps together everything that is neither agriculture nor industry. The diverse phenomena boxed into this category are, in fact, characterized by multiple, independent dynamics. This renders any overall, aggregated "trend" close to meaningless. For example, the rise of many service occupations in the social sector is primarily related to the expansion of the welfare state as it incorporates new social demands ("collective consumption"). It does not signal any profound economic transformation. Furthermore, many services are directly linked to industrial production, indicating its growth and increasing complexity, rather than its decline. Consequently, the impossibility of distinguishing the boundaries between "goods" and "services" renders the category "services" "ambiguous at best, misleading at worst."[7]

This is not the place to critique a theory which, despite (or more likely because of) its pervasive influence, has not been upgraded substantially in the last 30 years.[8] All it is necessary to note here is that Castells's theory of the economy, despite the aforementioned affinity with postindustrialism, has developed from a different, yet equally fundamental observation: the changing spatial organization of production. Rather than stressing the changes in the composition of the labor force, Castells's starting point has been the observation that by incorporating new technologies of communication, the spatial organization of production has been transformed profoundly. In the early 1970s he was already noting that

> the role played by technology in the transformation of the urban forms is indisputable. This influence is exercised both through the introduction of new activities of production and consumption and by the almost total elimination of the obstacle *space*, thanks to the enormous development of the means of communication.[9]

To take changes in the way physical space is organized as (one of) the foundational observation(s) on which to base a claim of the emergence of a new social system gives Castells a unique position among the leading theorists of the information(al) society. This perspective provides him with two of the major elements of his subsequent analysis. First, the realization of the translocal character of the emerging system and its dependence on information and communication technology as necessary means to coordinate itself across distances in *real time*. This leads to the formulation of the concept of the *space of flows* (discussed more fully in chapter 5) as the new material basis for economic organization in the late 1980s, almost a decade before the internet enters into his analysis. Second, Castells never understood internationalization as a one-way expansion, meaning that the rest of the world would follow the lead of the United States (as Bell assumed). On the contrary, different places, with their particular cultures and institutions, are being connected into an interdependent economic system. Thus this needs to be analyzed on two levels at the same time. If the system can be said to be integrated, then it must be possible to analyze its common features across regions and contexts. On the other hand, if we take internationalization seriously, the analysis needs to be *comparative*, analyzing how different cultural experiences, embodied in economic actors and their environments, react to, and shape, the emerging new system to which they all belong. This is also why, in Castells's view, it is impossible to analyze the economy, in anything but general terms, without reference to the social and political contexts in which economic processes operate. Finally, contrary to Bell, Castells argues that the initial trigger that set economic restructuring in motion was not the development of new technologies, but the crisis of the economic and political system that became manifest in the 1970s.

The Economic Crisis of the 1970s

The Western postwar economic order rested on three arrangements which created a highly controlled, hierarchized, and stable environment. The first was the social pact between capital and labor, epitomized by the German *Sozialpartnerschaft* (social partnership). This assured capital of a relatively peaceful working force at the price of recognizing the unions' position as representatives of the workers, and accepting their demands for steady increases in wages and social benefits for their members. Second, comprehensive regulation of, and intervention in economic and social processes by the state. This took many forms, ranging from state ownership of large economic actors, to subsidization of key industries, public expenditure to stimulate the economy, the expansion of employment in the public sector, and the provision of a widening range of services to citizens. The final aspect of the postwar system was the control of the international economy. It was exercised through new, multinational institutions such as the International Monetary Fund. This control extended to financial markets as well as to the supply of key raw materials and energy sources.

For roughly two decades these interlocking arrangements fostered economic growth at historically unprecedented rates. For those at the center of this system it brought rising standards of living in the form of consumerism. Yet, toward the end of the 1960s, the contradictions of this regulated capitalism started to become apparent. The virtuous cycle – high wages stimulating consumption and a boom in manufacturing – began to turn into a vicious one. Inflation was rising, disrupting the processes of economic circulation. The expansion of salaries and benefits for workers began to interfere with the rate of profit for owners of capital. The demands on the welfare system increased at a time when its income base began to shrink – not least since increasing taxation became politically difficult in the context of a falling rate of profit. The measures that were supposed to counteract this situation further increased inflation. The "oil shock," the massive spike in energy prices in 1974 and 1979, substantially increased the pressure on the state's finances and put severe limits on its ability to intervene in the economy successfully.[10]

The state was caught in a double bind. At a time when income was falling and inflation prompted the need for austerity politics to stabilize the economic environment, the leading economic theory, Keynesianism, suggested that spending should be increased. This was not only to stimulate the economy, but also to satisfy the growing demands of a welfare system that more and more people came to depend upon as unemployment rose. For Castells "the real crisis of the 1970s was not the oil prices shock. It was the inability of the public sector to keep expanding its markets, and thus income-generating employment, without either increasing taxes or fueling inflation."[11] Thus the state could no longer absorb the underlying structural contradictions that had been growing for a long time. This provided the economic pressure, and the political will, to begin a long, muddled process of change. And, for Castells, it was led by trial and error, with competition swiftly sorting successes from failures, rather than by grand vision.

This result was, Castells argues, a restructuring rather than a "simple" expansion of capitalism.[12] The latter would basically mean more of the same, whereas restructuring processes "modify the rules of the social system while preserving its fundamental logic."[13] This is a formulation quite typical for Castells, stressing the possibility of profound change within an overall framework of continuity. Consequently, the fact that the economic system is still capitalist becomes less important, or at least less analytically discerning, than the fact that it is a different kind of capitalism.

Internationalization of the Economy

Faced with regulated, saturated domestic markets that no longer supported economic growth as they used to, corporations began searching for new ways to grow. First, they secured and deepened existing markets. Only later did they start to enter new ones. In the US, the military market played an important part by providing a secure base from which to stage this expansion. In Japan, then in Korea, and most recently in China, the protected domestic market has played a similar role. Contradicting a simplistic free trade argument, Castells stresses that it was the existence of these shielded domestic markets that made it possible to build up a machinery that could be unleashed in the global markets. All advanced economies, using their home base as a launching pad, tried to export their way out of the crisis. In the process, they substantially increased their interpenetration. The particular nature of their bases even influenced what was being exported: high-tech from the US, consumer goods from Asia. Although internationalization *as such* is not new, "it has since the 1970s taken on much greater proportions, and has embraced new dimensions, in an attempt by corporations to overcome the structural contradictions revealed in the crisis of the world economy."[14]

The internationalization of production was not a one-way street. Rather, it deepened the interconnection between all economies in a pattern of multidirectional flows of goods and services, selectively creating winners and losers. During the 1970s and 1980s, manufacturing exports grew everywhere – even in the US, despite the fact that the balance of trade turned negative for the first time in 1971 and, with brief exceptions, has stayed negative ever since. In other words, other countries, initially Germany and Japan, then the so-called Asian Tiger countries (Hong Kong, Singapore, South Korea, and Taiwan) and now China, increased their exports much faster than the US. Indeed, the relative importance of manufactured goods in international trade has increased over the last 25 years to the point where manufactured goods now represent the vast majority of nonenergy trade, whereas it used to be primary commodities. Consequently, it makes no sense to speak of the decline of industrial manufacturing.

However, aggregated figures like these, Castells goes to great lengths to argue, mask as much as they reveal. Yet they are not useless. They point to a profound new reality: the framework of production is no longer the national territory but the entire globe. This is not just because ever more goods are being exported, but also because even domestically produced goods find themselves in direct competition with imported ones. This means that the integration into the global economy happens even for economic actors that remain entirely local. This is one of the many ways in which participation in the global economy is not an individual choice but a collective reality. In this sense, there are also no economies that are external to the new global economy, if only because lack of integration (or even active disintegration) is itself a major factor in economic development.

What such aggregates mask, however, is the fact that "integration" into the global economy says very little on its own. Not all trade is equal. What has been emerging is a new "international division of labor."[15] At the top are the "producers of high value," based on knowledge-intensive labor in production and services, followed by the "producers of high-volume," exploiting cheap labor, the "producers of raw materials," relying on their natural resources, and finally, "redundant producers," systematically excluded by the global economy. The most active members of the latter group are making their way back into the global economy through the global criminal economy. Establishing a "perverse connection," they provide "everything that receives added value precisely from its prohibition from the legal environment."[16]

Because of this division of labor, there are profoundly different levels – even if we only consider trade – at which individual countries and regions are integrated into the global economy. Castells has no patience with the happy notion that free trade creates fair opportunities for all. As he points out, at the turn of the century the economies of sub-Saharan Africa have a higher percentage of exports than OECD countries, 29 percent of their GDP. However, these exports are dominated by low value, primary commodities, effectively condemning these countries to remain at the bottom of the global economy into which they have been fully integrated. As a result, Castells writes, "the global economy is characterized by a fundamental asymmetry between countries, in terms of their level of integration, competitive potential, and share of benefits from economic growth."[17]

This asymmetry exists not only between countries. It extends to regions within countries, and to neighborhoods within large cities. The result is a patchwork of highly fragmented social realities and a variable geometry of inclusion and exclusion. Yet another fact masked by statistics still largely compiled on a national basis.

Key features of Castells's conception of the global economy are derived from his analysis of international trade. He notes that it has not only grown in size and relative importance, it has also developed from a system with a relative clear center–periphery structure (say, Europe and its colonies) into a multicentric system, internally highly differentiated, integrating more local economies than ever before. Yet this integration is highly specific and locks many of its constituent parts into positions of structural disadvantage.

Global informational capitalism is not only distinct from the old world economy by virtue of the speed, size, multidirectionality and complexity of its trading patterns. It is also different because of its systemic instability and essentially nonlinear character introduced by the relentless search for profit in the global financial markets.

Global Financial Markets

Perhaps as a consequence of Castells taking the spatial restructuring of production as an entry point into the analysis of the economy, the financial markets for a long time played only a minor role in his economic analysis. *The Informational City*, published in 1989, contains a detailed study on the restructuring of the American automobile industry, whereas the most substantive treatment of the financial sector concerns the issue of office automation.[18] Of course, with the benefit of hindsight, it is facile to point out omissions. Yet they are striking nevertheless. The transformation of the financial markets throughout the 1970s and 1980s has been anything but spectacular, starting with the abandonment of the gold standard by President Nixon on August 15, 1971. In the view of Barry Eichengreen, a preeminent economic historian, this event signaled a sea change, since this measure, long resisted for political reasons, "was a [first] consequence of the rise of international capital mobility."[19] It was a sign that financial markets, then still highly regulated, were already able to overwhelm the political controls of even the largest economy.[20]

Also in the 1970s, with the growth of "Eurodollars" – large amounts of US dollars based in Europe and therefore beyond the control of US regulation – big financial players began to operate in the cracks of the financial markets. Being outside national controls offered opportunities to achieve returns higher than those that could be realized in the regulated markets. During these years, the financial sector was the single most important civilian buyer of information and communication technology, initially in support of the internationalization of trade, but increasingly independently of it.[21] The 1980s were also littered with high profile events emanating from the financial markets, ranging from the headline-making rise and fall of financier Michael Milken,[22] to the stock market crash of 1987.

The development of new financial instruments, itself a major force in corporate restructuring during the 1980s, finds no mention at all in Castells's 1989 study. The stock market crash is briefly treated as an issue of the automation of services. This is not incorrect. After all, the crash was caused by computer-executed trading strategies entering into a self-reinforcing cycle of accelerated selling. However, such a focus misses the broader, and more substantial, point that financial markets had grown to such a degree that their internal dynamics, with little reference to the outside "real" economy, were playing an ever increasing role in the dynamics of the global economy. During the 1970s and 1980s, Castells analyzed the financial industry mainly as one of many sectors of the economy, with its own logic of spatial organization (concentration in the central districts of major cities). Not until the 1990s are the financial markets analyzed as the key actor shaping the development of the entire economy through its own internal dynamics.

Partly as a consequence of his own shift in perspective from national to global economies, partly prompted by the dramatic changes within the financial markets themselves, Castells has since put them at the center of his economic analysis. "If globalization is widely acknowledged as a fundamental feature of our time, it is essentially because of the emergence of global financial markets."[23] The financial markets share certain characteristics with the system of international trade: substantial quantitative growth, extreme diversification, structural interlinking of all aspects into a single interconnected system operating on a global scale in real time, and systemic volatility. It is not a coincidence that trade and finance, for all their differences, share key dynamics. For one thing, they are linked in multiple ways, for example by the practice of foreign direct investment (FDI). It has increased considerably faster than world trade. This is an indicator of the degree to which the interpenetration of national economies is driven by the financial markets. While multinational corporations are the main force behind FDI, the main mechanism by which money is allocated is the financial markets. They are continuously looking to shift money to better returns, or in times of crisis, to safe havens. Second, they are both based on the same technological paradigm, informationalism, which is good at supporting fast-paced change and the linking of entities, distributed across the globe, into functional units operating in real time. In other words, trade and finance are different aspects of the same integrated system: the global informational economy. However, now it is the financial markets, not trade or production, that are the core of the new economy. They are dominant in the sense that money for investment needs to be raised in financial markets, and that all money that is being made in the "real" economy ends up in the financial markets. Here profits are reinvested, because here returns can be higher than in any other sector of the economy. Thus the global financial markets are the source, and destination, of investment for virtually all sectors of the economy.

Castells highlights five developments that lead to this dominant position of the global financial markets. First, deregulation of financial markets in most countries throughout the 1980s and 1990s. Regulation was relaxed within markets, and perhaps even more importantly, regulation separating different markets from one another was also lifted. This increased the size and complexity of the markets rapidly *without* a corresponding expansion of the physical economy. It is to highlight the importance of deregulation that Castells chooses the "big bang", the simultaneous deregulation and computerization of London's stock exchange, in October 1987, as the beginning of the global financial markets. Second, over the last three decades, a new technological infrastructure was put in place capable of processing the rapidly increasing volume and complexity of market transactions, removing yet another set of limitations to expansion. Third, building on the first two developments, new financial products, from mutual funds to derivatives, significantly increased the interdependence of the various sectors of the financial markets. They effectively integrated the financial markets – previously segmented by region and equity – into a single, globally connected, continuously operating market. Fourth, this global market is internally standardized by market valuation firms, such as Standard & Poor or Moody's. Their ratings enable the comparison of the most diverse companies on the basis of unified and trusted metrics, such as the quality of their credit. Adding to this integration are the global media, both financial and general interest, distributing certain kinds of information around the globe without delay.

Finally, there is the growth of speculative capital, moving swiftly in and out of markets, increasing volatility and connecting, through their constant movement, various markets with one another. Castells points to two main sources for this capital. Large investors (including pension funds) are one source, seeking investments with a higher rate of return and the opportunity to operate outside what remains of government oversight (including taxation). The other is the laundering of money from the global criminal economy, seeking to mask its illegitimate origins through rapid movements across markets and jurisdictions.

The criminal economy as a source of destabilizing, speculative funds is an important and highly original aspect of Castells's otherwise relatively standard account of global financial markets. The reason why Castells emphasizes this aspect is not just the objective size of this shadow economy, which he estimates as accounting for as much as $750 billion per year (in the mid 1990s). It is also because these funds create a usually ignored link between the most advanced centers of the global economy and some of its least developed, say, coca farmers in Colombia and poppy cultivators in Afghanistan. These links not only connect the two extremes of the global economy, but through them the criminal economy and the excluded regions make their way back into the financial markets, "the backbone of the global economy": "where they amplify the speculative turbulences."[24] This is a crucial empirical element underpinning a core tenet of Castells's analysis. Due to the interconnected nature of the global economy, even the seemingly disconnected areas are an important part without which the whole cannot be understood. It is in fact only because of this "perverse connection" of excluded regions through the criminal economy that it is justified, in Castells's eyes, to speak of a global economy. Otherwise we would have a global economy which included only a minority of people and places.

These five trends have transformed the financial markets. They were once mainly a source of capital for industrial development, bound by relatively strict rules, vertically segmented and operating predominantly on a national scale. They are now a globally integrated machine, which operates beyond the control of even the most powerful institutions, largely following its own internal impulses.

Castells is very explicit on this point. He calls the global financial markets an "automaton" and fears that

> humankind's nightmare of seeing our machines taking control of our world seems on the edge of becoming a reality – not in the form of robots that eliminate jobs, or government computers that police our lives, but as an electronically based system of financial transactions. The system overwhelms the controls and regulations put in place [and] has established itself as a collective capitalist. Its logic is not controlled by any capitalist or corporation – nor, for that matter by any public institution. While capitalists, and capitalist managers still exist, they are all determined by the Automaton. And this Automaton is not the market. It does not follow market rules.[25]

It is not that the market performance of companies no longer matters, or that it is all a postmodern matter of perception. What companies actually do is still important. But it is only one of a myriad of factors determining the movement of capital financial markets. They are equally affected by speculation, herd behavior, and what Castells calls "information turbulences": the unpredictable encounter of multiple streams of information, independent in origin, but interacting in the unifying matrix of global investors. The ensuing dynamics are not following the supply and demand of underlying assets, but a "logic of chaotic complexity."[26] An example of this is the financial crisis of the late 1990s. It affected many economies, such as Thailand, Russia, and Brazil, whose fundamentals were rather different but which all belonged to the category of "emergent markets." Even though this category was created artificially only a few years ago by investment bankers to sell new types of investments, it nevertheless powerfully affected the realities of millions of people outside the financial markets. Similarly, the bursting of the dot.com bubble, which soured global investors in relation to the misunderstood promises of the internet and its "new economy," affected many companies that were economically healthy but happened to be in that same category ("tech stocks") being suddenly dumped by analysts and investors. In order to operate in an environment that is subject to such chaotic turbulences, companies need to be extremely flexible. The difficulties experienced by vertically integrated corporations in achieving such flexibility created the need to develop new organizational forms of production, contributing decisively to the transformation of capitalism.

The Network Enterprise

Private firms, relentlessly searching for profit, are the main engine of the restructuring of the economy. As the crisis of the 1970s revealed, established ways of organizing business were becoming less and less profitable.[27] Competitive pressures mounted, accelerating the search for new markets, new products, and new organizational forms to increase productivity. As we have seen, the search for new markets was one of the dynamics that led to the internationalization of the economy. Another was the development of new organizational forms capable of operating under the new market conditions. Castells's account of this process is basically "post-Fordist," though he modifies and extends the analysis in particular ways. The theory of post-Fordism centers around the observation that the crisis of the 1970s affected most deeply a particular type of business, namely "the large corporation, structured on the principles of vertical integration, and institutional, technical and social division of labor."[28] This type of business organization was epitomized by assembly line production in huge industrial complexes pioneered by Henry Ford (hence Fordism). The paradigm of Fordism was not specific to capitalism. It was also characteristic of industrial organization in most Communist countries. As Castells reminds us, Ford and Lenin were both inspired by F. W. Taylor's approach to the "scientific organization of work."

As became painfully manifest during the 1970s, this type of organization encountered increasing difficulties in managing the rising complexities of advanced industrial processes and emerging global markets. Importantly, as Castells stresses, this crisis of Fordism occurred under statism (the Soviet Union and its allies) and under capitalism at the same time for roughly the same reason. However, only capitalism was able to overcome the structural crisis of industrialism. Statism, on the other hand, stagnated for much of the 1970s, and then collapsed when attempting a belated reform in the late 1980s. In the West, a new type of business organization emerged, less hierarchical, more modular, and thus much more flexible. These organizations were able to react to and exploit the opportunities of fast changing markets. From the mid 1980s onwards, economic theory interpreted this development as a transformation from "mass production" to "flexible production," or from a "Fordist" to a "post-Fordist" paradigm of business organization.[29]

The focus of this type of perspective is on how business is organized (*mode of development*), rather than on the social character of this organization (*mode of production*). Thus it stresses change and discontinuities within capitalism, whereas Marxist accounts focus on the continuation of basic capitalist principles.[30] This focus on the transition from mass to flexible production has often been extended to diagnosing the crisis of the large corporations as such. Due to their size, they were deemed to be unable to move as swiftly as the new global, increasingly deregulated and integrated markets demanded. Small firms, it was argued, were more sensitive to changing market conditions which could not be controlled, not even by large corporations. This extension of the argument, however, Castells stresses, does not stand up to empirical scrutiny.

As importantly, though less visibly, it was not only large, Fordist corporations that came under pressure, but also independent small firms, despite their greater ability to adapt to changing market conditions. What they were lacking was the ability to successfully enter the new global markets, a venture demanding resources far beyond their reach.

The transformation of the organizational structure of the firm, then, has been taking place at both ends of the scale. It affected small firms as much as it did large and resource-rich corporations. In the process, Castells stresses, older forms of business organization have reemerged. In particular, family-based business networks, which had been pushed aside by industrial forms of organization, have been making a comeback, supported by advanced information technology. The most powerful example is the growth of family-based Chinese business networks, initially in Hong Kong, and now also in mainland China.

The incorporation of information technology, Castells argues – quite in line with much business literature – has been of fundamental importance to this process of organizational restructuring for companies of all scales. Yet, contrary to that literature, he is adamant that it was not caused by it. Rather, "organizational change happened, independently of technological change, as a response to the need to cope with a constantly changing operational environment. Yet, once it started to take place, the feasibility of organizational change was extraordinarily enhanced by new information technologies."[31]

The main trajectory of this organizational change has been to combine the flexibility of small firms, adapted to cope with continuous change, with the reach and resources of major corporations, able to exploit the economies of scale offered by global markets. This has been the general trend, because the strategy employed by every kind of firm follows the same trajectory: creating flexible networks capable of coordinating its constitutive elements in real time, across distances, according to changing tasks and opportunities. This trend can be observed across and within firms of all sizes. It connects major, competing multinationals to one another (through functionally limited, strategic alliances); it connects small companies to one another; and it connects small companies to large corporations for the provision of specialized goods and services. In large corporations, this restructuring is being carried out by internally transforming what were once vertical departments into horizontal operational units. In the process, these new units are given more flexibility and responsibility (by turning them, for example, into individually accountable "profit centers").

Of course, within large corporations, these units are not entirely independent. They remain aligned with the overall corporate strategy. However, the horizon in which they operate is not the corporation. The individual units are no longer primarily oriented toward other units within the same corporation, but are actively cooperating – always with the overarching goal of improving their own competitiveness, and ultimately profitability – with other units, whether they are part of the same or another large corporation, or independent small and medium-sized businesses. The transformation in the organization of production, Castells writes, "can be characterized as the shift from vertical bureaucracies to the horizontal corporation."[32] One of the most important consequences of this pattern of flexible cooperation is that production is no longer contained within one firm. Rather "the actual operational unit in our economies is the business project, operated by ad hoc business networks."[33]

Here we are at the core of Castells's justification for claiming the emergence of a new, informational economy. He writes, "global production of goods and services, increasingly, is not performed by multinational corporations, but by transnational production networks, of which multinational corporations are an essential part, yet a component which could not operate without the rest of the network."[34]

In other words, multinational corporations remain the strategic command centers of the global economy. Yet actual production is carried out through a diverse network of operational units, some belonging to the same corporate structure, some to competitors, and others nominally independent. Yet they are all functionally integrated on the basis of ad hoc needs and opportunities. How these different components are strung together depends less on the corporate hierarchy than on the particulars of the task to be carried out. This is why the productive unit is no longer the firm but the network, which is composed of parts of multiple firms. However, this does not mean the firm is somehow obsolete. Far from that, it remains the accounting unit, the legal unit, the place of employment (except for the self-employed), and crucially in a capitalist economy, the place of accumulation. Managing these different units, which are often locally dispersed, is complex, requiring sophisticated information technology and specialized services. Consequently, in Castells's account of contemporary capitalism, the rise of service occupations is not interpreted as a decline of manufacturing (as postindustrialism suggested), but as an indicator of a new, informational production process.

Using concepts such as "horizontal corporation," "e-business," or "e-enablement," Castells's analysis exhibits a clear affinity to management-oriented perspectives, as many critics have noted. Castells's adoption of the managerial view of the firm is directly related to his focus on the transformation of forms. Like managers, he takes what is being done in a firm (accumulation of profits) for granted and concentrates on how this is being done. The affinity between the two perspectives becomes obvious in Castells's identification of Cisco as the "archetypical expression" of the network enterprise.[35] Cisco has long been a darling of management theory, and Castells does not add much detail to the well-publicized story of a company focused on the beginning (research and development) and the end (sales and services) of the production cycle, while outsourcing the actual manufacturing process to the cheapest bidder. The entire process is connected by means of information technology, which defines how the different elements can interact. This approach is no longer unique to Cisco, and Castells argues that "the global networked business model, pioneered by Cisco, seems to have become . . . the predominant model for the most successful competitors in most industries around the world."[36] Out of this general trend Castells develops the ideal type of a network enterprise. He defines it as the

> organizational form built around business projects resulting from cooperation of different components of different firms, networking

amongst themselves for the duration of a given project, and reconfiguring their networks for the implementation of each project.[37]

The crucial point in this definition is that the network enterprise is not the same as what Geoff Mulgan identified in the early 1990s as a trend toward "firms like networks and networks of firms."[38] A network enterprise is less and more than this. It is less than an entire company, because it often involves only parts of it. It is more than one company because it is comprised of parts of multiple firms.

As with all ideal types the issue is less whether this is the perfect definition, but rather whether this general definition is useful in analyzing a variety of cases across different contexts. This is necessary, because for Castells social organizations never exist in the abstract, but always in concrete forms, created by people and reflecting their particular cultural experiences and resources. Consequently, there are different types of network enterprises which all fit into the above definition, yet realize these properties in distinct ways. Besides the American type, epitomized by Cisco and Silicon Valley more generally, Castells distinguishes a Japanese version (based on mutual ownership of companies), a Korean form (highly hierarchized and centrally owned), and a Chinese type of network (based on family ownership).[39] He also observes a distinctly Finnish type of network enterprise (with a mix of private and public elements).[40] None of these different types of network enterprises can be said to be more advanced than the others. There is no one leading example that others need to strive to emulate.[41] Yet they all fit the general ideal type. Here, in the area of business organization, Castells gives substance to his assertion of the emergence of a new social morphology which is simultaneously global and culturally specific.

Due to the affinity with management-oriented discourses, Castells has been accused of being too uncritical, or even apologetic, in his conception of the network enterprise.[42] He focuses on management favorites such as "efficiency" and "flexibility." The inefficiencies of corporate alliances are never mentioned. Yet a study of the performance of alliances in the airline industry – an industry with 401 alliances in 1995 – estimated that fewer than 40 percent of regional alliances and fewer than 30 percent of international alliances should be considered successes.[43] Furthermore, Castells's particular ideal type also has little to say about the persistence of hierarchies within supposedly flat organizations. According to Heiskala's criticism:

Castells's analysis of what he calls the network enterprise falls short because he is not able to distinguish between networks of equal co-operation between partners and networks that are actually hierar-chical chains, for example, of subcontractors of a multinational corporation. That is why his discussion of the network enterprise often ends up reproducing mantras borrowed from business consul-tants instead of analyzing the structures of economic power.[44]

This critique is a too harsh, though. For one thing, Castells is quite clear that domination and exploitation are not alien to the network form of organization. Rather, social polarization, as discussion of Castells's analysis of labor will elaborate, is shown to be endemic to this form of organization. Yet this critique is also not entirely unjustified. While Castells is obviously cognizant of the power dif-ferentials, he remains somewhat contradictory on this point. Focus-ing on morphology, he argues that production is characterized by "vertical disintegration of production along a network of firms . . . without necessarily altering the pattern of concentration of indus-trial power and technological innovation."[45]

Here the analysis gets a bit confusing, due to Castells's tendency to pack too many different issues under the same, very general headings. He seems to be arguing one thing and its opposite. How can we speak of a disintegration of production when it does not change the concentration of industrial power? The key difficulty Castells faces here is how to integrate two empirical observations featuring prominently in his work. On the one hand, the transna-tional character of production, where a single product, say a Nike sneaker, moves in the production process across multiple locations and firms. This is the very core of his definition of the network enterprise. On the other hand, there is the very obvious concentra-tion of the head offices and profits of multinational corporations in the G8 countries.

Castells's argument is the following: In order to cut costs and be able to take advantage of fast-moving markets, multinationals have been decentralizing production. However, in order to achieve maximum effect, they have been increasing the ability of manage-ment to leverage the expanded productive capacity in *real time*. This has two effects. On the one hand, the corporations are becoming ever more enmeshed in their environment. A myriad of relation-ships to subcontractors, consultants, and strategic partners extend the reach of the corporations. It is increasingly difficult to draw a boundary around these entities. As a consequence, even "the large corporation in such an economy is not, and will no longer be, self-contained and self-sufficient."[46] On the other hand, in order to able to survive in the ultracompetitive global markets, the leading corporations need to become bigger, and control is centralized. They need very significant resources to invest in research and development of new products (be it through scientific or market research). Perhaps even more importantly, they need very significant resources to be able to sell these products throughout the entire market within ever shorter timespans. The economies of scale are still with us, perhaps more than ever. Yet not even the biggest corporation is big enough to go it alone; hence there is a pattern of strategic partnerships among the leading corporations in the various markets. This marks an unmistakable tendency toward "oligopolistic concentration . . . not only in spite but because of the networked form of organization. This is because entry into the strategic networks requires either considerable resources, or an alliance with a major player in the network."[47]

Whether all of this amounts to a new, profoundly changed organizational environment, or just to an upgrading of the old oligopolistic tendency of industrial capitalism on a global scale, rests ultimately on how one judges what is perhaps Castells's boldest, and most controversial, claim in this area: "Overall, the networks are asymmetrical, but each single element of the network can hardly survive by itself or impose a diktat. *The logic of the network is more powerful than the powers in the network.*"[48]

What this means is the following: The various firms in the different markets – R&D, manufacturing, marketing and sales – which now constitute the production process are more powerful together than even the largest corporation by itself. Consequently, even the biggest actors are dependent for their own survival on their ability to cooperate within networks they cannot control. There is a contradiction here in Castells's argument. On the one hand, he stresses the "out-of-control" nature of the global economy due to its networked form of organization, yet he also sees this as responsible for a development toward "oligopolistic concentration." I will return to this contradiction toward the end of this chapter. But first, we turn to the final area that makes up Castells's analysis of informational capitalism: the changing realities of labor.

Individualization of Labor

The network enterprise as the embodiment of the new logic of global production and management is characterized by working conditions distinctly different from those of industrial firms. The issue is not the shift in employment from manufacturing to services.[49] Castells, as already mentioned, dismisses this analysis, because "the assumption of postindustrial theory that the advanced countries would specialize in service economies and the less advanced countries would specialize in agriculture and manufacturing has been rejected by historical experience."[50] Equally untenable is the popular thesis of "the end of work" through automation.[51] On the contrary, due to the massive incorporation of women into the *paid* workforce around the world, labor markets have actually expanded, nationally and worldwide.

Consequently, the transformation of work as a dimension of the informational economy needs to be located elsewhere. Castells's starting point is the observation that "the traditional form of work, based on full-time employment, clear-cut occupational assignments, and a career pattern over the life-cycle is being slowly but surely eroded away."[52] Consequently, the relevant indicators for the new conditions of labor are the flexibilization and individualization of work. Flexibilization increases along four dimensions: *working time* (more part-time, more overtime, less standardized working hours), *job stability* (employment is increasingly project oriented without long-term commitment on either side), *location* (people move more in the job), *social relationships between employer and employee* (decline of the old "social contract" where stability and social benefits provided by the employer were matched by the employee's loyalty to the firm).

Individualization of work is directly related to the new flexibility of work, but is experienced differently. On the one hand, due to the decentralization of the production process, different people involved in the various stages of an integrated production process are becoming disconnected from one another. Even though different groups of workers might be employed, directly or indirectly, by the same company, they no longer experience themselves as a coherent group. On the other hand, people who actually work directly together might no longer be employed by the same company, but be only temporarily collaborating on the same project. As Castells concludes, "the new model of global production and management is tantamount to the simultaneous integration of work process and disintegration of the workforce."[53]

The increasing flexibility and individualization of work, which can be observed on all steps of the occupational ladder, create very different realities for different segments of the workforce. Castells divides them into two groups. One he calls the "core labor force," the other the "disposable labor force." The core labor force provides what Castells calls "informational" or "self-programmable" labor, whereas the other, actually the majority of people, provides "generic" labor.[54] Across a survey of different trends that are multivaried to the point of being confusing, Castells's most general observation on the social consequences of this highly flexible and individualized labor market is that of a trend toward a polarization between generic and informational labor. The difference between informational and generic labor provides the basis for the new system of stratification characteristic of the informational economy. It is replacing, Castells seems to imply, the previous cleavage between capital and labor which characterized the industrial economy. The core labor force has changed its orientation and now sides with management and capital, condemning the generic workforce to political marginality (despite the fact that it is the actual majority). While there might still be something like a working class *by itself* it is no longer *for itself*.

Generic labor is provided by workers "who do not have special skills . . . other than those necessary to execute instructions by management."[55] They are not necessarily without responsibility or skills, but the skills do not depend on the particular abilities of the person and they do not improve over time. Generic workers do not increase their qualifications in the work process and experience gained counts for little, effectively locking them into a trajectory of unstable, poorly paid, dull jobs, always competing with the most recent entries into the work process. Security guards are an example of (semi-)skilled but generic labor. Others would include people working in call centers, low-level service and clerical occupations, and, of course, the classic factory job (now often located in developing countries). Much generic labor can be automated, outsourced, or located offshore, depending on the vagaries of business strategies. Given the global realities of production, working conditions at the low end of the scale, particularly in the advanced countries, have deteriorated under informational capitalism. There is a global race to the bottom, powerfully symbolized by the reappearance of "sweatshops," even in the most developed economies.[56]

For the "core labor force" the record is more mixed. For one thing, they have the crucial skills: the ability to organize innovation by creating and applying knowledge in whatever domain they happen to work. For Castells, they are the prime creator of economic surplus, because "innovation trumps production" as the source of value creation. Their skills are far more complex and scarce; hence they experience less competition from providers of low wage labor, and the threat to them of automation is less pronounced. Additionally, since they often depend on a large and complex infrastructure, these jobs are less mobile.[57] Consequently, as a general rule, their working conditions have improved. Second, given this higher level of skills, they receive more on-the-job training since it can be cheaper to retrain them than to hire new people, which might always be feasible, since certain skills are not readily available. In comparative terms, in the context of a general flexibilization, their job stability is still relatively high. At the upper end of the scale, flexibility can mean a more humane, because less routinized, work environment that demands, and rewards, a wider range of human cognitive abilities. In addition, the complex world of outsourcing and partnerships has increased the opportunities for small businesses, where the main employees are often also the owners, creating, for the most fortunate ones, a "historical revival of work autonomy."[58]

Yet even the core labor force is put under increased pressure by the "hardening of the capitalist logic." For example, the age span during which even highly skilled people are recruited into the core labor force is shrinking. Middle-aged workers, once laid off, not only face longer periods of unemployment than their younger counterparts, but they also are often forced to accept more precarious employment conditions and lower wages as a condition for reentry into the labor market. As a general trend, connecting the low end to the high end, the position of labor in relation to capital (management) has been weakened. It has resulted in "a world of winners and losers, but, more often than not, uncertain winners and losers who have no return to the network."[59]

Castells makes an at times tenuous distinction between those characteristics that are intrinsic to the informational economy, and others which are a consequence of public policy rather than business organization. The distinction corresponds roughly to the difference between the *mode of development* and the *mode of production*. Flexibilization of work is a direct consequence of new organizational patterns. The network enterprise is by definition flexible and so is the workplace it provides. Income polarization, on the other hand, is the consequence of the restructuring of capital–labor relations within the framework set by the state. Deregulation, the increased mobility of capital, and the flexibility of the production process tilted the scales in favor of capital. This was often, first in the UK and the US, achieved under heavy political pressure. Labor conditions have also worsened, because unions everywhere were unable to respond to the new composition of the workforce (more women and immigrants), attract the new (clerical) workers, and adapt to the transnational organization of production. As a consequence, whereas "capital is globally coordinated, labor is individualized."[60] Yet this is not intrinsic to the informational economy. For Castells, the case of Finland illustrates that it is possible to combine a collective, social welfare state with an individualized, globally competitive informational economy.[61] The difference is not to be found in the economy itself – which is as advanced, as networked, and as flexible as elsewhere – but in the conditions created by the state, reflecting historically determined values, shared by its constituency, the citizens.

Informational Capitalism: Critical Issues

Castells's account of the development of the informational economy proceeds along these four dimensions: trade, finance, business organization, and work. Each follows its own internal logic, yet they are profoundly related because of "the emergence of information processing as the core, fundamental activity conditioning the effectiveness of all processes of production, distribution, consumption and management."[62] Castells's theory of the informational economy shows very convincingly how common characteristics in all of these domains rely on the same processes of restructuring that have, indeed, created a new form of capitalism. Informational capitalism is distinctive because in its key dimensions it has a *global reach*, a *network structure*, and, enabling all of this, an *informational character*. Not all is global – particularly work remains predominantly local or regional – but the core activities of production, management and distribution, affecting all others, are global, in the sense that "they have the capacity to work as a unit in real time, or chosen time, on a planetary scale."[63] In order to achieve this, most of the leading producers in all domains – multinational corporations, service providers, scientific communities, or organized crime – have (re)organized themselves into networks with global linkages. It is only through their development of this new organizational morphology that they are able to combine a planetary reach with high flexibility, both of which are necessary to successfully operate in a global environment characterized by never-ending change and relentless competition.

The informational character stems from two facts. In the first place, global networks can only be organized at the current speed and degree of complexity through the incorporation of advanced information technology. Organized competently, they are able to operate in this environment more efficiently than other forms of organization, hence stepping up the pressure on others to reorganize themselves in the same manner. Yet, at the same time, the exponentially growing complexity increases the costs of organizing these processes. As the scale doubles, the possibilities square. This leads to the second feature. The main competitive advantages are not gained through fine-tuning old processes – the "lean production" model of the 1980s – but through qualitative changes in the productive process itself. Only continuous reorganization of processes allows the containment of the costs of organizing the ever changing, and ever increasing, complexities of production. Hence, the relentless search for new managerial models, scientific breakthroughs, synergies, and tie-ins. The goal is to produce more efficiently, for larger markets, and with faster turnovers. In order to control consumption, it is necessary to penetrate popular consciousness more deeply through intensive marketing campaigns. These are research-heavy undertakings, and consequently "the productivity and competitiveness of units or agents in this economy ... depend on their capacity to generate, process and apply efficiently knowledge-based information."[64]

With this account of the transformation of nationally bounded, vertically integrated corporations toward network enterprises operating in a highly dynamic global environment, Castells goes significantly beyond accounts of postindustrialism and post-Fordism. His argument for a "new economy" rests on the transformation of the organizational structure of capitalism, for both management and labor. The factor that makes all the difference is the superior productivity of the network enterprise as compared to vertically integrated, hierarchical models of organization. Competitive pressures diffuse this model, creating the global, multicultural reality of the informational economy.

Castells is on very solid ground here. The problems with his informational capitalism lie elsewhere. There is the difficulty we have already encountered twice: his implicit claim that the economy, both at the level of the global financial markets and at the level of networked production, is for all practical purposes beyond anyone's control, and, one must assume, on autopilot. The global markets, Castells concludes, are a chaotic system, whose properties are emergent, rather than designed. I will return to this point at length in final chapter. The second problem is that the analysis of the restructuring process is surprisingly incomplete. Castells focuses on the development of new markets and new forms of business organization. He analyzes their consequences in terms of the international division of labor and the individualization of labor. In these aspects, Castells's key thesis, the development of a new social morphology, is convincingly substantiated for the global economy. However, Castells's analytical project goes beyond the study of morphology. He claims to present an analysis of informational capitalism as a whole. What is missing is the development of new informational products, based on the creation of new forms of intellectual property, and a sustained analysis of the societal dynamics created by these new property claims.

Controlled chaos?

While Castells is not as radical as, say, Kevin Kelly, former editor-in-chief of *Wired* magazine, in stating that the economy is "out of control," this is suggested by his analysis of informational capitalism at least by implication.[65] The financial markets, as we have seen, are characterized as an "automaton" – driven by self-generated "information turbulences." Moreover, Castells maintains, the unpredictable character of the fast changing global markets makes it impossible for a global capitalist class to emerge, or at least has prevented it happening so far. Why? Because, Castells argues, there is an inverse relationship between control on the micro level and control on the macro level. He is categorical that

> managers control specific corporations and specific segments of the global economy, but they do not control, and do not even know about, the actual, systemic movements of capital in the networks of the financial flows, of knowledge in the information system, of strategies in the multifaceted network enterprises.[66]

Here, Castells points to what Geoff Mulgan once called the "control paradox." It is, Mulgan says,

> most visible in the financial sector where heavy investment in technologies designed to enhance the predictability and responsiveness has been blamed for exacerbating instability: when a multitude of different and competing actors seek to improve their control

capacities, the result at the level of the system is a breakdown of control. What is rational at the micro level becomes highly irrational at the macro level.[67]

As a result of this irrationality at the macro level, individual capitalists are effectively dominated by a "faceless collective capitalist," the global financial markets. These are viewed as a self-organizing system. They are a source of action – ranging from the enforcement of an imperative of relentless profit maximization, to information turbulences, bubbles, and crashes – but they are not, in a sociological sense, an actor. Capitalists are socially heterogeneous, globally distributed, and economically as much affected by the automaton as everyone else. Thus, Castells concludes, while there are global capitalists, "there is not, sociologically speaking, such a thing as a global capitalist class."[68] Indeed, the power of the out-of-control financial markets is viewed to be so significant that capitalists are "randomly incarnated" depending on who happens to win in the "global casino." "This scenario suggests," as Frank Webster points out, "that it is the accountants, system analysts, financiers, account investors, advertisers, etc. who run capitalism today."[69] And all they can do is skillfully administer, rather than steer or even control.

There are three things worth differentiating here. First there is the argument that the global economy, epitomized by the financial markets, is a chaotic system operating without central control. This is an uncontroversial suggestion, but only *from the point of view of individual market participants*. No individual actor, or group of actors, has control over the financial markets, not George Soros, once the most notorious of global speculators, not Alan Greenspan, the influential chairman of the US Federal Reserve Board. They may, in exceptional instances, exert substantial short term influence, but they cannot control market development. The sheer number of market participants, trying to outfox each other, makes this impossible. Castells's conclusion that individual market participants cannot control markets is empirically well grounded in the analysis of the internationalization of economy and the networked character of its organization. So far so good.

The matter is more difficult with Castells's second conclusion, that there is no such thing as a global capitalist class. The problem with this assertion is that it is not supported by any significant empirical research – even though it is a silent, yet sharp, departure from his earlier analysis. In 1991, focusing on the restructuring of New York City, he wrote:

The postindustrial era is no exception to the proposition that any epoch is characterized by the emergence of a dominant class (in his case, the managerial technocracy allied to the global financial elite) ... The new dominant class dominates the space of flows by having exclusive access to the most important information and by deploying powerholding organizations in these networks, which enable them, in theory, to execute unilateral decisions regarding the commitment of resources from any location.[70]

Fully consistent with his analysis that capital is coordinated but that labor is individualized, he concluded at the time that "an international-informational dominant class, supported by the upper professionals, has been formed, while the subordinate classes have been disorganized and their isolation reinforced."[71] What has changed in the intervening half-decade? Why was it justified to speak of an "international-informational dominant class" in 1991, but not in 1996? There is nothing in Castells's empirical analysis to suggest a sharp discontinuity. This shift in argument can also not be attributed to a cleaning out of the last vestiges of his Marxist legacy. By 1991, Castells was using the concept of class "in the Weberian sense to designate the social actors who, through the confrontation between their projects and interests, produce social values and political institutions."[72]

In this perspective, the empirically relevant questions would be: are there social values specific to a global (economic) elite, and are these values expressed in social institutions that are relevant to the global economy? If so, it would be justifiable to speak of a global capitalist class. Unfortunately, we find very little in the analysis of informational capitalism that could provide a basis for addressing these issues. In the revised edition of *The Rise of the Network Society* there is a brief section on "the political economy of globalization," in which Castells points out that "the mechanism to bring in the globalization process to most countries was simple: political pressure."[73] However, this small section contains no original research, and is poorly integrated into the overall argument. Thus it remains unclear how this political pressure was applied, or who applied it.

In terms of shared values, the first dimension of a Weberian class analysis, it seems reasonable to suggest as a hypothesis that there are cultural elements and sociopolitical values that are specific to the global elite. For example, the leading business schools of the world, all aiming at the same set of well-off students, play an important role not only in education, but also in creating the personal networks and a global business culture that permeate international institutions and gatherings. There is a famous joke that the World Bank is made up of people from a hundred countries who have attended six universities. Events such as the World Economic Forum, held annually in Davos, Switzerland, are politically ineffective. There is no world government. Their real value is cultural. They strengthen the social networks of the global elite. Vanity will hardly be the only reason why people, who are under high pressure to deliver results, attend such meetings. Rather, the events support what Castells calls the "social cohesion" and "cultural distinctiveness" of the global elite.

This is expressed, for example, in a common analysis of global affairs and political strategies. For much of the 1990s, the global consensus supported "free trade," implemented often against considerable resistance from local populations. Since the terrorist attacks of 2001, a new rough consensus has been established, supporting a renewed authoritarianism to fight the "war on terrorism." These common values are significant inasmuch as they are embodied in social institutions, the second dimension of Weber's definition of class. The most prominent embodiment of the free trade dogma is the World Trade Organization (WTO), founded in 1996 after years of negotiation. The creation of the WTO can be seen as a watershed event, which institutionalized and thus sharply increased the importance of trade issues for international, and even national, policy development. Unless we take free trade to be natural and self-evidently positive, which Castells clearly does not, the question remains crucial as to whose values such organizations represent. Leslie Sklair, based on empirical research on the tobacco industry, argues for the existence of a "transnational capitalist class" comprised of four main fractions: owners and controllers of transnational corporations and their local affiliates; globalizing bureaucrats and politicians; globalizing professionals (consultants); and consumerist elites (merchants and media).[74] Despite their obvious heterogeneity and global distribution, he argues that their interests are connected for the same reasons that Castells argues that the global economy is an integrated system. The point here is not to claim that there exists a fully fledged global capitalist class. Sklair's analysis is not without problems, not least because the tobacco industry is a rather biased choice as a representative of the global economy. At issue is the fact that, in the absence of solid knowledge, this question must be treated as open. It requires substantial empirical research. Castells does not offer much, yet he still draws very strong conclusions.

This particular lack of empirical research leads to the third aspect of Castells's problematic view of the global economy as a chaotic system. While there are important aspects of the economy that are fairly chaotic *as experienced by actors in the markets*, a substantial body of rules and regulations has been created over the last decade. They are the framework in which global markets constitute themselves. Like all rules and regulations, they are purposely designed. Over the last 30 years, the number of international organizations regulating the global economy has multiplied, establishing a dense regulatory regime centering around the WTO. While one can argue about the precise extent of their influence, it is very problematic to simply leave these organizations out of the analysis of informational capitalism. Yet this is exactly what Castells does. Despite his great emphasis on case studies, there is not a single study of any aspect of this emerging regulatory framework: neither of a governmental or private institution, nor of an international treaty. However, an analysis of these institutions, and of the processes through which they arrive at enforceable rules, would be necessary for a comprehensive account of informational capitalism. It would allow us to address the question of how the global economy consists, at one and the same time, of self-organizing and of purposefully designed dynamics. Castells's analysis is very one-sided in this respect. We are presented with a lot of adaptation to abstract dynamics and competitive pressures, but little purposeful design and with virtually no designers. I will return to this point in the discussion of Castells's conception of power. For now, let us turn to the second problematic aspect of Castells's theory of informational capitalism.

Information as a product?

In Castells's account of the information age, there is surprisingly little about how to understand "information." No general definition is provided. This is perhaps prudent as such definitions are notoriously abstract.[75] To skip a general definition is not a problem per se, as Castells's focus is more precise. He rarely speaks of information as such, but usually about "knowledge-based information." It is the latter that is the differentiating factor in the informational economy. But what is knowledge-based information? Here, too, Castells offers no formal definition, but he treats it quite consistently, so it might be justifiable to infer one. Knowledge-based information consists of codified, formal knowledge that can be applied in the pursuit of a concrete goal. In this sense, it is information about how to organize processes. It may lead to new ways of organizing production, improved algorithms for automating trading in the financial markets, the establishment of a tax shelter, a better way to manipulate genes, a new drug for suppressing the virus in HIV/Aids, or to more effective marketing strategies.

Surprisingly, though, Castells rarely treats information as a product in itself. By contrast with technology, he does not inquire how it is produced or how it is turned into a commodity. There is an extensive body of literature on the "commodification of information," usually from the perspective of political economy.[76] Castells barely mentions it. Yet such a perspective, as Bob Jessop argues, could help to

> understand "information" as both collectively generated knowledge and abstract intellectual property, as both social source of creativity and substitutable factor of production, and as both use-value and exchange-value. Posed in these terms we need to consider how information and knowledge came to be transformed into commodities and continue to be so transformed on an increasing scale . . . and the consequences of such appropriation for economic performance and economic justice.[77]

As something to be applied to value-generating processes, knowledge-based information appears primarily for its use value in Castells's account of the economy. While this is certainly important, it is hardly its only function in the informational economy. Increasingly, information itself, rather than just the material products, or the services, embodying it, is being treated as a commodity. In order to achieve this, fluid, collectively generated knowledge is turned into fixed, private property, which then can be exchanged in the market like other goods. The mechanism for this transformation is intellectual property law, most importantly copyright law and the patent system. Their critical role is widely and controversially discussed in the economic, legal, and sociological literature. It is also a key area of international treaty-making, carried out in well-established international institutions such as the World Intellectual Property Organization (WIPO). At the same time, it is a powerful dynamic in the ongoing overhaul of national legislation. These are not obscure issues. Rather, in the last decade, they have exploded into major political debates and battles, creating distinctly new political fault lines and coalitions in areas as diverse as science, public health, software development, civil liberties, international relations, agriculture, cultural industries, and many more. There is, indeed, virtually no aspect of the informational economy in which questions of intellectual property and access to knowledge-based information play no role.

This is not the place for a discussion of the role of intellectual property law in shaping the new global economy. What has to be noted, however, is that Castells has very little to say about it. A few disjointed remarks here and there, but no sustained treatment, no empirical study, whether of the processes by which a new legal and economic landscape is being created, or of its consequences in any of the areas mentioned above. In fact, the two main issues in Castells's economic analysis might relate to one another. The rise of new intellectual property regimes – based on WIPO's 1996 Copyright Treaty and the WTO's Agreement on Trade-Related Aspects of Intellectual Property Rights (TRIPS, 1994) – is increasingly seen as very central to the shaping of the structure of the global, informational economy. Peter Drahos, for example, in a detailed empirical study of the processes leading to the TRIPS agreement, shows the extremely narrow range of actors who were able to inscribe, almost literally, their interest into this treaty.[78] In fact, the number of actors was so small that Drahos was able to personally interview half of them! What Drahos concludes is that the emerging global intellectual property regime facilitates the formation of new, global informational cartels, giving the dominant players structural advantages which make it in effect close to impossible for new participants to enter the markets. At the same time, these international treaties are profoundly shaping the evolution of national legislation, across the globe, to favor these well-organized interests. All this in the name of free trade and open markets. In effect, this is not entirely different from Castells's "tendency towards oligopolistic concentration," but here it is not analyzed as a property somehow inherent in the networked form of organization, but as resulting from the political will of identifiable actors and an effectively coordinated strategy. In Drahos's account, there is little chaos but a lot of deliberate design in laying down the ground rules of the new economy, which then works like an automaton.

Whether this amounts to "control" over and "power" in the global economy, or whether these are just feeble attempts at regulating what cannot be regulated largely depends on how these terms are defined. Are control and self-organization, design and emergence, contradictory concepts or can they coexist? Castells uses these terms in ways that are particularly unsuited to grasping such processes in networks, a point which I will develop in the chapter focusing on Castells's conception of power. For now, it is enough to note that Castells offers little conceptualization of how a process can be out of control and purposefully designed at the same time. Castells resolves this difficulty by providing an analysis of the global economy that largely ignores the global regulatory framework and the politics shaping it.

Castells's analysis of the informational economy is an impressive achievement for its integrative capacity. Informationalism – the incorporation of the information technological paradigm into all aspects of production and distribution – is shown to transform the character of the economy to such a degree that it is justifiable to speak of a "new economy," despite, or perhaps even because of, the virtually unchallenged dominance of capitalism. Castells's theory of the informational economy is rooted in, but goes substantially beyond the notion of postindustrialism or post-Fordism, by providing a much more nuanced, multicultural account of key economic dynamics. However, its focus on the rise of a new form, the network, creates substantial problems when trying to grasp the political dynamics of the new economy, in particular the emerging system of regulation and control. In Castells's account, economic change is driven by seemingly objective issues such as efficiency and productivity. Normative questions concerning the standards of efficiency, or the values of productivity, have virtually disappeared. They have been relegated to the domain of "experience" to which we will turn now.

3

Experience

"Experience" is the second pillar of Castells's theory of the network society. Or, as he also calls it, the "relationships of experience," emphasizing their analytical position as equal to the "relationships of production." The term experience may be confusing at first, because its definition does not follow common usage. Generally, we take experience to be individual and internal. "Are you experienced?" Jimmi Hendrix once asked, questioning his listeners' (expanded) state of mind. In Castells's account of experience, individuals rarely appear, and their state of mind is something of no concern to him. Or, to be more precise, states of mind are something he puts off-limits, for methodological reasons. In Castells's toolbox of empirical sociology there is little that lends itself to observing what people actually think, or how they experience the world individually. Following his basic epistemological principles, he does not theorize about phenomena he cannot observe. Contrary to the work of, say, Richard Sennett, who shares an interest in the social consequences of the transformations of labor,[1] there is no trace of psychology in Castells's work.[2] Castells remains resolutely focused on groups and structures. Thus he concentrates on what people _say_ about themselves, not individually but collectively, about who they are and what they want from life, and on actions they take in order to advance their goals. Consequently, he defines experience, unusually, as "action of humans on themselves determined by the interaction between their biological and cultural identities."[3] By this, he means the way people give shape and meaning to their own life by drawing on the cultural and biological resources at their disposal.

The main advantage of this very open definition is not just the similarity to production ("action on matter"), but also that it highlights the role of deliberate, collective action within a culturally and biologically grounded framework.

In the following, I will first discuss Castells's notion of social movements as collective actors and thus the subjects of contemporary transformations through the construction of alternative identities. I will then discuss Castells's account of two movements: feminism and religious fundamentalism. I will do so in a fair amount of detail, because it is necessary to make visible the complexity, elegance and reach of Castells's conceptualization of social movements as a constitutive part of contemporary social dynamics, emerging from, and drawing on, the material structure of the network society. As central as social movements are to Castells's account of culture, they are not the only sources of its transformation. Castells highlights also those that are related to the electronic information environment, resulting in what he calls a "culture of real virtuality." It is the articulation of social movements in a culture of real virtuality that underpins Castells's bleak interpretation of a society that could be headed toward a fracturing of cultural codes and a breakdown of social communication. This chapter will conclude with a critique of Castells's theory of social movements, in terms of the particular construction of ideal types, and in terms of the place of social movements in the overall theory of the network society.

Social Movements as Subjects of History

Social movements, in Castells's account, are engines of change in contemporary social life. He echoes Alain Touraine's call for a new conception of social agency which would put "social movements at the center."[4] For such a perspective, though, not all movements are equally relevant. Those seeking to transform the individual – say, nonconflictive religious movements offering spiritual enlightenment – never enter Castells's analysis. In this perspective, what is relevant about the Chinese Falun Dafa movement is how it came to challenge the Communist Party, not its self-advertised "powerful practice to improve body, mind and spirit."

In short, what Castells packs under the broad heading of experience is a focused analysis of oppositional social movements. These have traditionally been studied from the point of view of the grievances they address (focusing on social conflicts), the resources they can mobilize (emphasizing internal organization), the opportunities they provide to participants (in terms of political processes and interaction with the state), or the meaning they create (social psychology).[5] Castells's early work in this domain focused on conflict and the political process,[6] whereas within the theory of the network society, social movements are treated first and foremost as sources of new (collective) identity. However, in this context, this means less a question of psychology than of social institutions. Social movements collapse the distinction between agency and structure. This is highlighted in their definition as "purposive collective action whose outcome, in victory as in defeat, transforms the values and institutions of society."[7]

This definition, brief as it is, contains almost everything that is central to his treatment of social movements. It deserves some unpacking. First, agency is always collective, never individual. This does not mean that individuals cannot or do not act. It is obvious that a social movement would not exist without the people who make it up. However, as long they act solely as individuals, without reference to others acting similarly, they do not form a social movement, even if they act in large numbers. For example, many people cross the street irregularly if traffic permits, yet they do not constitute a "jaywalking movement." A social movement is more than the sum of its parts; rather, it is a new entity, a collective actor. However, collective action alone is not enough. Hooligans rioting after a football game, even though their action is clearly collective, are not regarded as a social movement either. This is because the action, while being aimed at something – fans supporting the opposing team, for example – is not purposive in Castells's sense. Purposive means that the movement has self-defined long-term goals, and that the actions it takes are understood as advancing these goals, within the interpretative framework established by the movement itself.

Thus social movements are self-conscious. They actively present an analysis, of any kind, defining their members and their relationship to relevant outsiders. They put forward a strategy for collective action – sensible within their own particular frame of reference – to improve the conditions of their members. To paraphrase an old Marxian distinction, social movements are always "for themselves," never just "by themselves."[8] For Castells, "there is no social movement without a self-conscious definition by the movement of its own role."[9] This is a theoretical as well as a methodological point. Theoretically it serves to distinguish social movements from other collective action phenomena. Methodologically it defines how to study them. "When understanding a social movement, what is objective is the perception of the actors who constitute the movement."[10] Making this a central conceptual point indicates how far Castells has developed from his early approach as a structural Marxist. The advantage of the new position is that it "takes us away from the hazardous task of interpreting the 'true' consciousness of the movements, as if they could only exist by revealing the real structural conditions."[11]

It is this self-consciousness of the movement in terms of its trajectory, collectively pursued by its participants, that allows Castells, still following Touraine, to see social movements, and not individuals, as the real subjects of the contemporary historical process. He argues that "the subjects [of social transformations] are not individuals, even if they are made by and in individuals. They are the collective actors through which individuals reach holistic meaning in their experience."[12]

The self-consciousness of social movements is critical also in another sense. For Castells, social movements are what they say they are. In terms of individual agency, social theory has traditionally distinguished between subjective and objective factors, between what people intend to do and what they actually do. For Castells, focusing on collective agency, this distinction has no practical relevance. Since social movements attract people on the basis of what they say they are – thus giving meaning to their actions – subjective and objective dimensions of action are combined in what could be called "expressive action." Social movements are defined by themselves and act by themselves, irrespective of whether these definitions appear meaningful to outsiders, or whether their actions have the desired impact. Thus social movements are not the effect of something else. They are, analytically speaking, irreducible. There are no forces behind social movements to be uncovered by the analyst. They are genuine and authentic, in the sense of not being controlled or manufactured by third parties, or being necessary consequences of structural dynamics. Social movements, thus, are autonomous. Not in the sense that they are unconstrained by the larger social context in which they operate, but in the sense that they deal with these constraints creatively, reflecting their own logic and self-selected values. This is why social movements are an engine of change that can only be understood on its own terms, located, analytically, on the same level as production and power, and interacting with – but not derived from – them. This is the second important aspect of Castells's definition.

The third aspect is that the primary issue about social movements is not their success or failure. Rather, the most important point is their very existence. By putting forward an alternative analysis of the present, rallying people around it, and proposing a course of action, they are key engines of social innovation. The very attempt to change social reality transforms it: to varying degrees, depending on the size of the movement and the goals/strategies pursued, but irrespective of whether the goals initially put forward are ever fully realized or not. In this sense, social movements need not be realistic within the dominant framework of "realpolitik." The famous slogan of the French student movement of '68 – "soyez realistes, demandez l'impossible" – is more than a catchy paradox. It is an astute recognition of the specific character of social movements, operating outside the established channels of politics. Castells sees social movements as being primarily about formulating cultural values. Contrary to political parties, they are not about taking over the government or managing social affairs. They are about ends, not means. For example, if the ecological movement is aiming to define a new balance between nature and culture, green parties are working on reforming the tax code to promote ecofriendly investment.

The fourth point encapsulated in Castells's definition of social movements is that they always aim, directly or indirectly, at changing social structure, even though their native territory is culture, not politics or the economy. For Castells, culture is not "just" a set of values or norms shared by a group of people. On the contrary, "cultures manifest themselves fundamentally through their embeddedness in institutions and organizations."[13] This is crucial because it brings together voluntary social action and structural transformation. Social movements center around cultural values, but in order to protect/advance them, existing social institutions need to be changed. In other words, social movements are the subjects of change, the content of their struggles are cultural values, and the object of change are social structures, as represented by specific institutions and organizations, such as heterosexual marriage, a nuclear waste storage facility, or regional self-government.

The final point contained in Castells's definition is that social movements are conflictive and/or oppositional. There is no dominant social movement. If they succeed, they are absorbed into the renewed power structure. Social movements reflect their members' dissatisfaction with the dominant culture and its ways of organizing their lives. They are fueled by the conviction that the aspirations of their participants cannot be fulfilled within the established institutional framework. They advocate "nonmainstream" values. If we take it that cultures are embedded in institutions and organizations, any serious advocacy of alternative values will, sooner or later, need to aim at changing the relevant institutions so that they protect/ enable those values. Sooner or later they will come into conflict with those social groups whose values have been inscribed in the dominant social institutions.

This aspect of Castells approach to social movements becomes clearer when considering how the current definition evolved from earlier ones which put more emphasis on this conflictive aspect. In the 1980s he viewed social movements as "able to produce qualitative change in the [social] system, local culture, and political institutions in *contradiction* to the dominant social interest institutionalized as such at the societal level."[14] A decade before that, he saw social movements not just as being in contradiction to the dominant values materialized in social institutions and organization, but as going directly "against the logic, interests, and values of the dominant class."[15] Any attempt to establish nonmainstream values will end up upsetting the balance of power underpinning social institutions. It challenges the dominant social groups, who will not accommodate newcomers without resistance.

Castells's definition of social movements – collective action self-consciously aimed at changing social structure – has remained deeply Tourainian and largely unchanged over the years. What did change, though, was how he conceptualized the relationship between dominant social institutions and the movements challenging them. Within the 1970s Marxist framework, social institutions reflected the particular class character of their societies. Consequently, social movements under capitalism were seen as anticapitalist because they challenged, if not in spirit, then in effect, the class domination which was thought to manifest itself in all institutions. For some time, Castells put great hopes in social movements as providing not a revolutionary but a "democratic road to socialism," reflecting the experience of the transition to democracy in Spain. But, as discussed earlier, successive instances of empirical research made it impossible to maintain that social movements *per se* were anticapitalist, even if they were oppositional. The fact that they challenged the status quo did not automatically imply that they were challenging capitalism. Social reality turned out to be far more complex and the sources of resistance far more heterogeneous. Consequently Castells broadened his framework. Nevertheless, he continued to view social movements as essentially progressive forces, aimed at transforming dominant, hence well-established and conservative, social institutions. This reflected the "freedom orientation" of the major social movements of the 1960s and 1970s. Yet his assessment of their potential turned pessimistic in the early 1980s. He detected an increasing mismatch between the globalization of the economy and the local character of these movements. Thus in the early 1980s he was no longer hopeful, but concluded that "urban movements do address the real issues of our time, although neither at the scale nor terms adequate to the task. And yet, they do not have any choice, since they are the last reaction to the domination and renewed exploitation that submerges our world."[16]

Things changed again during the 1990s. Castells abandoned the view of social movements as an emancipatory force addressing the "real issues." He now sees them as transformative, aiming at and effecting change of any kind. The fact that they have globalized themselves has increased their potential effectiveness, for better or worse. This new, more ambivalent assessment reflects not only the growth of reactionary/fundamentalist social movements,[17] but also Castells's increasing distance from the political process and generally ambivalent analysis of the social potential of network society.

Social Movements beyond the Local

Social movements have traditionally been understood as local phenomena: concrete forms of protest and civic engagement centering around issues of direct interest to a community whose definition almost always contained a strong geographical element.[18] This also characterized Castells's view until the 1990s. During the 1970s he analyzed "urban social movements" aiming at changing specific aspects of the local urban environment. Issues of "collective consumption" – such as public housing, public transport, and public education – constituted the core of these movements. As such, their character was somewhat ambiguous. On the one hand, Castells saw them as reacting to more fundamental contradictions within capitalism. Hence he understood them as part of radical, if not revolutionary, political struggles. On the other, it was clear that their focus was not the "relationships of production," but the concrete local manifestations of social policies. Consequently, they were addressing local governments as a way to effect local and immediate change. Their cumulative, structural effect was to drive the expansion of the welfare state nationally and internationally in the 1960s and 1970s, though their actions and horizons were usually locally bounded.

Analyzing social movements as predominantly motivated by economic issues (even defined broadly to include social services as "collective consumption") was too narrow a conception to capture complex empirical realities. In *The City and the Grassroots* (1983a) Castells saw social movements as centering around not one, but three major themes:

1 *Collective consumption*, that is goods and services directly or indirectly provided by the state.
2 *Defense of cultural identity*, associated with and organized around a specific *territory*.
3 *Political mobilization*, in relationship to the state, particularly emphasizing the role of *local government*.[19]

While Castells broadened his analysis to include additional issues around which social movements could form, their essentially local character was still taken for granted. Also cultural identity, even in the case of the immigrant cultures, was seen as being local, in fact, usually articulated within a single neighborhood. Only in exceptional circumstances, such as the end of the Franco era in Spain, were the different movements seen as "linking up," though still primarily within one city (for example, Madrid).[20] Even the gay movement was framed through its interaction with a specific local government and its construction of alternative urban spaces (in San Francisco), rather than, say, its appeals to fundamental rights, alternative culture, and solidarity within a translocal community. To be fair, Castells's focus at the time was urban change, so his approach to social movements must be understood within this framework.[21] Yet it is indicative that the economic dimension of urban transformations was characterized, from the beginning, by international trends and pervasive structural changes. Social life, on the other hand, was conceptualized to be primarily locally generated. To some degree this difference reflected the actual, uneven incorporation of technology into society. The economy was becoming interconnected across large distances at least a decade earlier than civil society. Yet, the same time, issues of translocal cultures were already being established as a topic of research.[22] Castells's concentration on the local was also based on the long-held theoretical distinction between structural change, particularly through the concept of the "mode of development," which was seen as translocal and technology driven, and social change, seen as local and nontechnical. There is, for example, in Castells's analysis of gay culture in *The City and the Grassroots* of 1983 no mention of gay media, either in terms of the first gay characters appearing in mainstream media (in the mid 1960s), or of gay (underground) cinema, and we find little about the gay press and other fundamentally nonlocal aspects of culture.

Since then, Castells's perspective on the (spatial) character of social movements has changed quite significantly. Analytically their main importance is no longer that they address specific problems, or lobby governments (though they still do that). Rather, their most pervasive influence is through raising, and proposing answers to, the most fundamental questions: about who we are, and how we should lead our lives. They are now seen less as locally bounded and more as identity driven. Of course, people still live in specific places and act within the cultural frameworks characteristic of those places. Yet by placing the (re)construction of identity at the center of the analysis, it becomes much easier to draw out how these different social movements relate to one another across time and space, how they manage, in fact, to be local and translocal at the same time. In Castells's analysis, as we will now see, social movements are increasingly rooted in ideas, not in places, though these ideas become effective only when embodied in (material) organizations.

Social Movements and the Creation of Identity

The need to create meaning in life is a primary social force. Life without meaning is unbearable. All cultures we know of have created explanations, with varying degrees of comprehensiveness and rigidity, about themselves and others, where they come from, what the purpose of life is, and how to organize everyday life within this grand narrative. For Castells such meaning is constructed around issues of identity, that is, the definition of certain cultural characteristics as constitutive for a person in the context of a shared culture.[23] One could call this a process of "essentialization," of creating a stable core within a context of change. Creating an "essence," an identity, is a collective as well as individual undertaking. Castells builds his definition on Giddens's notion of individuation. This is the process of selective internalization and transformation of social values by which individuals differentiate themselves from others, as well as position themselves within the larger social context. One of the hallmarks of modernity, accentuated in what Giddens calls "high modernity," is that this process of individuation is carried out with a high degree of self-consciousness. It requires from the individual continuous monitoring of himself or herself in relation to a larger social context. Today, even the most basic forms of identity, say, what it means to be a woman or a man, are no longer a given, but a "reflexive achievement,"[24] leading to a "deepening of the self."[25] While from a sociological perspective it is easy to agree that identities have always been constructed, this process of construction has become more open, contentious, and consequently more fragile in "post-traditional societies."[26]

Unlike Giddens, Castells focuses only on the collective aspects of this construction of identity.[27] Individual and collective aspects are of course related, because identity is anchored in individual people, yet as a source of shared meaning, the construction of its basic patterns is a collective process. Castells does not enter into a debate about the relationship between the collective and individual aspects of identity, but sidesteps this issue by arguing that new sources of meaning only become socially relevant if they are expressed in a shared culture, that is, in social organizations and institutions. These are, by definition, collective. There is, of course, never a full fit between collective and individual identity; "identity correspondence" is always imperfect. Giddens's process of individuation is a process carried out by the individual, with an uncertain outcome. The sociological, rather than the psychological, aspects are crucial to Castells's approach. It is precisely the gap between official forms of meaning – anchored in the traditional institutions of social life – and the desires and needs of a growing number of people that has provided the space for social movements to flourish.

The construction of identity and meaning (that is, of culture and social life) always stands in some kind of relation to the dominant institutions of society. Castells uses this relationship between the social movement and dominant values as the distinguishing characteristics of three ideal types of identity, each affecting society in a different way. He calls them "legitimizing identity," "resistance identity," and "project identity."

The first type receives only cursory treatment in his analysis, because it contributes to the reproduction of the status quo, including its officially sanctioned forms of conflict articulation.

"Legitimizing identity," he writes, "generates a civil society; that is, a set of organizations and institutions, as well as a series of structured and organized social actors, which reproduce, albeit sometimes in a conflictive manner, the identity that rationalizes the source of structural domination."[28] Some of the carriers of this type of identity used to be social movements but are now part of the institutionalized power structure. Unions in the capitalist welfare state are an example of an organized social actor whose sometimes conflictive behavior contributes to the overall stabilization of the status quo. Official churches and all kinds of civic association also belong to this type by being, at one and the same time, sanctioned by the state and deeply rooted among people.[29] These institutions have succeeded in imbuing social structures, and their differential creation of constraints and opportunities, with positive connotations. Unions legitimize the unequal appropriation of surplus between capital and labor by promising to make it more equal, a mission they have been carrying out with varying degrees of success. Churches sanction some forms of social arrangements, for example privileging the marriage between husband and wife over other forms of intimate partnership, by connecting secular, contemporary laws to divine values and deep traditions. These sources of legitimacy for the status quo have never been unchallenged. Revolutionary parties have frequently accused unions of abandoning the "historical interests" of the working class, and the history of organized religion is also a history of heretics. Yet, in the decades after World War II, such institutions contributed significantly to a more or less smooth reproduction of the power structure in Western democracies. They were able to do this, Castells argues, because they provided a continuity between the logic of power making in society and the logic of association and representation of mainstream culture. Enough people recognized themselves in the dominant values of society to accept the institutions that embodied them, not least by sticking to the accepted ways of articulating discontent.

This continuity between the institutional and the cultural logic of society began to show signs of serious strain in the late 1960s. The authority of the established civil society institutions started to erode and new social movements began to "fill the gap left by the crisis of vertically integrated organizations inherited from the industrial era."[30] What is crucial is that the social movements were not simply advocating change (unions and political parties had been doing this all the time), but were doing so *outside* the channels created for this purpose by the dominant social institutions. The difficulties of the official institutions in integrating the new social movements and their demands further undermined their legitimacy as connectors of power making and culture making. The result was a crisis of legitimacy of the state built with and around institutions of civil society. We will return to this point in the following chapter.

In Castells's ideal typical construction, the new social movements are distinguished by the type of identity they produce: resistance or project identity. To the first (ideal) type belong social movements which are characterized by their resistance to the dominant institutions and the values embodied therein. Such movements are carried by "actors who are in positions/conditions devalued and/or stigmatized by the logic of domination, thus building trenches of resistance and survival on the basis of principles different from, or opposed to, those permeating the institutions of society."[31] The social basis of such movements are those to whom the dominant institutions have nothing positive to offer. For them, it is either cultural obliteration, that is giving up their shared identity and trying, individually, to reestablish one more favorable within the dominant matrix, or accepting the structural disadvantages pressed upon them. The only positive, in the sense of self-respecting, alternative is resistance to this form of negative domination by widening the gap between the marginalized groups and the mainstream of society. Castells calls this strategy "the exclusion of the excluders by the excluded," echoing Marx's famous line about "the expropriation of the expropriators." This strategy is used by indigenous movements, by religious fundamentalists, extreme nationalists, and cults. All of these groups situate themselves outside the dominant culture, holding on to something precious – the source of their identity – which exists only inside their own community. They do not demand integration but separation, and the social vision they advance centers around more or less self-contained communes.

The second (ideal) type of social movement develops what Castells, again in line with Alain Touraine, calls "projects." These are carried out by "social actors, on the basis of whatever social material is available to them, [to] redefine their position in society and, by doing so, seek the transformation of overall social structure."[32] Projects aim to change mainstream society in order to find a place in it. The most significant projects, in his view, are feminism (and the gay/lesbian movement), which is challenging patriarchy, arguably the social institution with the deepest historical roots, and environmentalism, seeking to establish a new relationship between humankind and nature. Contrary to resistance movements, projects demand integration into the mainstream of society, but integration on their own terms, through changing the dominant values and institutions.

If competition in the never-ending quest for profit is what drives the evolution of capitalism, then value conflicts are what transform social institutions. This is a remarkable "cultural turn" in the location of primary social conflicts. The problematic aspects of this turn I will discuss at the end of this chapter. In Castells's analysis, capitalism is proceeding without much effective, organized resistance in the sphere of production. Organized labor has been weakened to such a degree that it has lost the ability to impose its own goals and values on the organization of the economy. This does not mean that Castells sees the economy as free of social tension, or somehow socially equitable. Far from it. Castells argues that economic exploitation and inequality continue and powerful social contradictions are still produced. Nevertheless, the stage on which social conflicts are carried out is no longer the factory, or the workplace more generally. The new zone of conflict is culture, understood as a broad set of social institutions (including economic ones). Conflicts are no longer articulated around the question of who owns the means of production. This question, thanks to the role of the financial markets, is more opaque than ever. Rather, the central question, Castells contends, has become much more fundamental, namely: how can we lead a life with meaning and dignity?

Two Case Studies

The power of Castells's analysis of social movements, and its embeddedness in a broader analytical framework, only becomes visible in his case studies, many of them representing significant contributions in their own right. In the following, I will concentrate on the challenge to patriarchy, and on the rise of fundamentalism, which in part can be understood as a violent reaction to this challenge.

The erosion of patriarchy

For Castells, one of the major deficiencies of Marxist analysis, including his own, was that "the oppression of women in the patriarchal structures was simply 'forgotten.' "[33] Castells has since turned women's resistance against patriarchy into a core aspect of his theory of the network society. This is more than justified, since patriarchy is, quite arguably, the most pervasive social institution in recorded history, and certainly characteristic of all contemporary societies. For Castells's analysis, two elements of patriarchy are essential: the dominance of men over women, and closely related, "compulsory heterosexuality." Its institutional core is the family (nuclear or otherwise) in which the dominant positions are assigned to men, above all the *pater familias*. Adopting a feminist perspective, Castells stresses that the influence of patriarchy extends far beyond the private. It pervades all institutions of life, including those of culture, the economy, and politics. Over the last three decades, in the West, the foundations of patriarchy have been shaken in all of these domains by the women's and gay/lesbian movements. Its legitimacy has been severely weakened and its transmission across the generations is becoming less pervasive, as more women and children, but also men, live their lives in nontraditional arrangements. This adds up to nothing less than a historically unprecedented "undoing of the patriarchal family."[34]

Why now? Women have challenged patriarchy throughout history, and at the beginning of the twentieth century the women's movement won important victories in a relatively short timespan, above all, universal suffrage as a precondition for democracy. For the validity of Castells's basic thesis – that we are in the midst of an epochal transformation related to informationalism, of which the rise of social movements is a constitutive aspect – it is important to show that the challenge to patriarchy does indeed relate to structural changes *and* to deliberate social movements, including, as a backlash, religious fundamentalism.

Structurally, the most important change comes from the massive incorporation of women into the paid labor force, and the technological changes affecting human reproduction. The integration of women into salaried employment has quantitative as well as qualitative aspects. Quantitatively, more women than ever before are earning their own money and gaining a greater degree of economic independence (from their husbands/fathers). And not just in the developed countries. Due to globalization and networked production, large numbers of women are drafted into the Mexican *maquiladoras* and the sweatshops of Asia, where they are often the majority of the workforce on the shopfloor. Paradoxically, one of the reasons for this development is that women are still discriminated against. They have to accept to work under worse conditions, stricter supervision, and for lower wages than their male counterparts. Even in the West, the closing of the gap between female and male wages has been very slow and the basic demand for equal pay for equal work has still not been fulfilled, except in a few privileged contexts. In a ruthlessly competitive economy, hiring women is a strategy to keep costs down and – thanks to the persistence of male domination – managerial control up.

Under such conditions, the incorporation of women into the productive economy is in itself, apart from the geographic aspect, not particularly new. Castells goes further. He argues that informational labor – with its demands for flexibility, networking, and social skills (even at the low end, for example in call centers) – holds unique chances for women. In advanced economies, statistical indicators show that women's employment grew particularly strongly in the two key areas of the informational economy, business services and social services. He argues that, apart from their labor being cheaper, women's "relational skills [are] increasingly necessary in an economy where the administration of things takes second place to the administration of people."[35] This is a continuation of the traditional gendering of social skills, yet these skills are no longer associated with the private world of women, but have become essential in the management of the informational economy.

It is hard to quantify this argument, which is a gendered version of the classic postindustrial theme of the economy becoming a "game between persons." How do these "soft skills" relate to other factors? To which jobs are such traditionally female-gendered qualities actually relevant? Castells doesn't go into much detail here apart from stating the basic thesis and citing statistical indicators that show a certain degree of correlation. He is on empirically firmer ground when he notes that another key aspect of work in the informational economy, flexibility, also facilitates the increased incorporation of women. Women account for the bulk of part-time and temporary employment. This fact has many faces. Often the flexibility is forced on women, reflecting general social discrimination. Young women are hired into sweatshops not just because of their lower wages, but also because they are easier to replace if they fall ill, which invariably occurs given the poor conditions, or if they begin to organize for better working conditions. Also, flexible or part-time work is necessary for many women who still have to carry the burden of raising children, with little help from their husbands or social institutions. Childcare facilities are insufficient, even in the most advanced countries (with the possible exception of the Scandinavian countries). All in all, women are entering the workforce under conditions of discrimination through still largely patriarchal structures, but they do so thanks to access to educational opportunities, at all levels, particularly also including the areas central to the informational economy. The economic balance between men and women is shifting around the world, though it is still tilted in favor of men. Nevertheless, the consequences are profound: a broadening of the economic basis for challenging male domination beyond the privileged few (who sustained the bourgeois women's movement of the late nineteenth and early twentieth centuries).

The second structural change that Castells foregrounds are new technologies, ranging from accessible and reliable birth control to *in vitro* fertilization, with genetic engineering looming on the horizon. They are providing women with unprecedented control over when, how, and under what conditions they want to give birth to children. There is a secular trend in all developed countries for women to have fewer children and to have them later in life, usually after having gained substantial experience in the workplace, which they often cannot, and don't want to, fully give up once they become mothers.

Yet structural change doesn't make for a new society. All it does is introduce stress into the existing institutions. And stress there is, as conservative observers tirelessly lament.[36] What is necessary for a new society to emerge are new values. A new culture, in Castells's view, is built through social movements. Modern feminism, defined as "the commitment to ending male domination,"[37] was born as a social movement in the late 1960s in the US, and in the early 1970s in Europe. Among other things, it reflected a disappointment with the male dominated radical organizations, in which women's demands were either ridiculed (as a "bourgeois problem"), or relegated to the status of a "secondary contradiction," to be addressed after the primary one – capitalism – was overcome. Women didn't want to wait that long and began to organize autonomously, "applying the logic of the desired freedom to themselves."[38]

Over the last three decades feminism, as a social movement with a diverse organizational base, has gone through its ups and downs, and has developed a great richness of discourses and institutions. Castells groups them into three broad groups based on their central demand: equality, difference, and separation. Across all internal tensions they are united in their "(re)definition of women's identity." This is as much a "discursive" undertaking – critiquing the traditional models of female behavior and developing alternative identities – as it is a practical one – building institutional contexts in which the new identities can be lived as everyday practice. Within feminism there are widely diverging ideas as to what these new models should be, but it is clear that they are not to be defined by men, and that they do not take the patriarchal family as their central reference point. Equality – equal rights and chances in all aspects of life – has been the core theme of the "liberal" women's movement. Legislative change and the challenge of discriminatory practices in the courts have been key strategies to advance this goal. Many important victories have been won. The female identity offered here is that everything that men can do, women can do as well. What is most necessary is to remove the structural barriers that prevent women from actually realizing their potential. In parallel to this, other feminists developed the argument of women being fundamentally different from men, arguing for the profound reality of the "female way of being." Both strands, overlapping and internally diversified as they are, have attacked the cultural, legal, and institutional foundation of the first pillar of patriarchy: domination of men over women. They aim at reducing the gendered aspects of society, or at reevaluating them by recreating femaleness as distinct, autonomous, and positive.

Questioning the second pillar of patriarchy – compulsory heterosexuality – has been more difficult for women (as a social movement) than for men. During the 1970s the gay movement gained significant visibility and strength, not least by creating their own neighborhoods, most famously in San Francisco, a process which Castells analyzed in the early 1980s under the perspective of urban renewal.[39] Within feminism the more visible expression of lesbianism was the result, Castells argues, of a generational change in the movement during the 1980s. Many of the early pioneers hesitated to foreground sexual liberation beyond the limits of heterosexuality, fearing for the credibility of the movement. In the 1990s a new generation of women, for whom the idea of equality had become a given, were taking the basic demands – the rights of women to determine their own life outside the strictures of male domination – one step further: the affirmation of the full range of female sexuality and lifestyles. A lesbian movement emerged with sometimes uneasy relationships to both the traditional feminist and the gay movement.

Feminism and the lesbian movement, while born in the West, are not restricted to it. Castells analyzes this transcultural element through the Lesbian movement which shocked (and shook) the very patriarchal culture of Taiwan in the late 1990s.[40] New gender images reflecting previously marginalized experiences and invisible sub-cultures halfway across the world were creatively appropriated and translated into the Taiwanese context. The ease with which these experiences, embodied in people and images, could travel across the globe is cited as yet another indicator that the challenge to patri-archy is directly connected to the development of informationalism.

Yet, particularly in less developed countries, the redefinition of women's social identities happens largely independently of the feminist movement. Rather, a large number of small-scale social movements and informal social organizations are sustained by women. In the process, they assume roles other than those en-visioned by their traditional, patriarchal cultures. Yet they have no access to the elite discourses of feminism, though recently, with the increasing availability of two-way electronic communication (via the internet) and affordable air travel (and sponsorship from nongovernmental organizations from rich countries), a new discur-sive sphere is developing that is no longer restricted to privileged actors. Feminism, as a multifaceted discourse, is inspiring, and being inspired from, a broad range of local practices. In short, is becoming a truly global phenomenon.[41]

In all these ongoing debates and struggles, the moral authority of patriarchy is being questioned. In the West, the patriarchal family has been fundamentally weakened, yet it has not been replaced. "There is no new prevailing form of family emerging: diversity is the rule."[42] For Castells, what makes this moment so extraordinar-ily fragile is the difficulty men have in developing for themselves new models of nonpatriarchal masculinity. Of course, the gay move-ment has been doing just that for the last 30 years with increasing sophistication and visibility, not least in the global flows of media images. Heterosexual males have been slow to catch up, reacting with a mixture of violent backlash ("fundamentalism"), evasion ("flight from commitment"), and uneasy adaptation ("renegotia-tion of the marriage contract") to the new demands that con-fronted them.

For Castells, at issue is the reconstruction of one of the most basic elements of identity: what it means to be a woman and what it means to be a man (and everything in between). It is undertaken by feminism (and the gay/lesbian movement), thus giving mean-ing to, and deepening, structural changes which are simultaneously decreasing women's economic dependence and increasing their control over their own bodies. Yet the reconstruction he sees under-way is radically different from what conservative analysts perceive. Francis Fukuyama, for example, analyzes the same development, relying at times on the same statistics, as a decline in morality during the period from the 1960s to the 1980s. For him, this decline produced all kinds of negative effects, from a rise in the crime rate to the breakdown of the family unit. The reconstruction he sees underway is a return to patriarchal values, an argument he bases on, among others, genetic factors as a force beyond culture brought into decline by "moral miniaturization."[43] For Castells there is nothing natural about patriarchy. Rather, he sees it as a system of repression and, by and large, welcomes its weakening. Yet he is keenly aware that a shift in the construction of identity at such a fundamental and intimate level is a tremendous challenge. Not everyone is up for it. In his view, religious fundamentalism is fueled by fear over the erosion of old certainties, not the least of them being the relationship between men and women. This backlash is itself a social movement, battling for influence over the (re)construction of values in the network society. For Castells, contrary to Fukuyama, there is no easy return to patriarchal values, yet this does not mean there could be no hard return under the guise of divine law.

The rise of fundamentalisms

Over the last three decades, the fundamentalist element has grown stronger and more articulate in all major religions, including Christianity, Judaism, Islam, Hinduism, and even Buddhism (for example, in Sri Lanka). The critical questions in terms of Castells's theory are not whether this is a good or a bad development (though he clearly has no sympathy for it) but, why now? And, how does fundamentalism relate to the transformation of society under the impetus of informationalism?

Fundamentalism is defined as "the construction of collective identity under the identification of individual behaviour and society's institutions to the norms derived from God's law, inter-preted by a definite authority that intermediates between God and humanity."[44] This definite authority, in the case of Judaism, Christianity, and Islam, is a book (or a scroll) read literally as an ahistorical text with a single meaning that needs no interpretation, laying down, without distortion, God's eternal laws and com-mandments. Within all three religions, there is a conflict between those emphasizing the historical context of the production of the

founding text and the need to interpret its meaning for contemporary application, and those who refuse to do this. It is easy for crit-
ically trained Westerners to argue that any reading, even that which
professes to be literal, is an interpretation, but for those adhering to
a literal reading, this argument itself is reproachable. Yet an anti-
critical and anti-intellectual stance is hardly new; in fact, it is as old
as enlightenment itself, as Isaiah Berlin has shown in his brilliant
analysis of the "counter-enlightenment."[45]

Castells's argument takes a different direction. The rise of contemporary fundamentalism is fueled by the structural and cultural
transformations of the last three decades, particularly by two of
its most fundamental aspects: capitalist globalization and the challenge to patriarchy. For religious fundamentalists, economic globalization is a secular force which profanes even the most sacred
aspects of life by turning them into a commodity (intimacy, for
example, is turned into pornography). Globalization is viewed as
an alien, threatening, and profoundly immoral process, led by a
godless group (Jews, bankers, the US government, world government, etc.) bent on enslaving and degrading the planet for their own
material gain. To counter this whirlwind of change and meaninglessness, ahistorical, absolute values under divine authority are
propagated. Thus fundamentalism is "an attempt to reassert control
over life . . . as a direct response to the uncontrollable processes
of globalization."[46] On the micro level, this means the reestablish-
ment of the patriarchal family in its extreme form as both divine
and natural (which is viewed as the same). Fundamentalism offers
clarity and simplicity in a world full of confusion and complexity:
good versus evil, believers versus infidels, pure versus corrupted.
A Manichean battle will sooner rather than later enter its decisive
phase in which the "just" will triumph over the "wicked." In this
battle (and in its preparatory phase, now) it is impossible not to
choose sides: one is either on the side of God, or on the side of the
devil. Fundamentalism, contrary to pietism or mysticism, is a political project. It is not just about saving one's soul, but about bringing society – defined as the community of believers, the *umma*, for
Islam – into a state of grace through strict adherence to God's laws.
The ultimate goal of all fundamentalism is a theocracy, that is, the
subordination of all aspects of social life to religious imperatives.

The argument of fundamentalism as a backward reaction to the
forward movement of globalization has often been made, by com-
mentators as diverse as Thomas Friedman, who captures it in the
image of the "Lexus and the olive tree," Benjamin Barber, who

condenses it into "jihad vs. McWorld," and Samuel Huntington, who warns of a "clash of civilizations."[47] Yet, contrary to Castells, they all identify fundamentalism as primarily Muslim and globalization primarily with the West, usually on rather a skimpy empirical basis. Castells disagrees sharply. For one thing, fundamentalism is a growing feature of all major religions, including Christianity, particularly in the US. At the same time, contemporary fundamentalism should not be understood as "backward." On the contrary, as rooted in history and holy texts as fundamentalism tries to appear, its current form is often "hyper-modern."

A paradoxical relationship between transhistorical imagery and hypermodern strategy is widespread, but nowhere more pronounced than in Islamic terrorism, For Castells, the extreme radicalization of Islamic fundamentalism is a direct consequence of its failure as a political project. In the Arab world, the crisis of the 1970s was seen as a crisis of Westernization in its three major forms: socialism (Algeria), capitalism (Persia), and nationalism (Egypt). They have come to represent the failing ideologies of the postcolonial order. Despite a relatively successful modernization of the state during the first phase of independence, in the 1950s and 1960s, all Arab countries failed in the modernization of their societies and economies. Their underdevelopment became more pronounced as the advanced economies restructured themselves during the 1970s and 1980s. The gap widened.

Not only did Arab nations fail to enter modernity collectively, but the individual route through immigration was also, on the whole, not a successful option. The experience of social segregation and exclusion (say, of young Arabs in the French *banlieues*, or Pakistanis in Britain) contributed to undermining the attraction of the West as a model to follow. A new generation of young Muslims grew up who knew the West, and were literate and educated. They realized all the more keenly that the West had no place for them: rather, they were locked into structural discrimination, experienced as long-term unemployment and daily racism. Yet economics is not all, Castells stresses. The emerging Arab middle class, while growing rich from its contacts with the West, did not integrate either. Just at the time when contacts were intensifying in the 1960s, the West took, culturally speaking, a direction unacceptable to the cultural traditionalism of the Arab elites. The conservative elites in the West were also challenged by the new social movements, but they were forced to deal with the new cultural demands. After all, they were expressed by their own children.[48] Those in the Arab upper middle class, however, reduced their contacts with the West and stayed outside the (corrupt) centers of political power in their own countries. These were the structural conditions, economic and cultural, under which a revival of political Islam could flourish. Depending on the local context in which it operated, political Islam, a social mass movement led by intellectuals, either took over the government (in Iran, the country most open to the West, in 1979), triggered a civil war (in Algeria), was ruthlessly oppressed (in Egypt), or uneasily acknowledged (in Indonesia). Yet nowhere was it able to substantially improve the lives of the people. As Castells points out, "Islamism in fact failed as a political force in most Muslim countries. And . . . it is precisely because of this failure that radical terrorist groups emerged as a desperate alternative to impose their utopia by the violent means of a global revolutionary vanguard."[49] Islamic terrorism, then, is a reaction of an elite to Western dominated globalization, following the failure of political Islam as a *mass movement*. This distinction is crucial for Castells's analysis, despite connections between the Islamic elite and the wider population in Afghanistan (under the Taliban) and other places.

Like other governments, the Arab ones paid for their integration into the globalized networks of money and power with an increasing distance from their constituency.[50] This is most visible in Saudi Arabia, particularly after the decision to allow US troops into the country during (and after) the 1991 Gulf War. As Castells puts it, the contradictions in its double role as "the guardian of the holy sites and the guardian of Western oil reserves" became all too transparent. For Bin Laden, the presence of American troops on holy soil was the ultimate proof of the corruption of the Saudi state, of which he has firsthand knowledge as a member of one of its leading families. While his background of extreme wealth clearly distinguishes him from other key figures of al-Qaeda, virtually all of them, including those who carried out the attacks on the World Trade Center in New York City in September 2001, come from privileged backgrounds. Many of them know the West, have years of education, have traveled significantly, and are using advanced technologies skillfully. They operate with a global vision – uniting Muslims across all nations into a community of believers, the *umma*. It is to this goal that the American presence in the Muslim world, directly through troops on the ground, and indirectly through its backing of corrupt regimes in Egypt and Saudi Arabia, is seen as the major obstacle.

For young Muslims brought up in a conservative culture, the increasing integration of their societies into the global culture has come at an unacceptable price: "to be modern, and therefore accepted, came to be tantamount to renouncing the codes and values that were meaningful for people at large, particularly the traditional elites."[51] This feeling of denigration was accentuated by the fact that the Western stereotypes of the "oriental" saw nothing of value in this alien identity, in contrast to its enduring fascination with Eastern exoticism.[52]

For radical Muslims, the most significant event of the 1980s was the victory over the Soviet Union in Afghanistan. This built the case that it is possible to win a war against infidel invaders, though the strategy has been appropriately upgraded and adapted to the new goal and enemy. Already before the 2001 attacks on Afghanistan as the territorial hub of al-Qaeda, but even more so afterward, the terrorists built an organization uniquely suited to carrying out "asymmetrical warfare." In Castells's view, the overthrow of the Taliban regime was an ambiguous success. It did remove many of the leading figures of the first generation of al-Qaeda, but it prompted the organization to rely even more on its key organizational principles: loose coordination, local autonomy, and a simple overarching strategy – strike the enemy as hard as possible, where ever possible. As an organizational form it relies extensively on the resources of global networking: electronic communication and international travel, based on a shared culture providing trust and orientation.

Despite their orientation toward holy sites, their involvement in struggles for local self-determination (for example, in Bosnia and Chechnya), and their rejection of the West, Islamic terrorism's focus is not territorial. It is about cleansing the Muslim community from the degrading influence of the West, embodied in, as Margalit and Buruma put it, "the city," "the bourgeois," "reason," and "feminism," and symbolized by America.[53] Today, Western culture is global and so is the resistance to it.

The success of this resistance, Castells maintains, like that of all social movements, is not whether it is able to take over the state, but in its ability to "change minds, to challenge dominant values, and to alter global power relationships."[54] This is also why the media play such an important role in al-Qaeda's tactics. They carry the images of the attacks into the Muslim communities around the world and the fear into the hearts of the infidels. Their actions, violent as they are, are primarily symbolic, they are "propaganda by action," a tactic pioneered by nineteenth century anarchists. The goal is to create images of powerlessness at the heart of the most powerful Western institutions. The force of these images is testimony to the cultural dominance of the West, as well as to al-Qaeda's skillful handling of the global media.

That this is enough to revive the project of political Islam, and to connect to the masses of dispossessed Muslims, is following Castells's analysis, not very likely. For now, Islamic terrorism takes its identity from an extreme and primarily negative resistance against Western cultural domination ("the Americans love Pepsi Cola, but we love death"[55]). It can be interpreted as an attempt to "exclude the excluders" on a global scale. It pursues this goal with murderous creativity, using the full range of the material basis of the network society: electronic communication, air travel, as already mentioned, plus advanced technical knowledge, mass media, and the global financial markets. Indeed not a backward mode of operation. It is not a coincidence that many terrorists are trained engineers.

Castells's analysis of fundamentalism is one of the strongest applications of the theory of the network society. He is able to show how even movements which reject (hyper)modernity and its ways are themselves emerging from the very dynamics they fight against. One of the great strengths of his analysis is that it is, here as elsewhere, intrinsically multicultural. He sees deep structural similarities between Christian and Muslim fundamentalism. This makes it impossible to fall into facile, and self-serving, analyses, either identifying fundamentalism with the *other* (clash of civilizations), or as a backward reaction by those who misunderstand globalization (who cling to the olive tree instead of driving a Lexus). On the contrary, Castells argues, fundamentalists understand, and know how to use, the resources at their disposal, but they also understand that mainstream society has nothing to offer them. Fundamentalism, then, is seen as a phenomenon of a hyperconnected global society that structurally disconnects and devalues entire regions and populations, not just economically, but, perhaps even more importantly, culturally. To stretch Castells's analysis a little bit, one could say that fundamentalist terrorism and globally organized crime establish, on cultural and economic levels respectively, "perverse" connections through which regions and people who are systematically excluded from the network society make their way back in. In doing so, they constitute a key element of contemporary, globalized societies.

Social Movements and the Culture of Real Virtuality

The theory of the network society gives a central place to social movements. They are the vehicles through which people develop and promote new values and are thus changing social institutions. Furthermore, Castells sees a deep relationship between the character of social movements and the structural transformation taking place at the same time. They are both cause and effect of the same general trend: the transformation of the morphology of social institutions from vertically integrated hierarchies to flexible networks. Networks facilitate a new balance between diversity and coordination. Thanks to the internet (and similar technologies), social movements can accommodate great heterogeneity yet still maintain a sense of identity. They can be local and global at the same time. They are able to address creatively highly textured cultural questions which require sensitivity to the particulars of the local contexts in which people live, and integrate them into a broader framework through which personal experience can be shared with, and enriched through, others. The old forms of organizations, created in the industrial age, are too monolithic to be able to accommodate so much heterogeneity without fracturing. They are losing their ability to provide meaning for people's lives. Social movements are addressing this deficit of meaning, enabling previously marginalized cultures to (re)affirm themselves. The cultural orientation, and the reliance on information flows (one-way through the mass media, or two-way through the internet) connect social movements with the broader cultural transformation characterizing the network society.

The underlying argument has distinct postmodern resonances. As more and more aspects of life are coordinated through electronic information flows, the space of mediation is becoming increasingly important. Power, as Castells puts it, is "primarily exercised around the production and diffusion of cultural codes and information content."[56] Hence the impact of symbolic violence. This is not just a question of the production of symbols and cultural codes, but is, through these symbols, a strategy for shaping the development of material reality. In fact, in Castells's view, there is no gap between the symbolic and the material dimensions of social life. He calls the idea of unmediated reality "absurdly primitive." Rather, the two are inseparable because "all realities are communicated through symbols."[57] To stress the reality of the symbolic, particularly in its electronic form, Castells introduces the term "real virtuality."

The meaning of cultural symbols is never unambiguous. People, Castells stresses, have always interpreted media messages creatively. Cultural studies have established this point convincingly. Even what appears as passive reception (say, by the proverbial couch potato) in reality involves at least some measure of active decoding. In fact, processes of coding, decoding, and recoding symbolic messages are always taking place.[58] While this decoding/recoding of cultural messages has always occurred, in a culture dominated by one-way mass media this used to be a relatively isolated activity. In the era of broadcast media, the sharing of messages created by individuals was difficult and thus rarely reached beyond small, dedicated groups, often locally isolated from one another.

With efficient many-to-many communication tools becoming widely available, people can communicate much easier about their particular way of experiencing reality. In fact, this decoding can now take place collectively, or, perhaps more accurately, collaboratively. This facilitates the rebuilding of identities around specific, community-based interpretations/creations of reality. Thus the mainstream – the single, accepted way of representing reality – is being fragmented into an ever growing multiplicity of culturally specific symbolic and material discourses. They are taking place in parallel, often without any intersection. What is historically new is that this happens not just locally, but globally, and not just in a few specialized subcultures, but for culture in general. Mass media, following and accelerating this trend, are developing a universe of targeted channels, effectively changing from a "broadcast" to a "narrowcast" paradigm. Thus "the unifying culture of mass television is now replaced by a socially stratified differentiation, leading to the co-existence of a customized mass media culture and an interactive electronic communication network of self-selected communes."[59] People around the world have gained a new ability to receive, send, and create communication codes relevant to their particular context, using the full range of the global media system. The effects on culture, locally, nationally and globally, are profound. Castells concludes that

> cultural expression becomes patterned around the kaleidoscope of a global, electronic hypertext. . . . The flexibility of this media system facilitates the absorption of the most diverse expressions and the

customization of the delivery of the messages. While individual experiences may exist outside the hypertext, collective experiences and shared messages – that is culture as a social medium – are by and large captured in this hypertext. It constitutes the source of real virtuality as the semantic framework of our lives.[60]

This provides a fertile ground for social movements. After all, they are centering around the definition of new collective identities and using the new electronic communication infrastructure to produce their distinct cultural codes. This process, Castells suggests, takes place, first and foremost, *within* social movements and communities. Their communicative actions are aimed at increasing internal cohesion, creating a common project, a shared vision of the world, however rough. From this, a set of shared cultural values can be derived, and on these the trust and respect can develop without which the loose coordination within the networks that make up the social movements would break down. Resistance movements use the development of cultural codes, for example reviving traditional customs and indigenous languages, as a way to exclude the dominant cultures and increase the sense of community. The development of new cultural values within project movements has, at least initially, the same effect of creating a demarcation between inside and outside. Even though, contrary to resistance movements, this is not necessarily their goal. Environmentalism wants to save the planet for everyone. As a process, such cultural differentiation is not new. Professional groups, for example, have always developed a specialized vocabulary (technical jargon, acronyms) as one of the ways to differentiate who is "in" and who is "out." What is new is that this fragmentation doesn't just concern specialized roles, but reaches down into the construction of identity for an ever larger number of people.

As a consequence of this, Castells sees a fragmentation of culture that no longer follows traditional metapatterns (nation-states, languages, religions, classes, etc.). What is emerging is a new, discontinuous pattern of subcultures. Some of them are locally bound, others are physically distributed. All of them are communicatively integrated. Social movements, and the mutually incompatible value systems they develop, are only part of this development. The same trend can also be observed in the interlinking of immigrant communities across the world, where films, newspapers, satellite TV, and the internet play a very significant role in maintaining connections to the culture of the homeland while living abroad. How much such developments, which cannot be attributed to social movements, are contributing to the development of new values and new practices in everyday life is left open. Castells's theory of culture becomes a bit murky when we move beyond social movements and examine the full range of communicative practices that pattern everyday life. Yet the combined effect of these developments is quite clear: the fragmentation of experience through the construction of self-contained communicative universes.[61] For Castells, this is a worrisome situation, because, as he writes, "the more we select our personal hypertext, under the conditions of a networked social structure and individualized cultural expression, the greater the obstacles to finding a common language, thus common meaning."[62]

This fragmentation and the difficulty of finding common meaning is nowhere more consequential than in the crisis of the democratic institutions. They have been built around the ideals of deliberation leading to widely shared compromises on how to administer public affairs. As cultures fragment into value systems that are ever more differentiated, the basis of the legitimation of liberal democracy – rational discourse and compromise between interests – is eroding.

By and large, Castells's analysis of social movements as the sources of new values and institutional change succeeds in combining an analysis of social action with an analysis of the transformation of social institutions and structures. It is flexible enough to be applicable to social movements of any kind, irrespective of their cultural origin or progressive or reactionary goals. Conceptually, Castells remains indebted to Alain Touraine, Craig Calhoun, and Anthony Giddens, but goes beyond any of them by locating social movements within the wider theoretical matrix of the network society.

Yet, for all its strength, there are two main problems. One is with the construction of ideal types, the other with the place of social movements within the overall theory. Castells differentiates social movements according to the formal type of identity they create: resistance or project identity. In practice, however, the difference is often much less clear, and more fluid, than the ideal types suggest. The Zapatistas, for example, can be seen equally as a resistance movement (focus on indigenous culture) and as a part of a project movement (focus on antiglobalization). Depending on the action, and the interpretative framework, the Zapatistas, and many other locally defined social movements, are defensive (resistance) or transformative (project). In fact, the antiglobalization movement seems to have made this very distinction obsolete, or at least rather fuzzy in many instances. Thus the ideal types as constructed by Castells do not seem to be particularly productive in actual research, and it is indicative that he doesn't use them in his own recent treatment of the antiglobalization movement.

More substantive are the issues related to how social movements are integrated into the general theory. As already mentioned, they are seen as the real, and as it seems the only, subjects of history, in the sense of being self-aware, purposive actors. They are the sources of new values and the transformers of institutions. This puts them, rightly I think, at the center of attention, but it also skews the analysis. We now have subjects on one side, and processes on the other: self-conscious people fighting against dynamic systems, or, more in line with Castells own terminology, collective actors versus informational flows. These systems have no actors in the sense that the actors we can identify, say, global corporations, governments, international institutions, are themselves subject to dynamics they cannot control, caused by stepped-up competition, financial markets operating as an automaton. Hence even they are driven, rather than drivers.

Except in his most recent discussion of American unilateralism,[63] Castells does not investigate how other self-conscious, purposive actors might aim at changing social institutions. He argues that new social values are formulated primarily from below. This has not always been the case. In his analysis of the crisis of capitalism during the 1970s, Castells was quite clear that the internationalization of the economy is a conscious strategy to liberate capital from the control of national regulators.[64] This perspective was based on a dialectical model of conflict between social classes. There are good reasons to abandon such a simplistic framework, yet as a consequence of Castells's "cultural turn" social movements are left in a void, facing anonymous, uncontrolled processes. This is not a minor aspect of the theory of the network society, but its very core. The presumed tension between the "net" and the "self" is one of the main themes of the trilogy. This might be an adequate rendering of the self-description of most social movements (for example, indigenous people fighting against neoliberalism), but as an analysis of political processes and of institutional transformation it is far from complete. This will become more visible as we move to the analysis of power in the following chapter.

4

The Network State and Informational Politics

The third major engine of change driving the development of the network society is the transformation of the "relationships of power." Power, as defined by Castells in classic Weberian terms, is "the relationship between human subjects which imposes the will of some subjects on others."[1] The capacity of imposing one's will is "founded upon the ability to exercise violence."[2] The control over the means of violence is the root of power. Still in line with Weber, Castells sees the state as the primary locus of power, defined by its exclusive control over the means of violence, within a given territory. Consequently, Castells's treatment of the "relationships of power" revolves, first and foremost, around an analysis of the state as a set of institutions holding a territorially bounded monopoly of legitimate violence. Castells examines what happens to this "bordered power-container," to use Giddens's expression,[3] in an environment where borders of all sorts have become leaky, and control over the means of violence is slipping out of the hands of the state. As we will see, this focus on the state is both productive and problematic. Productive because it brings into sharp focus how the historic constellation that produced the nation-state as the apex of power is coming to an end, and how this is putting the institutions of liberal democracy under considerable stress. Problematic because by focusing on the transformation of the existing institutions of the nation-state, Castells remains vague on the new sources and forms of power arising in the network society.

In 1648 the Treaty of Westphalia ended 30 years of religious wars that followed the Reformation and established a new international system centering round the nation-state. This new type of state was a territorially fixed entity whose borders marked unambiguously the domain of its absolute control, and governed by a secular authority which also represented the state beyond its borders. Power was based on territory which provided the resources to maintain a standing army. The nation-state was the pinnacle of power, with no authority, secular or religious, above it. The separation of domestic and foreign politics was established, as well as the principle of non-interference with the internal affairs of other states.

Castells concurs with what is now the mainstream view among scholars of international relations: all of these principles, and the institutions of the nation-state which embody them, are fundamentally challenged in the globalized world.[4] However, he rejects the notion of the "end of the nation-state,"[5] which had gained popularity in the exuberant 1990s, as "a fallacy." Clearly the nation-state does not go away. Rather, the nation-state, as Castells puts it, "seems to be losing power, although, and this is essential, *not its influence.*"[6] Unfortunately, he does not expand on the difference between power and influence, even though that would be crucial. Sticking, like Castells, to standard definitions, we can say that influence is the ability to shape outcomes (rather than impose them). Influence, in this view, is a weaker form of power, one which is not sovereign.[7] It is power that cannot act alone. In this sense, the fate of the state in the network society is a dual one. On the one hand, there is a loss of sovereign power. States can no longer manage their affairs, internal or external, alone, not even the US. On the other hand, there are attempts to create new arrangements, which Castells dubs "the network state," through which state institutions continue to exercise influence over the fate of their citizenry. In short, what Castells sees is a transformation of nation-states from "sovereign subjects into strategic actors." In the process of this transformation, the political institutions of the nation-state are thrown into a crisis.

In the following I will outline Castells's argument of how the nation-state has been weakened (loss of power) and how it is reaffirming itself in a new role (asserting influence). On this basis, I will examine what I perceive as some serious shortcomings in Castells's account, which ultimately remains centered round the nation-state and the Weberian definition of power. But first a look at the theory of the state which Castells offers, somewhat hesitatingly, in a brief sketch in the revised version of the second volume of *The Information Age* trilogy.

The Theory of the State

Castells's theory of the state is expressed most crisply in the following two sentences:

> The state [is] the institutional system that mediates and manages the dual relationships between domination and legitimation, and between development and redistribution, under the influence of conflicts and negotiations between different social actors. This set of relationships is territorially differentiated, so that each state institution in each locality or region expresses at the same time the dynamics of the local and regional society . . . as well as the overall set of relationships present in the nation-state.[8]

What Castells means is the following. The state is a system of domination. Some values and interests are promoted whereas others are suppressed, by various means, based on the historic ability of some groups to inscribe their particular interests into the institutions of the state. This is a continuous and ongoing process. Political power struggles are never really won, domination is never complete.[9] Not least because the state needs a minimum of legitimacy in order to carry out this domination efficiently. Even in non-democratic states, a system of legitimation is necessary to justify the privileging of some interests over others. Having to fall back on overt violence (as the Chinese government was forced to do with the students' movement in 1989) leads to significant friction. Even if it is successful in terms of the short-term survival of the dominant elites, it cannot be maintained over a longer period (hence, as Castells argues, nationalism is promoted as an "ersatz" ideology by the Chinese rulers). In sum, the balance between domination and legitimation determines the stability of the state.

The more the values embodied in public institutions lose their legitimacy, the more fragile the state becomes. This is not only an objective question of their actual performance, but also, perhaps even primarily, a subjective question of the acceptance of the fundamental values expressed through the state by the population at large. These subjective aspects, as always in Castells's theory, are personal and collective at the same time. They are shaped by the confluence of tradition (the state as carrier of a historic national project), charismatic leadership (the exceptional personality), personal expectations (the state's influence on one's own future), and, I would add, propaganda (management of collective perception).

Managing this dialectic of ensuring domination while building legitimation is a complex and expensive task. In order to carry it out, the state needs access to resources through which to finance itself. Today, the most successful means of increasing the pool of available resources is to foster economic development, that is, the growth of material wealth. Since territorial expansion is no longer an option, the preferred way to foster economic growth is to strengthen the position of a country as a node in global economic networks. Once raised, the state's resources are allocated to various social groups that have been able to institutionalize their interests with regard to the state. This redistribution is an important source of legitimacy, particularly for the welfare states created in the second half of the twentieth century. The management of these "dual relationships" is carried out through a layered ("territorially differentiated") set of institutions, each shaped by their own internal balance among different social groups and by their relationships to the institutions on the other layers. The modern nation-state has typically been structured in three layers – local, regional, and national. They were ordered hierarchically, like Russian dolls. The localities were fully contained within one region, the regions were contained within a single state. There were relatively few horizontal connections (say between regions of different nation-states). This ensured the domination of the interests organized at the highest, the national, level over those organized below.

Somewhat surprisingly, Castells has begun to draw again explicitly on the Marxist theory popular in the 1970s, though now his main reference is no longer the structuralist Poulantzas. Rather, he goes all the way back to Antonio Gramsci. In particular, he uses Gramsci's concept of the "power bloc," by which he means the aggregation of heterogeneous actors which together control the development of the state's institutions. In the same way as the institutions are territorially differentiated, so are power blocs. Contrary to what the term "bloc" might suggest, Castells (following Gramsci) points out that the "power bloc" is not monolithic, but a result of negotiations between social groups – sometimes smooth, sometimes conflictive. Not all of them represent dominant values (for example, unions, environmentalists), but their inclusion helps to achieve the balance of domination and legitimation on which the state is based.[10]

Despite his renewed references to Gramsci, Castells has moved away from Marxism for good. His use of existing theory, here as elsewhere, is very pragmatic, and not particularly faithful to the original source. For Gramsci, there was a direct relationship between the notion of a "power bloc" and the theory of "hegemony." By the latter he meant the comprehensive system by which the dominant social group is able to inscribe its values into the culture at large and thus make the dominated groups accept their fate as "common sense."[11] As detailed in the previous chapter, for Castells contemporary culture is precisely characterized by a lack of any such "hegemony." Through the increasing fragmentation of cultural codes, common sense is eroded. For Castells, then, the idea of the "power bloc" is a way to put the complex relationships between social groups that shape state institutions into a black box – whereas for Gramsci the notion of the power bloc served as an entry point to the analysis of its composition. Furthermore, contrary to Marxist assumptions, and jarring a bit with the idea of the "power bloc" as the force shaping the state, the state is now seen as an actor in its own right, with relative autonomy in relation to the social groups that constitute it. For Castells the state is still crucially important for the economy, and vice versa. Rather, the state is not now seen primarily as supporting capitalist exploitation, but the economy as providing the basis for the state's ability to support social welfare. In this sense, it is in the state's own, genuine interest to support the expansion of the (capitalist) economy to finance redistribution. Politically speaking, even though Castells is careful to maintain a distance, this analysis supports the "third way" approach advocated by center left politicians (Clinton in the US, Blair in the UK, and Schröder in Germany) in the late 1990s.[12]

In Castells's view, the historical development of the nation-state can be read as an overall increase in the power of those interests that were organized at the highest, that is the national, level over those incorporated in local and regional institutions. Additionally, the institutions of the state have been adjusted continuously to the changing composition of the power bloc, allowing new values and interests to be integrated in an evolutionary fashion.[13] This centralization of the power was legitimized by arguing that the most significant forces operated at the national level, and hence that it was at this level that the dual relationships could be managed most effectively. Additional, or perhaps even primary, legitimation for this particular power structure arose from fusing the cultural concept of the nation with the administrative structures of the state, or, as Castells puts it, from combining "identity" with "instrumentality." This has been extraordinarily successful, to the degree that today it is still hard to think of the two as separate entities. This fusion extends all the way down to the conventions of grammar, inserting a hyphen between "nation" and "state" to add extra emphasis on their connection: nation-state. One of the key contributions of Castells's discussion of power is to show how this pair of nation and state is coming under stress, and sometimes even coming apart, with very mixed results.

In a nutshell, this is Castells's theory of the state as it pertains to the nation-state as a sovereign entity. Its crisis stems from the erosion of the central claim of the nation-state – that it can effectively manage these "dual relationships." The most significant social forces no longer operate on a national level and the claim of national institutions to represent the people rings hollow as citizens articulate increasingly diverse interests, values, and demands for institutional reform through social movements. There is a fourth layer emerging, above the nation-state, which is calling into question the efficacy of the institutional arrangements on all three levels, at the same time as their legitimacy comes under attack from below.

The Crisis of the Nation-State

The crisis of the modern nation-state in the network society stems from two sources. The first is the loss of sovereignty. Many of the key processes (economic, social, political, cultural) are no longer contained within the nation-state; rather they operate on a global, or at least interregional, scale through the space of flows (see the next chapter). The other factor in the crisis, which is only partially related to the first, is the loss of legitimacy of the institutions of liberal democracy. This loss occurs despite the fact that, since the collapse of the Soviet Union, representative democracy has become the only template for legitimate government throughout the world. In other words, while the institutions of democracy are in a state of crisis, other forms of governance – political Islam (Iran), absolute monarchy (Saudi Arabia), Communism (Cuba), one-party rule (China), or military dictatorships (Burma) – have even less legitimacy. The national institutions of liberal democracy may be bruised and battered, but, for Castells, there is no serious contender to replace them, for better or worse. This perhaps helps to explain why his analysis of power remains focused so thoroughly on the state.

For national governments, the process of globalization has dramatically undercut their ability to act autonomously. Yet, as Castells points out again and again, they still play an important role in shaping the fate of their citizens. However, they do so in an environment that is very different from, say, the 1960s. The key difference is that many of the most central aspects of national policy are now determined by processes shaped as much, or even more, outside than inside its national borders. Yet policies have traditionally been formulated, and legitimized, within these borders. Highly visible are the economic dependencies through the global financial markets. They seriously constrain the sovereignty of national governments in managing their monetary policies. Traditionally the main determinant of monetary policy was the national economy; today it is the global financial markets. This loss of sovereignty is most explicit in the European Union. National governments of the eurozone have delegated monetary policy and the setting of prime interest rates to the European Central Bank, a transnational institution explicitly set up to be beyond the reach of national governments. As a consequence, "the budgetary autonomy of nation-states is limited to allocation of resources between different items of the budget within parameters . . . imposed by the independent monetary authority."[14] What is explicit within the eurozone is also, though not as formalized and strict, the case worldwide. Not even the US, the most self-sufficient economy in the world, can set its monetary policy without regard to the global financial markets, though its room for maneuver is much wider than that of other states. Yet, even for the US, the state of the financial markets is a key determinant of monetary policy.

The nation-state's control over the economy is further weakened by the globalization of production, not just by multinational corporations, but by production and trading networks that exist on all scales. They create a "contradiction between internationalization of investment, production, and consumption, on the one hand, and the national basis of taxation systems on the other."[15] This contradiction makes it increasingly difficult for national governments to locate within their territories the productive basis from which to generate taxes. Not just because of the existence of fiscal havens offering their services for tax evasion to corporations and wealthy individuals, but also because of the general difficulty in accounting for value added in global flows of money, goods, and services. This induces systemic financial pressures on governments which have been increasing their borrowing on the international financial markets (with Japan and the UK as notable exceptions), and hence their exposure to global financial flows. While this argument is supported well by statistical indicators, it remains unclear if this systemic pressure on government budgets is really such a new reality. Niall Ferguson's historical analysis of the financial structures of governance suggests that budget deficits and dependence on the financial markets have been pervasive, if not crucial, features in the development of advanced nation-states over the last two centuries.[16] The question, of course, is whether the financial markets of the nineteenth century were not more dominated by governments than those of the twenty-first century. According to Ferguson, the answer is less clear-cut than the dichotomy between economic sovereignty and its loss would suggest.

Castells points out convincingly that the difficulties in raising revenue on a national basis from a global economy put pressure on the state either to increase productivity dramatically (thus creating a surplus that can be taxed without reducing competitiveness), or, if that is not successful, to cut labor costs (social benefits) and government expenditure (social welfare costs). The globalization of production creates "negative competition" between states to provide the most favorable environment for capital investment (either through low labor costs, or through high productivity, or both). This competition has accelerated sharply over the last two decades because it can no longer be offset by protectionism (tariffs) or reliable productivity differentials between developed and developing countries. What used to be "third world" countries, China and India most prominently, have increased their international competitiveness dramatically, not just by providing cheap labor, but also through an expanding pool of highly skilled labor. Both strategies for economic development – increasing productivity and entering the race toward the bottom, in whatever combination – push the national economies deeper into the global economy by increasing their exposure to competition and reducing government control over the conditions under which they operate.[17]

Politically, Castells relates the loss of sovereignty to the rise of problems which cannot be addressed effectively on a national basis, ranging from environmental degradation to migration, the global criminal economy, and global epidemics such as AIDS or SARS. These are not issues of traditional foreign policy, yet they all contain significant cross-border components. They demand internationally coordinated action in a widening range of areas, though prevailing national interests make such coordination exceedingly hard to achieve. As a consequence of the inability of nation-states to act effectively in these areas, which broadly concern a new class of "global common goods," a host of new actors, NGOs such as

Greenpeace, Médecins sans Frontières (MSF), Amnesty International and scores of others, have entered the international domain, challenging the nation-state's historical monopoly on international policy making. By doing do, they are undercutting the claim of advanced democracies to be the locus of humanitarianism, draining another, important source of their legitimacy.

Militarily, the loss of sovereignty has two main aspects. With the major exception of the US, no national government can fight an external war without major international support. This international support is not only a question of coalition building for the pursuit of war, but extends deep into the makeup of high-tech armed forces. They rely on technological infrastructure that only the US can generate domestically. For Castells, this technological self-sufficiency is a major reason why the US can justifiably be called the last superpower.[18] Yet the loss of sovereignty in the area of violence is not just a question between states. Rather the control over the means of violence is increasingly slipping out of the hands of governments and into the hands of nonstate actors. The main new actors controlling relevant means of violence are the terrorist networks and organized crime. The latter is supporting guerrillas whose original political goals have been replaced by, or fused with, their new economic function to secure the ground for criminal operations. To retain its monopoly of violence, the state has to use it more and more against its own population, from which terrorists and criminals are hard to separate – not least because the categories can be a matter of contested definition. However, establishing internal and external warfare as a permanent *modus operandi*, Castells points out, seriously threatens the state's legitimacy, in relation to its own citizens and as an actor in an interconnected political system. I will return to this last point later in this chapter. For now, I'll continue with Castells's account of the erosion of national sovereignty.

The final element that contributes to this trend is the state's loss of control over the media. Up to the mid 1980s, the mass media, particularly television, were everywhere closely regulated, if not directly controlled, by national governments. A relatively small number of media outlets, for example three major TV networks in the US, controlled the markets, which were national or regional. In the course of a decade this changed radically because of the intertwined dynamics of technological change and political deregulation. Media markets became global, new players emerged, and competition became more pronounced, despite the fact that the market is dominated by only a few global conglomerates. So far, so good. However, Castells's analysis of the relationship between political power and the new media environment is more specific, and, in my view, problematic. To survive competition, he argues, the media need to gain a certain distance from the political process, that is, they need to appeal to a market segment that is broader than any clearly defined political camp. If they become too closely associated with a particular political position, they will not remain attractive to advertisers, who are their main source of income, and who want to reach the broadest market possible. From this it follows that "independence and professionalism are not only rewarding ideologies for the media: they translate into good business."[19]

This conclusion is contrary to almost everything the political economy of communication has been arguing on this subject for the last two decades. Herman and McChesney, for example, in the subtitle to their book on the global media, call the newly formed conglomerates *The New Missionaries of Global Capitalism*.[20] They highlight the close alignment of the main actors in the media, economy, and politics. Scores of studies have pointed out the bias in the way the mainstream media present political issues. If anything, political economists tend to argue, the range of opinion in the mainstream media has narrowed rather than widened, and the opinions published there consistently promote certain values over others.[21] Here, Gramsci's concept of hegemony might still be useful for an analysis of the political role of the media. Thomas Frank, for example, argues that the idea that (financial) markets are fundamentally democratic has been repeated so often on television that is has become "hegemonic," establishing a new common sense that leads people to favor economic policies that are against their own material interests.[22]

Castells is on stronger ground when he argues that the loss of control stems from a particular kind of diversification of the media landscape. One aspect of the diversification is the rise of non-Western satellite TV, most notably the Arab news networks *Al Arabia* and *Al Jazeera*, challenging the domination both of national, government-controlled TV stations in the Arab world and of Western globalized media. The other aspect is the rise of ethnic local TV. These channels are bypassing the standardized national/global media and are only addressing very particular constituencies, fostering their experience and expression of cultural particularity. For Castells, "the new pattern of interaction between media and the state is characterized by the tension between globalization and identification."[23] The state is seen as unable to match the reach of the global media outlets and unable to match the specificity of the local, ethnic media channels.

This is complemented by the fact that computer-mediated communication flows are largely outside the control of the state. While states are trying to establish control over this domain, they are forced into a dilemma. When they disconnect their population from the internet (or fail to connect them), they interfere with their ability to foster economic development, yet when they promote the use of new technology, they abdicate control over what their citizenry reads or writes. Of course, just as the control was never ironclad, the loss of control is not absolute, but overall Castells sees attempts to (re)establish state control over the information citizens can access as a "lost battle." Unfortunately, it remains unclear over what timeframe Castells imagines this battle to be lost. This vagueness makes his assertion problematic, not least because the empirical record on "open networks, closed regimes" has so far been much less straightforward.[24]

These, then, are the four key areas in which nation-states have lost sovereignty in the network society: domestic economic policy, international policy making, the military, and the media. While some of the points of this analysis are problematic, the general conclusion is unquestionable: the nation-state is no longer a sovereign political actor. The weakening of state authority has led to, and is aggravated by, a loss of legitimacy of some of the key institutions of political democracy, namely political parties and governments. They are caught in a double bind. On the one hand, more and more problems vital to their constituencies are negotiated on an international level. On the other hand, as the cultural realities of their constituencies fragment, they are confronted with ever more specific, and contradictory, demands. Yet in order to be able to act effectively in an international arena, governments need a certain degree of independence from their constituencies, otherwise there is not enough room for maneuver. "Thus, the more states emphasize communalism, the less effective they become as co-agents of a global system of shared power. However, the more they triumph in the planetary scene, in close partnership with the agents of globalization, the less they represent their national constituencies."[25] The loss of sovereignty of the nation-state is reflected directly in the politicians' inability to represent the particular interests of their constituencies, which, from the point of view of the people who vote for them, undermines their legitimacy as their representatives.

Informational Politics

The crisis of the state, Castells stresses, is also caused by the transformation of politics from party politics – centered around political parties with diverging ideologies representing different social classes – to "informational politics," that is politics "fundamentally framed, in its substance, organization, process and leadership, by the inherent logic of the media system, particularly the new electronic media."[26] And this "inherent" logic corrodes politics in the traditional sense, for two main reasons. First of all, media politics is extremely expensive. Buying advertising time, staging spectacular yet highly controlled events, continuous polling, information processing, and maintaining rapid reaction capacities require substantial resources, not just in the US but everywhere. Politicians need to spend a significant amount of their time on fundraising, for themselves and their political parties. This not only gives monied interests undue access to politicians, but it also creates systemic corruption. Without private donations, no politician (or political party) can survive. The ensuing practice of fundraising at the edge of legality creates the popular assumption that politicians can be bought, which is, Castells concludes, by and large accurate. Even though, in advanced democracies, the motive is rarely personal financial gain, but securing the resources necessary to compete for power.

Systemic corruption, in a competitive media environment that is not under state control, creates material for endless scandals. And the media thrive on scandals, of any kind, because they sell media products. The scandals are neither, as Castells stresses, because politicians were more virtuous in earlier times, nor because the media are fulfilling their roles as independent watchdogs. Rather, they occur because "scandal politics are the weapon of choice for struggle and competition in informational politics."[27] This struggle is carried out as a complex game of leaks and counterleaks, with political actors trying to instrumentalize the media as much as the media turn politics into a show, competing with entertainment and sports, in the pursuit of audiences and profits. However, since the politician who replaces the one who has been caught in illegal fundraising is subject to the same pressures, the situation is unlikely to change, and hence the status of the entire *classe politique* is undermined. This is one side of the problem of informational politics.

The other side is that all politicians, irrespective of their positions, must communicate through the same medium: commercialized television (and other commercial media channels). This forces them to speak the language of television: short, personalized statements ("sound bites"), supported, or even driven, by powerful images. All of this makes them more vulnerable to the corrosive effects of scandals which are as personalized as the politics they engulf. However, for politicians there is not much choice. Without mastering the basic language of TV, it is impossible to reach a relevant size of population in pursuit of the next electoral victory. Other media, print or the internet, still play only an auxiliary role (even if the internet is becoming an important tool in organizing and fundraising). Politicians can bring up certain issues, but unless TV picks them up and digests them into short punchlines, the issues remain politically marginal. Politicians, aided by professional "spin doctors" who help them to operate under these constraints, are not only becoming more and more alike, but the showlike aspects of politics are more visible, further undermining their credibility. The showlike aspects are reinforced by TV shows about the practice of selling politics and media manipulation.[28] The circle closes.

Up to this point, Castells's analysis of informational politics is solid, if somewhat conventional. That television transforms politics has been argued since Kennedy won the first presidential TV debate against Nixon in 1960. However, Castells's argument is more specific, and the many issues that made his analysis of the media in terms of the loss of political sovereignty problematic reappear in his analysis of informational politics. The media, while introducing a set of structural constraints, are more or less agnostic about the interests of the politics for which they provide the stage. Indeed, there are supposed to be strong commercial interests in staying above politics, and thus Castells argues that "*mediacracy* is not contradictory to democracy because it is as plural and competitive as the political system is. That is, not much."[29] Castells knows that he is on thin ice here, and he hedges his bet on both sides. Media provide the all-important stage for politics, a stage that has very particular constraints, yet the fact that pluralism in politics is at an all-time low is unrelated to the media system. For Castells, the media shape the message they transmit but are profoundly disinterested in the content of these messages.

Castells remains here essentially within his McLuhanite reading of electronic media, and their culture of "real virtuality," as "a multisemantic text whose syntax is extremely lax."[30] This is a worthwhile observation about TV in general (which is what McLuhan spoke about), because it can help to highlight the transformation of the style of political communication (independent of the political goals) into shorter and shorter sound bites and symbolic images, as news meshes with entertainment. This leads to a style of communication far removed from the reasoned debate in the public sphere that is central to the theory and legitimacy of liberal democracy. This observation is hardly new.[31]

Yet this kind of analysis is insufficient for understanding the concrete relationships between TV and politics in the media-saturated network society. The fact that the medium of TV affects the format of all messages equally does not preclude the owners of TV channels having an interest in, and a certain degree of influence over, how the content of those messages is framed. Form and content, the medium and the message, are two very different levels of analysis. Castells has little to say about the fact that the media corporations are themselves major economic actors, either in their own right, or as part of even larger conglomerates, with very distinct economic interests in a broad range of political issues.[32] It is not a coincidence that corporate scandals are much less reported than political ones, or labor interests far less present than those of financial investors.[33] Furthermore, for Castells the main effect of the high cost of media politics is the endless string of scandals over fundraising, and not the narrowing of political opinions conducive to raising significant amounts of money.[34]

This is not the place to assess the political bias of the news media, but to note that for Castells this is simply not relevant for the analysis of informational politics. Indeed, he dismisses the argument that mass media can significantly influence their audience. To support this thesis, he refers to cultural studies which have pointed out that audiences actively and subjectively interpret media messages, rather than passively receiving them. With respect to critical theory and its critique of "culture industry," he goes so far as to conclude that "it is one of the ironies of intellectual history that it is precisely those thinkers who advocate social change who often view people as passive receptacles of ideological manipulation."[35] As an analysis of the actual dynamics of "mediacracy," this does not suffice.

In certain ways, Castells's analysis of the media is similar to his analysis of the financial markets. He sees them both as highly particular environments, with their own internal dynamics and constraints which produce systemic volatility (rapid price fluctuations there, scandals here). Nevertheless, he sees them as basically politically neutral as to what happens through them. Both the media and the markets are independent of politics because they are so internally differentiated and competitive as to be, by and large, beyond the control of anyone, particularly national governments. They both contribute to a sphere of global information flows which is, in essence, determined by its internal, blind dynamics rather than by any particular political will or strategic action. He writes: "the flows of power generate the power of flows, whose material reality imposes itself as a natural phenomenon that cannot be controlled or predicted, only accepted and managed."[36]

In both areas, this conclusion that global flows are beyond the reach of political actors directly relates to Castells's conceptualization of power, which is still seen as primarily working through direct control and coercion. I will come back to this point at the end of this chapter.

The Reaffirmation of the State

The basic principles of the nation-state – set out in the mid seventeenth century and still operational deep into the second half of the twentieth century – are coming apart. They are increasingly ineffective and are losing legitimacy. Yet, Castells stresses, nation-states are not passively descending into obsolescence. On the contrary, they are still very resourceful actors, nationally but also internationally, and as such their response to these developments is an essential aspect of the developments themselves.[37] They cannot withdraw from the global networks because outside these networks there is only marginality, yet they can and do act within and upon them in a variety of ways, determined by the resources they have at their disposal, accumulated in the course of their history.

For Castells, there are really only two sets of strategies available to states, and they are both a direct reaction to the new global realities. Economically speaking, the options are either to integrate into the mainstream of global exchanges, or, bypassed by the global flows of wealth and opportunities, to establish informally a "perverse connection," that is, to allow the most aggressive segments of society to enter the global criminal economy. Politically speaking, the choice is between becoming adept at managing the messy processes of competition and cooperation in the arenas of international/interregional policy making, or opting for a unilateral strategy, usually based on a renewed form of aggressive nationalism, or a redefinition of "national interest."

Of course, and Castells is clear about this, these options are not mutually exclusive, nor is there, for many states, much of a choice.

For poor developing countries, for example, integration into the mainstream global economy is either not possible (because they are treated as "redundant producers"), or often possible only on disadvantageous terms (as producers of "high volume" or "raw materials"). Weak states may not have the capacity to prevent the growth of the perverse connection, even if a newly elected government initially may have the will to do so. However, within the ambit of these two directions, there is enormous variety in the way states reorganize themselves in order to keep and even increase their influence, in what Habermas calls "the postnational constellation."[38]

When Castells speaks of the need to integrate into the global economy, he positions himself against both the right-wing doctrine of deregulated free trade (that all countries will profit from free trade, and the less state intervention, the better) and the left-wing dependency theories (no sustained economic growth is possible for dependent states). For Castells, the empirical record points in a different direction. Those states that have been most active in supporting their economy so that it can enter the global economy *at its own pace* have been the most successful in strengthening their national economies to become powerful nodes of the global economy. Castells distills two models from this observation, both with clear positive connotations: the "developmental state" and the "informational welfare state."

The developmental state – chiefly the "Asian Tigers" (Hong Kong, Singapore, South Korea, and Taiwan) but also Japan and China (since the 1980s) – "establishes as its principle of legitimacy its ability to promote and sustain development," in the sense of economic growth.[39] By using a mixture of state intervention and deregulation, of protectionism and free trade, the developmental state

> focused on linking up the country with the global economy to industrialize and dynamize the national economy . . . The developmental state was based on a premise of a double edged, relative autonomy. Relative autonomy *vis-à-vis* the global economy by making the country's firms competitive in the international realm, but controlling trade and financial flows. Relative autonomy *vis-à-vis* society, repressing or limiting democracy and building legitimacy on the improvement of living standards, rather than on citizen participation.[40]

This strategy was, by and large, very successful, securing the state's legitimacy despite high social costs in terms of systemic corruption, cronyism, and sustained autocratic rule. Castells stresses that this model has been successful because its aims were not just economic but served simultaneously as a "nationalist project of self-affirmation of cultural/political identity in the world system."[41]

A nationalist project also underlies the successful creation of the informational welfare state, for which his prime example is Finland, but which arguably applies to all northern European states (and the Netherlands). Here, the welfare state has been able to transform itself into a key factor in increasing productivity. Extensive social policies in the areas of education, health care, cultural development, and social security contribute to providing the human resources necessary to compete successfully in the global economy. In Finland, in particular, the transition toward an informational economy was the result of a comprehensive political strategy, initiated and coordinated by the state, connecting policies in a wide range of areas into a common national project. This was facilitated by a strong national identity, based on language, geography, and a tradition of cooperation against outside forces that are seemingly overwhelming (the climate, the neighbors). It is this increase in productivity that enables an extensive social welfare system to be financed without reducing global competitiveness. In fact, the informational welfare state is what sustains its competitiveness.[42]

In sum, "the state survives by connecting the nation to the global context, adjusting domestic policies to the imperatives of global competitive pressures. . . . This requires that the state becomes interdependent within a broader network of economic pressures out of its control."[43] This creates the contradiction that the more deeply the economy is integrated into the global flows, the less the underperforming sectors of the economy can be shielded against the "whirlwinds of the space of flows," as was indicated by the structural problems of the Japanese economy throughout the last decade, or the Asian financial crisis of 1997. In addition, relying too much on nationalism as the "legitimizing identity" to hold society together against the centrifugal forces of transition brings the danger of xenophobia, leading to cultural closure at a time when multiculturalism has become a key source of competitiveness. As Castells and Himanen write in their analysis of the Finnish informational society, "Finland cannot choose a non-multicultural world, but the multi-cultural world can choose a world without Finland."[44]

Castells argues that the state remains a crucial actor in the informational economy, and that there is a range of different models for the informational economy. Silicon Valley, he insists, is not the future of all advanced economies. However, the ability of the state to play an expansive role relies on above average productivity in the economy (that is, an above average rate of profit for investors, after taxes), thus forcing the state to accelerate the transition to the informational economy. In a sense, the best defense for the state is offense. Castells's argument for a diversity of models of equally advanced informational societies, adapting to and driving forward the development of a globalized informational economy, is convincing and original. He is able to demonstrate that different forms of governance, drawing from distinct national cultures, can survive and even prosper in the globalized economy.

Yet the structural reality of pervasive economic integration does not necessarily create the will for the political integration characteristic of the developmental and informational welfare state. On the contrary, a range of states are opting for renewed political unilateralism. To understand this movement as a constitutive part of the contemporary dynamics (rather than an anachronism), it might be worth reviving a line of analysis that Castells proposed in the late 1980s but has not taken up since. Focusing on the US at the end of the Reagan era, he diagnosed a shift "from the welfare state to the warfare state." For Castells, the concept of the warfare state, introduced by Herbert Marcuse for somewhat different reasons,[45] signals "the replacement of the state's principle of legitimacy as an economic regulator and social redistributor [with] the old conservative justification for the strength of the state as the rampart of national security and domestic law and order."[46] In this view, the warfare state is the (neo)conservative answer to the crisis of the liberal welfare state, a crisis that manifested itself in terms both of accumulation and legitimacy. The military (and the other security apparatuses) are put at the center of the state, not just in terms of its legitimacy, but also in regard to its economic policies. Large budget deficits, abhorred by traditional conservatives, are justified on the basis of "national security." These, in turn, provide the need to cut back social redistribution even further, and thus weaken its role in legitimizing the state. But this does not imply a generally reduced role for government. In fact, the defense spending provides the basis for renewed state-led economic policies – what Castells calls a "perverted Keynesianism" – made up of military expenditure and a regressive income distribution.

It seems in line with Castells's general argument, though he does not say it explicitly, that this transition – somewhat obfuscated during the 1990s, with its optimistic ideas of a social democratic "third way" and hopes for democracy in post–Soviet Russia – has sharply accelerated after the recent series of terrorist attacks. Governments around the world, most explicitly in the US and Russia, are using the "war on terror" to relegitimize authoritarian, nationalistic policies, centering round a broadened notion of national security. For Castells, this is a direct reaction to what are seen as the negative consequences of a world that has become too integrated, and individuals, that is terrorists, who have become all too powerful. On a smaller scale, the transition from a welfare to a warfare state could also be seen in Serbian politics under Slobodan Milosevic during the 1990s. Here too, the state tried to relegitimize itself as the guarantor of national security, that is, the integrity of the national territory. Indeed, a renewed authoritarianism, which, particularly in Europe, goes hand in hand with multilateralism, might be one of the most powerful reactions to the crisis of liberal democracy.[47] Thus internal violence of the state against some of its own citizens might not be, as Castells supposes, a factor in the erosion of the legitimacy of the nation-state, but, on the contrary, a key apsect of its resurgence under the guise of security.

Castells's conclusion is clear: There is still room for national policies and they can make a decisive difference, for better or worse. Yet states no longer create their policies, even unilateral ones, as a sovereign actor, but as part of a new power-sharing constellation which forces their transformation from (modern) nation-states to (postmodern) network states.

The Rise of the Network State?

In terms of Castells's theory of the state as an integrated set of institutions organized on three layers (local, regional, national), what has happened over the last decades could be characterized as the emergence of a fourth, supranational layer. What differentiates the situation today from what political theorists discussed in the 1970s as "interdependence" is not just the density and intensity of the cross-border relationships.[48] What is really new is that nation-states are no longer alone in the arena of international policy making. The arena has become crowded. Yet the states' tasks have not changed. They still have to manage, with respect to their domestic constituencies, the dual relationships between domination and legitimation, and between development and redistribution. However, they have to do so within a constellation that is "characterized by the plurality of sources of authority, the nation-state being just one of these sources."[49] Unfortunately, Castells is less than clear what these other sources of authority and power are. As far as his conception of the network state is concerned, this plurality is rather limited. Its components are primarily "other states, or fragments of states, or associations of states."[50] Most interesting here are the "fragments of states," by which Castells means local and regional institutions which no longer accept being represented internationally by national governments. Rather, they pursue their own interests in horizontal associations with other local or regional governments, sometimes in support of their national governments, sometimes to lobby against them. They can do so not only because their legitimacy has risen – being closer to the citizens, they are better able to represent specific identities – but also because many national governments, particularly in Europe, have delegated competences back to the regional and local level as a way to increase their own legitimacy.

Castells observes that in Europe, for the first time in 300 years, there is room for a positive expression of the difference between the nation and the state. Renewed regional identities, be they Catalan, Scottish, or Northern Italian, are gaining power by networking among themselves and intervening directly at the supranational level. Whereas the nation-state is in crisis, Castells sees the potential for a renaissance of local and regional governments, which, in the best of cases, are being reinvigorated by a combination of the power of identity (representing the specificity of their constituency) and the power of networking (by creating new forms of lobbying and resource sharing). This is a hopeful development, because

> the articulation of society and economics, technology and culture in the new system can be arranged with greater efficacy and fairness on the basis of reinforcing local societies and its political institutions. The global and the local complement each other, jointly creating social and economic synergy, as they did back at the beginnings of the world economy, in the fourteenth to sixteenth century, a time when city states became centres for innovation and commerce on a worldwide scale.[51]

This renewal of local autonomy offers, for Castells, the most promising prospect of a positive transformation of the state as a bottom-up recreation of democracy in the network society. By comparison, the establishment of a global civil society (in Gramsci's sense, as the space where state and society intersect) is a much more complex undertaking and one that requires new forms of articulation and representation, currently being developed, with uncertain success, by social movements and NGOs.[52]

Yet it is also clear that not all regions benefit equally from this renewed subsidiarity. On the negative side, local autonomy can be interpreted as a desolidarization of national societies, at a time when fiscal pressures are high and certain problems (for example, the fate of immigrants in the large housing projects) are tacitly regarded as unsolvable. Abandoned local minorities are pushed further into developing their own communal identities, defending themselves against this renewed, and highly effective, marginalization by exclusion. As an effect, the integrative capacity of the national level is decreasing, further weakening the legitimacy of the national institutions.

At the supranational level, we now find all kinds of state institutions, not just national governments, immersed in complex games of alliances, trying to use their position within the network as a whole to advance their own specific goals. The result is "the de-centering of the nation-state within a realm of shared sovereignty."[53] The Russian doll has been transformed into a chess game. The fact that power is shared among all actors in the network state, Castells stresses, should not indicate that it is shared on equal terms and that the internal constellations of the network state do not reflect power differentials between the various nodes of the network. They do. But the power of the network, he maintains, trumps any particular actor within it. This forces nation-states into a situation in which they have to accept the dominant interests formulated within the network (often, but not always, aligned with the interests of the dominant nodes), irrespective of how they relate to the interests of their own constituencies. This is a condition of gaining access to, or remaining in, the network.

This is a crucial point about the contradictory nature of power in global networks. On the one hand, global networks are defined by rules – say, the trade agreements of the World Trade Organization – that can override national policies and national law. On the other hand, major nodes in these networks, particularly the US and the EU, have a disproportionate weight in determining those very rules. Whether this amounts to a weakening of the major powers, who have to negotiate continuously, or whether this indeed extends the power of the G8 countries, who are now able to reach deep into the national policies of other countries, is a matter of considerable debate.[54] Castells does not really address this question, but by focusing on the loss of autonomy he seems to imply the former.

Global governance is a problematic issue in Castells's theory of the network state because he uses the concept in two different ways. On the one hand, the network state is understood as the *practice* of power sharing in which nation-states are continuously engaged in an attempt to manage global problems. However, at times, he also equates it with "the international system of governance built in the aftermath of World War II, centered around the United Nations."[55] Unfortunately, Castells puts very little emphasis on the institutions and instruments of global governance, which he sees as little more than the effect of "the negotiated convergence of national governments' interests and policies."[56] Yet he also argues that international institutions, such as the World Bank, take on a life of their own and "tend to supersede the power of their constituent states, instituting a *de facto* global bureaucracy."[57] Such a contradictory stance is repeated several times in the very few paragraphs which he devotes to questions of global governance. For example, he argues that it would be wrong to think of the International Monetary Fund as an instrument of American political domination, while also maintaining that it is not a coincidence that the economic theory underlying its policies is labeled the "Washington Consensus" because of the influence of the US government. He goes so far as to state that during the 1990s "most of the developing world, as well as the transition economies, became an economic protectorate under the IMF – which ultimately meant the US Treasury department."[58]

Clearly something is happening here that is both empirically novel (a global bureaucracy) and theoretically complex (heterogeneous actors of global governance, shared sovereignty). Yet surprisingly, despite the enormous scope of Castells's work, there is not a single case study, however brief, of a branch of this global bureaucracy – not of the United Nations (or any of its organizations or programs), not of the World Bank, not of the World Trade Organization, not of the World Intellectual Property Organization (WIPO), nor of any other. This is certainly not due to a lack of knowledge or access. Castells frequently speaks and consults at this level. He personally knows some of the most senior staff quite well. Yet all of these organizations appear only in passing in Castells's theory of the network society. And then they are often lumped together in a single paragraph, leading to entirely uncontroversial conclusions such as "the growing role played by international organizations and supranational consortia cannot be equated with the demise of the nation-state. But the price paid by nation-states for their survival as nodes of states' networks is that of their decreasing sovereignty."[59]

If this sounds confusing, it is. The confusion arises from deep tensions between Castells's theoretical model of the state applied to global/transnational governance, and the empirical reality he observes. Within the theoretical model, the trajectory of development would be, loosely speaking, toward a federal superstate. In the same sense that regions banded together to form a nation-state (for example, in Switzerland in 1848, or in Germany in 1871), nation-states are now forced to cooperate intensively and extensively. It is their recognition, however insufficient and obscured by ideology, that many problems need to be managed on a higher level which leads to the creation of governance structures above the nation-state. Instead of three, we now have four layers of government. Castells goes as far as hinting at the existence of a "global power bloc" – in an analogy of the regional/national power blocs that dominate the institutions of governance – he does not elaborate on its constitution. Similarly, in the same sense that national civil societies create a zone in which the logic of power making and the logic of experience can meet and adapt to one another, he sees it as an urgent matter to support the emergence of global civil society to fulfill the same function supranationally.[60]

If there is one case that fits the trajectory of this model, then it is the development of the European Union. Of all the international governance mechanisms, this is the one most resembling a nation-state. And, indeed, it is the only empirical case in which the supranational elements of the network state are examined at all. In a revealing offhand remark, while sketching the theory of the state, Castells sees the EU as evolving toward a "super nation-state."[61] This is a surprising remark which reflects neither Castells's personal political views, nor his actual research. Rather it seems driven primarily by the internal logic of his theoretical model, which conceives the network state as a set of governance institutions operating on different layers (local, regional, national, global).

Characteristically, the conclusion he draws from his empirical study is quite different. Rather than detecting the rise of a "United States of Europe" – despite the fact that the EU has a president, a parliament, a currency, and a court – he finds that the actual arrangements are better characterized as "neo-medievalism."[62] This term, coined in the late 1970s,[63] indicates that political power is, again, becoming territorially ambiguous. Member states of the EU no longer have exclusive control over their territories; rather they have to share and negotiate it with the claims of others, some formulated at a regional, some at a European, and others at a global level. In short, governance functions are no longer monopolized by the vertically integrated nation-state.[64] In short, also on this level, we have the transformation of vertically integrated hierarchies into flexible networks, a development fully congruent with what Castells has identified as the general trajectory characterizing the rise of the network society.

The new political reality is incompatible with traditional notions of national sovereignty, and it makes it almost impossible, or even redundant, to distinguish between foreign and domestic politics.[65] Multiple power claims and regulatory regimes coexist at the same time, and their interrelation is a matter of continuous negotiation. The resulting indeterminacy of the institutional arrangements characteristic of the EU is a critical, constitutive feature. It creates the necessary flexibility to accommodate the endlessly shifting coalitions and interests. Castells notes that "the network state, with its geometrically variable sovereignty, is the response of the political systems to the challenges of globalization. And the European Union may be the clearest manifestation of this emerging form of state, probably characteristic of the Information Age."[66]

This conclusion that the European Union is the clearest expression of a far more general trend is, however, problematic. On a very general level – governance functions are shared among nationally based institutions of governance in a process of flexible and continuous negotiation – it is consistent with the empirical record presented by Castells. On a more specific level – the EU as a model for other regions, or perhaps the globe – it directly contradicts Castells's own conclusion that the kind of integration characteristic of the EU would be impossible, for historical reasons, elsewhere. Asia, he maintains, will not integrate under the leadership of Japan (or China), nor will Latin America under that of Brazil, as Europe did under the leadership of France/Germany.

It might well be justified to characterize the EU as a new form of state, a network state. However, it is entirely unclear how the institutions of global governance, the UN and the countless branches of the global bureaucracy, are to be integrated into this notion of the network state. Particularly since Castells still sees the capacity to impose legitimate violence as its hallmark, something that not even the EU is capable of, with no army or community-wide police force (though that might change in the future).

All in all, Castells's analysis of the evolution of power, centered round states in process of transformation, is highly uneven. It is best at the level of the region and the nation-state. Multiple and seemingly contradictory trends, such as the crisis of democratic institutions, the split between nation and state in some regions, and a rise of aggressive nationalism and informational welfare states, are convincingly related back to what have been identified as the fundamental tension of the network society: the tension between the dynamics of global networks of economic, cultural and political relationships, and the particularities of local identities. His argument that the network society is simultaneously shaped by global and local dynamics, and that it is consequently a multicultural reality is convincing and the conclusion is certainly valid: national politics can still make a difference, for better or worse.

Most wanting is an analysis of global governance, which is, by and large, simply absent. Above the level of the nation-state, Castells's theory of power loses its purchase. It yields little beyond relatively chaotic, ad hoc arrangements reflecting the tenuous balance of national agendas. In such a context, sovereignty is lost, power diffuses and politics becomes powerless, because the "flow of power" is overwhelmed by the "power of flows." This is theoretically unsophisticated and the lack of empirical grounding is fatal, all the more because of Castells's basic methodological premise of grounding theoretical abstractions in an iterative process of empirical research. What we are left with is a set of overly general propositions. Somewhere in between sits his account of the evolution of the EU. This is not surprising, since the EU is the supranational project that is the most like a traditional nation-state. But even here the theory of the state only partially fits the analysis of the empirical processes ("super nation-state" versus "neo-medievalism"). All in all, the analysis of the weakening of the old levers of powers, particularly the nation-state, is not balanced by an analysis of the new character of power operating not through national hierarchies but through global networks.

Power and Networks

This is not the first time we have reached the conclusion that the treatment of the new forms of power, broadly understood as rule setting and governance in networks, is the single most problematic part of the theory of the network society. The same problem has already been encountered in the analysis of the "relationships of production." As I have argued, the economic analysis is most convincing at the level of the firm and networks of firms (including the associated changes in the constitution of labor), but weakest in regard to new global regulatory regimes, private or state-supported. For Castells, the most significant aspect of the global economy is that it is driven by fierce competition among global production networks. Many are dominated by multinational corporations which act as networks of tight coordination within networks of loose coordination. Yet even global corporations are found to be powerless relative to the chaotic fluctuations of the global financial markets, conceived as a faceless enforcer of relentless profit-maximizing. These markets are more powerful than any actor, or even any group of actors (say, national banks trying to support a currency). Yet, for all their force, these markets are conceptualized as blind, as an efficient "automaton." Such a perspective stresses the out-of-control nature of the processes at the global level, described by Castells with a recurring metaphor as "whirlwinds." This is an important point, characteristic of the new global landscape created by complex systems. In such self-adjusting systems, as John Urry puts it, "change can occur without a determining 'agency' producing different outcomes."[67] True enough. Nevertheless, this is hardly a complete picture of the (political) forces shaping the network society.

Of course, Castells's sprawling work is more complex and empirically sensitive (not to say, contradictory), so that elements of what is missing can be glimpsed here and there. For example, he is quite clear that economic globalization has also been a political process that has been forced on many countries by the most powerful ones. Unfortunately, not the mechanisms, nor the arenas, nor the actors of this political process are explored. All we get are generic references to the deregulation spearheaded in the 1980s by Thatcher and Reagan, and to pressures brought to bear in negotiations in asymmetrical networks of states. Or there is a casual remark that there is a global bureaucracy emerging, yet it is not investigated at any length. So the glimpses remain just that, tantalizing allusions to otherwise absent processes, hidden actors, and unexplored realities.

The point here is not to criticize the empirical grounding of the theory as incomplete. Per se, this would not be problematic. On the contrary, if the theory lent itself to exploring areas neglected so far, its explanatory value would be increased. As we will see in the next chapter, this is the case with Castells's rudimentary analysis of the transformation of time. However, here, in respect to questions of power, the opposite is the case. Castells's definition of power is particularly unsuited to the very process he focuses on: the transformation of institutions of governance from fixed hierarchies to flexible networks.

Let us recall Castells's definition of power, here in a slightly different version: "the action of humans on other humans to impose their will on others."[68] He insists on a very strict separation of "power" from "influence," and then proceeds to focus on power exclusively.[69] There are two things that are problematic in this definition of power when trying to understand network processes. First, power is conceptualized as being applied by one person and directly affecting another one, as, for example, a police officer arresting a suspect. The problem is that this notion of power does not lend itself to investigating how power operates in the absence of a person exercising it. Second, power is thought to be unidirectional in the sense of flowing from the person who exercises it to the one who is subjected to it. Again, this is hard to apply to network processes characterized by feedback and mutual adaptation.

It is worth remembering that such a definition of power, even though it has become entirely standard and can be found in every handbook and dictionary, was developed some hundred years ago by Max Weber for a very precise purpose: to analyze administrative bureaucracies, which he saw as the hallmark of modern societies. As such, Weber was interested in formal processes and the chains of command through which orders could be relayed without much regard to the will of the particular person receiving the order. These chains of command were held together by an explicit or implicit threat of violence in the sense of "if you don't obey me, I have the authority to punish you." The key here is the direct, ultimately physical connection between two subjects, one coercing the other. In short, power operated through (the threat of) repression.

Weber was offering less a universal definition of power (which, one can assume, would be relatively meaningless anyway), and more something more precise: an operational tool to analyze the formation and processes of integrated, hierarchical bureaucracies. Castells, of course, is right that this kind of power, based on the legitimate means of violence to enforce formal orders, remains ultimately within the hands of the nation-state, even though the state may have growing troubles exercising it. From this emerges one of the contradictions of the network state, precisely identified by Castells. The power of international institutions remains dependent on the support of the nation-state. Because of this, Castells seems to imply that the nation-state remains the beginning and the end of governance. What has changed is that its sovereignty is no longer absolute but shared. This, as we have seen, is not a small matter. But is it all there is?

The central argument of the theory of the network society is that the role of such formal hierarchies is decreasing, and the role of flexible networks is increasing. This has a substantial impact on the relationships of power, as Castells argues, because power

> is no longer concentrated in institutions (the state), organizations (capitalist firms), or symbolic controllers (corporate media, churches). It is diffused in global networks of wealth, power, information and images, which circulate and transmute in a system of variable geometry and dematerialized geography. Yet, power does not disappear. *Power still rules society, it still shapes, and dominates, us.* Not only because apparatuses of different kinds can still discipline bodies and silence minds. This form of power is, at the same time, eternal, and fading away. It is eternal because humans are, and will be, predators. But in its current form of existence, it is fading way: the exercise of this kind of power is increasingly ineffective for the interests it is supposed to serve.[70]

What Castells maintains is remarkable: There are fewer instances in which a representative of a formal organization can tell someone else: "You must do this, or else . . . !" If accurate – and it seems like a conclusion that is reasonable but hard to substantiate empirically on such a general level – this constitutes a very significant reversal of the secular trend that Weber identified as central to modernity. Weber feared bureaucracies would lock society in an "iron cage" of instrumental rationality. For Castells, informationalism has shattered that cage. Whether that is to be seen as an improvement is less than clear. Weber was undoubtedly very worried about the growth of administrative bureaucracies, whose cold rationality would lead society into a "polar night of icy darkness." This is no longer the primary danger. As Castells details in his tour through the "fourth world" and the "black holes of informational capitalism," large sections of the world population are not so much repressed – rather they are abandoned, declared worthless, and bypassed, as he states repeatedly, by the global flows of wealth and power. The time of gulags is over. The intense, if repressive, attention totalitarian regimes paid to their citizens has been replaced by the extensive neglect of informational capitalism, which has declared entire populations to be "redundant," to be ignored or treated as undesirable migrants if they show up at the gated communities of the rich.

The latter issue, however, remains underdeveloped. Castells barely mentions how the state intervenes in the lives of ordinary citizens, whether in the form of the "prison-industrial complex," or through the various means of regulating transnational migration, or more recently, through the extensive measures connected to "homeland" security.[71] Rather, Castells, in line here with a growing chorus of analysts, argues that power today operates more through exclusion than through repression.[72] But if the Weberian definition of power is based on repression, and if contemporary power's most potent threat (and practice) is exclusion, would that not indicate the need for a new definition of power, rather than simply arguing that power has somehow diffused into processes, or automata?

Unfortunately, Castells has very little to offer on this crucial point. In his account, processes are indeed autonomous. The bypassing has no agency. It is not done by identifiable agents, say, multinational corporations managed by tightly knit networks of board members, consultants, and public bureaucrats. Rather, he uses the passive voice, referring to flows of power and wealth. While this can seem like the reification of processes as actors, as Peter Marcuse argues,[73] for Castells this is justified because even these corporations are disciplined by the intense pressure to maximize profits imposed on them by their dependence on the global financial markets. Consequently, the chief executive of a pharmaceutical company is not to blame for not investing resources in finding a cure for malaria. After all, it is a disease that predominantly affects people who are too poor to buy medicine. Under pressure to create profits, it would be unwise, and untenable in the long term, to address a demand where there is no market. Nothing personal, just deadly.

Such a perspective is not so much incorrect, as incomplete. What it fails to grasp is how the very dynamics which constrain the players in the global markets are following certain rules that have been written, and are enforced, by specifiable agents to serve particular ends. Whereas Castells seems to imply that free trade is indeed trade under the absence of rules, shaped primarily by direct, raw competition, a burgeoning literature on global governance has been analyzing the new regulatory mechanisms that underpin, and decisively shape, the global economy.[74] These authors report a number of noticeable shifts which do not confirm the picture of "deregulation" in the sense of less regulation. Rather, there are new and different regulations, less nationally based and more globally coordinated.

For example, Saskia Sassen points out that a new kind of global governance regime is emerging, so that "we are headed for a situation where international law will be predominately private law, that is, international economic law."[75] In parallel to the globalization of the economy we have also a globalization of law. One of the institutional loci of this reregulation is the WTO, which is based on a very expansive notion of international trade. The issue is not whether this regulatory regime is fully coherent and fully enforced. For now, what needs to be noted is that it comprises extensive legal agreements between transnational production and service networks, a proliferating number of international treaties and organizations, and multiple global enforcement mechanisms. Of course, particularly the latter remain ultimately tied to the nation-states, but in their day-to-day operations they cannot be reduced to that. Even for the US, the room for unilateralism in trade issues is limited, more so than in military affairs (because in the area of trade the US is not the sole "hyperpower," and hence one could argue that the WTO is more important as an arbiter than the UN).

Consequently, the fact that it can be justifiable to call certain networks "automata" does not preclude that they operate under specific rules that are far from arbitrary or simply emergent as unintended consequences. In one remarkable passage Castells writes that

> it all depends on the goals of a given network and the most elegant, economical, and self-reproductive way to perform these goals. In this sense, a network is an automaton. *In a social structure, social actors and institutions program a network.* But once programmed, information networks, powered by information technology, impose their structural logic on their human components.[76]

This section is noteworthy not only because it is a rare reference to the programming of networks, but also because the key idea is sandwiched between two sentences that talk about something rather different. Are networks programmed or are they autonomous? This passage reads like a crime report that focuses on ballistics and the path taken by the bullet as constrained by the laws of physics, only to mention, in passing, that someone aimed and pulled the trigger. What Castells refers to in this one short sentence is that networks are programmed to be specific automata, and the programming is done by social actors and institutions. But he goes no further. If the issue of programming were developed, it would help to clarify the nature and organigation of power specific to the network society.

The key concept in grasping the new constitution of power, I would argue, is the *protocol*. In general, a protocol is "any code of conventional or proper behaviour" to use the definition of the Oxford English Dictionary. In diplomatic circles, where the term originated, it also refers to a set of behavioral norms regulating the interaction between the head of state and foreign ambassadors. A protocol is necessary because there is no formal hierarchy between the two. Indeed, what is distinctive about ambassadors is that they are not subject to the power of the foreign state in which they are located. Because the head of state cannot simply impose his will on the ambassadors, a protocol has to be agreed on which allows the two sides, each independent of the other, to interact smoothly. In computer science, where the term is currently most used, a protocol is a set of standards which enables computers to interact with one another. Or, as Galloway puts it metaphorically, a protocol is "the etiquette of autonomous agents."[77] This is the core of the matter: a protocol regulates the interaction of social and technological actors which are formally independent of one another. In short, a protocol enables interdependence on the basis of independence.

Networks are held together by protocols. The internet, for example, is based on a technical protocol called TCP/IP (Transmission Control Protocol/Internet Protocol). Any application, be it a file-sharing client or a corporate intranet, that wants to run on the internet must adhere to this protocol. This "must" does not stem from Weberian coercion: this is the key point. Rather, it flows from the simple fact that outside this protocol, there is no internet. Take it or leave it, that is if you can afford to leave it. In the same sense, free trade is based on a set of rules defined by, among others, the WTO. Any country that wants to participate fully in the official global economy needs to accept these rules and regulations, just as any developer of internet applications needs to accept the TCP/IP standards. Put generally, a protocol is what allows autonomous agents to interact in a network, thus "without a shared protocol, there is no network."[78]

A protocol is very different from a chain of command. Whereas a hierarchy defines the role and functions of all its elements – there is no member of a military organization without a rank – a protocol structures the space in which each actor needs to decide for itself what to do. Despite the autonomy of the network agent, the protocol is crucial, because it is what enables actors to constitute the space, a network, through their interactions. Thus protocols, even though they are simply a *formal* set of rules, are never neutral. Rather, by defining the "rules of engagement" they are an important aspect of the quality of the engagement itself, even if they do not prescribe the content of the interaction. Protocols are the grammar, not the syntax of communication. They are constraining and enabling at the same time, constituting another conflation of the distinction between structure and agency so characteristic of networks.

Actors in networks are simultaneously autonomous and highly constrained. This is what is specific about the network form of organization and marks its difference from a formal hierarchy. In this narrow sense Castells is right when he argues that even powerful corporations and states are no longer sovereign actors, but subject to the logic programmed into the networks through which they operate. Yet, despite pointing out that that networks are programmed by social actors, which, I assume, have their particular social agendas, Castells pays no attention to how this programming is done. He stresses relentless, if not Darwinian, competition which forces all actors to adapt, yet the conditions under which this competition takes place remain unexamined. However, it is through setting the rules of the games and then letting the individual actors figure out for themselves how to deal with the constraints – rather than in old-fashioned command-and-control hierarchies – that power operates in a network. This is precisely the point where we can locate the transformation of power operating through repression to power operating through exclusion. Actors are no longer told what to do. Rather, they are left to fend for themselves in the network created by the protocol. If they cannot do that within the constraints of the protocol, they drop out of the network. Plain and simple, and there is not even anyone actively pushing.

Only very recently has Castells begun to recognize the problematic conceptualization of power within the theory of the network society. He has taken the first steps in refining his analysis precisely to focus on this question of how systems of domination can be self-organizing and designed at the same time. He writes:

> Perhaps the question of power, as traditionally formulated, does not make sense in the network society. In the world of networks, the ability to exercise control over others depends on two basic mechanisms: the ability to program/reprogram the network(s) in terms of the goals assigned to the network; and the ability to connect

different networks to ensure their cooperation by sharing common goals and increasing resources.[79]

These processes of setting the rules of interaction in a network ("programming") and of connecting the different systems of networks ("switching") are extremely complex and require the ad hoc coordination of a large number of people and institutions. This complexity seems to be the main reason why Castells argues that it makes no sense to speak of a capitalist class, or a power elite, anymore. In other words, rather than being concentrated in the hands of a few, power is constantly reconfigured in changing networks and strategic alliances, formed around, and held together by, short-term projects. So, he concludes,

> it is precisely because there is no power elite capable of keeping under its control the programming and switching operations of all the important networks that more subtle, complex and negotiated systems of power enforcement have to be established, so that the dominant networks of society have compatible goals and are able, through the switching processes enacted by actor-networks, to communicate with each other, inducing synergy and limiting contradiction.[80]

This certainly points in the right direction and is testimony to Castells's willingness to rework his theory when it comes into conflict with empirical observation. However, there has not been a real test so far of any of Castells's theoretical conceptualizations. Neither he – nor any of his close collaborators[81] – has (yet) followed up with research on any concrete programming of a major global network generating wealth and power. In terms of an empirical analysis of power operating in networks through protocols, the basic questions are: Who writes the protocol? What are the rules codified in the protocol? And what are the cumulative effects of these rules enacted by autonomous agents in the field created by the protocol itself? Without such studies, it has to remain an open question how subtle, complex, and flexible these arrangements really are, and whether they do not, in fact, point to the formation of a global elite, or capitalist class.

In the literature on the design of technological networks, it is commonly understood that some of the most significant decisions are taken when protocols and standards are defined. Or, more generally, that the specifics of the architecture itself matter. Individual decisions taken later on are often much less effective (hence the difficulty for governments in trying to censor the internet on top of the prevailing architecture). Lawrence Lessig has forcefully argued that "technical codes" are often more effective in shaping people's behaviors than "legal codes," despite the very real threat of violence that stands behind the law.[82] Technical codes exercise power that is not based on the threat of physical violence, but on the ability to set the conditions for interaction, for access to the network.

The vast literature on the social construction of technology has convincingly pointed out that the setting of standards and design decisions are themselves political processes.[83] The medium might be the message, but this message has a grammar, and authors. A similar analysis can be done, and has been done, on the social construction of the protocols that shape the global networks, and the turbulent, chaotic competition that unfolds through them. One of the most impressive of these studies, Peter Drahos's *Information Feudalism*, has already been mentioned. In minute detail he analyzes empirically how, and by whom, a particular notion of intellectual property has been inscribed in multiple international agreements, most importantly in the 1994 Agreement on Trade-Related Aspects of Intellectual Property Rights (TRIPS). It is true that this treaty is about free trade and global flows of wealth largely outside the control of the nation-states, but it is free trade that results, not coincidentally, in "a huge structural shift in the world economy to move monopoly profits from the information-poor to the information-rich."[84] This is not a conspiracy that secretly controls the world markets. Rather, these are conditions which structurally favor some independent actors over others. The whirlwinds are still blowing, and they can take down the most powerful corporation if it is unable to adapt to the changing currents. Yet the structural bias of the protocols that enable competition to be chaotic and relentless virtually guarantees that the fall of a mighty corporation will be most profitable to other mighty corporations, rather than to those who suffer from structural violence.

Castells is, of course, aware that economic globalization is not a self-unfolding process. "Neither technology nor business," he writes, "could have developed the global economy on its own. The decisive agents in setting up a new, global economy were governments . . . and their ancillary international institutions." Yet, in the very next paragraph, he dismisses this question, saying: "How and why it happened is a matter for historians."[85] This is odd, particularly since he dwells happily on the historical minutiae of technology in his discussion of the internet.[86] What we have here is a strange combination of a poorly fitting theoretical tool, the Weberian definition of power in hierarchies, and a tacit lack of interest in exploring certain research questions. Whatever the cause of this concurrence might be, the results are crippling to Castells's analysis of power.

Rather than concentrating on issues of network programming, Castells has tried to sidestep the constraints of the Weberian notion of power by using a different notion of power in his analysis of global social movements. In terms of coercion and control, they have no power at all. Particularly as, Castells stresses convincingly, they are not interested in "the long march through the institutions." How can they exercise any influence? Well, there is old power and new power, and

> the new power lies in the codes of information and in the images of representation around which societies organize their institutions, and people build their lives, and decide their behavior. *The sites of power are the people's minds.* This is why power is at the same time identifiable and diffused. We know what it is, but we cannot seize it because power is a function of an endless battle around cultural codes of society.[87]

For Castells's social movements are the primary producers of cultural codes and images, and governments' "mighty, rigid apparatuses will not be a match, in any reasonable timespan, for the minds mobilized around the power of flexible alternative networks."[88] Again, this is not so much incorrect as incomplete. Castells does not consider the state, or large institutions generally, as producers of cultural codes, or to be more precise, he asserts that the only types of cultural codes they produce – those leading to legitimizing identity – have lost their grip on the minds of the people. The question here is, can the state not produce any other codes? Do advertisements and state-induced propaganda, while clearly not brainwashing people into total submission, have any symbolic power? Not for Castells, because the structure of media politics – as we have seen – is taken to make sustained propaganda impossible, or at least ineffective.

Additionally, Castells does not analyze the production of cultural codes as a material process, one in which resource-rich institutions might have advantages over resource-poor institutions or social movements. It is not clear how the Weberian type of power relates to this new symbolic power. The two seem to spring from radically different sources and one does not really help or gain from the other. The state's codes are anemic; social movements do not aim at taking over the state. As a result, perhaps, power dissipates in networks. One tenuous connection between the two forms of power is that they are both based on violence. Classic power is based on physical violence, cultural power on "symbolic violence," that is, "the capacity of a given symbolic code to delete a different code from the individual brain upon whom power is exercised."[89]

Thus we have a duality of power both versions of which are based on their own sources of violence. In what can only be described as a secular trend (with strong postmodern overtones), the balance between the two is shifting, because within the new sphere of power – the space of flows – cultural codes play such an important role. They influence minds. Physical power on the other hand, is where the bodies are, in the space of places. And, over time, control over bodies is less effective than influence over minds. What is here a duality of violence as the basis of two distinct forms of power is often thought of as a triad. One element is missing in Castells's account. This is the element of *structural violence*. The term was coined by Johan Galtung in the late 1960s to refer to situations where violence is inflicted on someone without the direct, violent agency of someone else.[90] Classic examples of structural violence are discriminatory laws which repress people in the normal course of events without anyone doing anything that is not perfectly within the order of things. Other examples are policy-induced famines where people starve without someone violently taking away their food.

The concept of structural violence has been criticized as overly broad, but in the context of the present discussion – focusing on the nature of power in the network society – it might be useful as a way to introduce a term such as *structural power*. This would denote the ability to threaten with, or inflict, structural violence. In terms of the global economy and global governance, it would indicate the ability to create conditions which induce people to behave in ways such that their actions, taken as independent actors, produce highly differentiated results. In other words, it would point back to the question of the programming of network protocols, just identified as the new locus of power in the network society.

Castells is very concerned not to reduce the programming of networks to control over the networks. For good reason. The relationship between protocols and the applications built on top of them is an indirect one. As Phil Agre points out in a discussion of the social character of peer-to-peer technologies, "decentralized institutions do not imply decentralized architectures, or vice versa. [Yet] architectures and institutions inevitably coevolve."[91] While network architecture does not determine the types of applications running on the network, it does introduce important constraints on their creation/development. Without considering how these constraints are produced, often very deliberately, we cannot understand the particular character of the networks created on the basis of particular protocols.

Castells's account of power in the network society is very uneven. Convincing is the analysis of how the old levers of (state) power are becoming creaky. He is also on strong ground in pointing out that inside the networks of the global economy and politics, the pressure on actors is relentless and even powerful actors can be more driven than they are drivers. Yet Castells's account makes power disappear far more than necessary. Instead of actors, we have only powerful processes. We have programs and protocols, but still no programmers and no designers. This leads to a strange imbalance. Castells is no apologist of neoliberalism; he is very clear that an intolerable number of people are excluded and reduced to abject poverty. Yet, as Peter Marcuse remarked, Castells presents "the excluded without the excluders."[92] People face processes whose political origins remain nebulous. The element of their chaotic self-organization, driven by the need to survive dog-eat-dog competition, is systematically worked out, whereas the elements of their deliberate programming are almost systematically neglected. Without taking into consideration the network architecture, any analysis of the dynamics of the network remains incomplete. This applies also to Castells's political analysis of sociotechnical networks of production and power. Here, in the incomplete analysis of the relationships of power characteristic of the network society, due to a lack of attention, theoretically and empirically, to the programming of the various intersecting networks of commerce and politics, lies the single greatest weakness in Castells's theory of the great transformation of social morphology. It is, as we will see in the final chapter, directly related to his specific notion of the network. However, in the meantime, let's turn to what I believe to be Castells's most profound theoretical contribution, the analysis of the transformation of time and space.

5

Flows and Places

The relationships of production, experience, and power are material processes that relate people and things to one another in historically specific ways. They constitute the fabric of society, realized, and contested, in space. The particulars of their spatial forms are neither accidental nor without consequences. Rather, they are a central aspect of the overall character of society. The analysis of the complex interaction between the structural logic of these relationships and the concrete materiality of their realization in and through space provides the organizing structure to Castells's entire work. People, as long as they are physical beings, cannot but live and act in space, and the spaces they create reflect and shape social life in its totality.

The transformations of space are, quite literally, the grounding of Castells's holistic perspective on interrelated social dynamics. All social processes have substantial spatial components, which in one way or another are materialized, and thus rendered empirically observable, in physical places, in particular cities and regions. A theory of space is therefore an essential element of a comprehensive social theory, and vice versa. In fact, Castells has always taken them to be coextensive. Quite simply, "there is no theory of space that is not an integral part of a general social theory."[1] In such a perspective, space is not a container. Space is not a given, nor is it stable. Rather, space is constituted by social relations and transformed along with them. In the following, I will sketch Castells's theory of space, with particular emphasis on the theory of the space of flows. Along with the emergence of a new type of space, Castells argues that time has taken on new characteristics in the network society. I will focus on this argument in the second part of this chapter. In the final part, I will look at how Castells conceptualizes the interaction between the space of flows and the space of places, leading to a transformation of the urban landscape.

The analysis of the particular character of time and space provides the framework that integrates the various domains of the network society into a coherent theory. It constitutes the single most original aspect of Castells's entire theory.

Castells's Theory of Space

Philosophically speaking Castells's theory of space as a (social) relation stands in the lineage of Gottfried Wilhelm Leibniz (1646–1716). Leibniz argued against the notion of space as an absolute entity which had just been proposed by Isaac Newton (1642–1727). Newton had conceived space as "God's boundless uniform sensorium," implying that the reality of space is prior to the existence of things. Objects are located in space, which is unvarying and infinite with no relation to the objects in it. In contrast, Leibniz argued, that space is created in between things, and therefore there can be no such thing as empty space, not the least because this would be a substance without properties. It is the objects that create space. Space is constituted by the relationship among these objects. Without objects, there is nothing in between, hence there is no space.[2]

It is not a coincidence that debates concerning the nature of space preoccupied many of the leading thinkers of the late seventeenth and early eighteenth centuries. It was a time of profound change, not unlike our own. From the perspective of McLuhan's media theory, Newton's notion of space – absolute, infinite, and stable – betrays a "visual" bias, characteristic of "print culture" in general. The Leibniz–Newton debate took place at a time when European societies were deeply transformed, a process which laid the foundation for modern science and politics. Or, as McLuhan described it, Europe was entering the "Gutenberg galaxy." Leibniz's notion of space – relational, finite, and flexible – is closer to what McLuhan called an "acoustic" conception of reality, characteristic in preprint, or more generally, oral cultures. In this sense, Leibniz defended an older sensibility against Newton's new, scientific worldview.

The same theoretical perspective suggests that today we are witnessing a similarly profound transition, resulting in the decline of print culture. It is not that printed works disappear; after all, you are probably reading these words printed on paper. However, print is no longer the dominant medium of social communication. With this decline, certain key ideas that characterized print culture are being called into question, and notions that were once tied to oral cultures are being revived. This is not a cyclical return back to old concepts, as McLuhan sometimes seemed to suggest. Rather, following Walter Ong, this revival is better characterized as the "secondary orality" of electronic communication. For Ong the new orality is secondary because "the orality of telephones, radio, and television . . . depends on writing and print for its existence."[3] In other words, the now dominant informational mode of communication is giving new meaning to ways of conceptualizing the world which are in many of their aspects much older.

Thus it is also not a coincidence that today notions of space (and of time) are being reconceptualized simultaneously in many intellectual disciplines, after the domination of Western thinking by the Newtonian vision of stability and infinity for some three hundred years.[4] Rather, one can argue that this is again connected to profound cultural transformations related to the rise of new communication media. This "today" must be understood in a historical dimension. For McLuhan the exit from the Gutenberg galaxy began with the introduction of the telegraph (mid-nineteenth century) and accelerated with radio and the telephone (early twentieth century). The dominance of print culture was finally brought to an end with the rise of television as the preeminent medium of communication. This is why McLuhan argued in the early 1960s that we had left the Gutenberg galaxy. Almost 40 years later, Castells proposes that we have entered the internet galaxy.[5]

For Castells the contemporary transformation of space is directly related to the increasing importance of electronic communication. However, contrary to McLuhan, who concentrated on the transformation of perception (the shifting "balance of the senses"), Castells's focus has always been on the social ordering of things, much closer to Leibniz, for whom space was "an order of coexistence." "Space, as a social product," Castells has argued consistently since the early 1970s,

is always specified by a definite relation between the different instances of social structure, the economic, the political, the ideological, and the conjuncture of social relations that result from them. Space, therefore, is always an historical conjuncture and a social form that derives its meaning from the social processes that are expressed through it. [Consequently,] it is absolutely necessary to study the production of spatial forms on the basis of the underlying social structure."[6]

Space, then, is a product of society. We cannot understand the specifics of space without understanding the society as a whole which creates this space; consequently, a space-centered analysis must always be holistic. This is so not only because space is not a fixed container, but also because space is not simply a mirror of social relations. Space is as much a product of society as it is a source of social dynamics. It is both a way in which the past reaches into the present, and raw material to build the future, used by social actors according to their own objectives and abilities. Many of the political disagreements within the New Urban Sociology of the 1970s can be traced to the fact that some (for example, Castells) focused on how the past reaches into the present, creating structural determinants, whereas others (for example, Lefebvre) focused more on how space could provide a resource to build an alternative future.

Space, in the last resort, cannot be conceived without time. They are expressed through one another. In Castells's perspective, their relationship is such that "space is the material support of time-sharing social practices. . . . [It] brings together those practices that are simultaneous in time."[7] If social actors are not present in the same space, they cannot share time, that is, interact in real time. For much of history, the only space that allowed for time-sharing was a place, that is, "a locale whose form, function, and meaning are self-contained within the boundaries of physical contiguity."[8] If it takes time to get from place to place, time cannot be shared across places. This does not mean places are not connected to one another, or that they are independent from one another. But their connection is defined precisely by the fact that they do not share the same time, for better or worse.

For a long time, this proposition seemed such common sense that it could be assumed without ever being specified. Indeed, Castells, for all his interest in space, regarded time as entirely unproblematic until quite recently. The space of time-sharing was assumed to be a place because time and space were taken to be coextensive. Analyzing the restructuring of capitalist production during the 1980s, Castells concluded that this common sense was no longer justified. Rather, a new type of space had been created. It enabled social actors to share time across places. Suddenly social actors could be in the same temporal space without being in the same physical space. More importantly for a sociological analysis, key social institutions were being restructured to take advantage of this fact, thus gaining competitive advantages over those who continued to follow the conventional logic of time/space. In this restructuring process, these institutions, mainly capitalist firms, actively expanded the space of flows to the point where it became the material basis for the dominant processes in the network society. According to Castells, the threshold was passed in the second half of the 1980s.[9]

The Space of Flows

Technologies have always shaped the social reality of space and time. Comparing ancient Egypt to ancient Greece, Harold Innis was the first to propose that the historical organization of space and time was closely related to the type of communication media dominant in a particular culture. He argued that writing in stone, characteristic of Egyptian culture, created a bias toward time, that is, a concern with the organization of deep traditions and long lines of ancestry. The management of time, and thus of society, was in the hands of a caste of priests, who interpreted the events of the present in relation to the divine flows of time. Writing on paper (or parchment), on the other hand, created a bias toward space, that is, a concern with organizing territory, with much less emphasis on tradition and ancestry. The management of space, and therefore of society, was organized by secular authorities which managed armies and trading routes whose meaning was determined within a human timescale.[10]

The great historian Fernand Braudel, and many others, showed how writing letters, keeping accounting books, and advances in maritime technologies were essential to extending commerce across land and sea from the sixteenth century onward, thus again affecting notions of time and space.[11] Alfred Chandler detailed how the introduction of the railway and the telegraph allowed, for the first time, the integration of the entire country into a single market. These technologies were key elements in the emergence of new organizational forms and new managerial approaches in late nineteenth-century America. To exploit the new economies of scale, economic enterprises of unprecedented dimensions and complexities emerged within a few decades. These giant corporations, and the social conflicts they created, were decisively shaping the social, cultural and political development of the period.[12]

Anthony Giddens theorized "time-space distanciation" – the stretching of social relationships across time and space – as one of the hallmarks of modernity.[13] At the end of the 1980s, the geographer David Harvey summarized this historical trend in the concept of "time/space compression," and noted a significant acceleration of social, in particular capitalist, dynamics due to new global communication networks.[14] Postmodern theorists, particularly Paul Virilio, have been paying close attention to changes in the social structure of time and space. Taking the notion of "time/space compression" to its logical conclusion, Virilio argued that space is being annihilated by computer networks, establishing the "dictatorship of speed," leading, paradoxically, to "total inertia."[15]

Castells concurs with the now conventional wisdom that social relationships have been expanded across distances at an ever greater rate and speed. However, he suggests that there is a historical limit to the process of "time/space compression." Contrary to postmodern visions of finality, time and space are fundamental categories of social life and cannot disappear. Computer networks are not black holes. At one point, the negative, quantitative dynamic of compression (less space, less time) turns into a qualitatively new condition (a new type of space/time). This is exactly what Castells proposes with his concept of the space of flows: a new material basis for time-sharing on which the dominant social processes are reorganized and managed through flows. That is, through "purposeful, repetitive, programmable sequences of exchange and interaction between physically disjointed positions held by social actors."[16]

It is worth going into the detail of the construction of the argument before looking at how it is applied. In Castells's theory, time and space are inseparable and coextensive. In order to be in the same time (that is able to interact in real time), actors need to be in the same space, which, up to now, has always been a place. Consequently, the fact that two actors can be in different places – say, one broker working in New York City and one in London – but share the same time – the present of the financial markets – indicates that the social reality of space has been transformed. A new kind of space must be present which brings those brokers together in time without contiguity of physical space. Since time and space are coextensive, this new space is fundamentally different from physical space, yet connected to it. After all, our brokers are physical beings, one located in downtown Manhattan, the other in the City of

London. This new space, the space of flows, does not replace the geographical space; rather, by selectively connecting places to one another, it changes their functional logic and social dynamics.

For Castells, the emergence of the space of flows signifies, more than anything else, that we have passed a historical watershed and have, indeed, entered a new era. The notion of a watershed, with its thin line of separation, is always a bit problematic, since nothing is created in an instant, not even the space of flows. After all, the telephone has enabled real-time communication across distances for more than a hundred years,[17] and the financial markets have operated across continents in real time since the early 1970s.[18] So, what's new? New, Castells argues, is the relationship between the different time-sharing practices with their distinct material foundations. Until some time in the 1980s, Castells implies – without stating it explicitly – the social practices that relied on physical places for time-sharing were dominant over those built around time-sharing across distances. The effect of the growth of the latter was that they changed the social distance between physical places; hence time and space was compressed. To use a metaphor popular in the 1970s, the world was shrinking. Not anymore. As advertisements in the 1990s announced, "your office has just expanded."

The space of flows does not indicate a linear shrinking of distance, but the establishment of an environment with a completely different, nonlinear spatial logic. Being part of the space of flows means being part of a context whose functional logic is based on real-time interaction, no matter in which places its constitutive elements are located. Though, crucially, not all places are able to provide the infrastructure required to become part of the space of flows. Generally speaking, the more complex the time-sharing activities are, the smaller the number of places which can master the necessary resources to provide the material basis for carrying them out. While it makes no sense to ask whether the financial markets are located in London, New York or Tokyo, it is no coincidence that the centers of twentieth century capitalism were able to transform themselves into the key nodes of the global financial markets in the twenty-first century.

The key to Castells's conception of the space of flows is its materiality, because it foregrounds how expensive and complex it is to create, maintain and navigate that space. In this particular sense, Al Gore's metaphor of the "information highway" is more apt than it was given credit for at the time. This extensive materiality introduces new sources of social exclusion and social stratification that are manifest in new spatial patterns of urban development. Before considering its effect on geographical places, it is important to look at the materiality of the space of flows in more detail.

Castells differentiates between three dimensions that make up the space of flows. The first is the "circuit of electronic exchanges." These are the global information and communication infrastructures that enable real-time interaction across the globe. Importantly, this infrastructure does not just transport digital information around the world, but it is also the foundation of the accelerated movement of people and goods. Consequently, it is made up of information networks, but also of high-speed transportation links through air, land, and water. This infrastructure creates potentiality. These are the pipes and conduits of the flows. The ability to hook up to this infrastructure is the precondition for entering the space of flows. Disconnected from the technological networks, social institutions, places, and people are being marginalized. Even places which prosper by promising disconnection, say vacation resorts, do so on the basis of fast transportation links and deep information flows to selectively maintain those links deemed necessary. Rather than disconnection, they offer particular filters.

The massive, material infrastructure of the space of flows is highly maintenance intensive and requires advanced knowledge and services to work efficiently. Hence the network is not evenly distributed, but clustered in nodes and hubs, the second dimension in Castells's model. In such places, multiple services are provided and consumed, thus creating critical mass for a self-sustaining ecology capable of continuously (re)producing the material basis of the space of flows. The interlocking clusters of financial and administrative services created and managed in global cities are the best analyzed example. They provide the major nodes of the global financial markets, and much of their material and social basis.[19] However, Castells points out that, depending on the types of processes managed in the space of flows, the geography and functionality of its hubs and nodes differ. For example, the hubs producing academic and industrial knowledge, concentrated in what Castells calls "milieux of innovation," exhibit a different spatial distribution than those managing the production and distribution of cocaine, though there are certainly connections between them.

Yet, in all of these networks, the most important nodes require a certain size without which it is impossible to manage the intricacies of advanced processes that make up the space of flows. As Saskia Sassen has shown, advanced financial services are located in a complex and extensive ecology, composed of other high-end legal and cultural services but also of low-level clerical and services labor, and close proximity to a major transportation link.[20] It is this size and complexity of the nodes that explains why the distribution of nodes follows a historical logic, and why the major cities still play a central role, despite the placeless logic of processes organized within the space of flows. It is difficult to create such a complex ecology from scratch, though it certainly can be done, as indicated by development of "technopoles," government-sponsored innovation centers, some of them located outside major metropolitan areas.[21]

But network nodes are not just an agglomeration of circuits and abstract, automated services. Crucially, they are also places were people meet and elites constitute themselves, Castells argues, as a cohesive social group. A particular spatial distribution of, and specific spatial forms created for, this elite provide the third dimension of the space of flows. The territory occupied by these people is separated from the territory of other social groups, first and foremost, by the very real barrier of pricing. They work in expensive offices, live in the most prestigious residential neighborhoods, eat at high-end restaurants with international cuisine, spend their leisure time in secluded clubs, and travel to exclusive resorts for vacationing. If pricing is not enough to keep out the local population, then walls, security services, and other forms of enforced separation are created. Gated communities provide the most visible physical expression of this trend. Around the world their construction has boomed in the 1990s, in direct relation to the growth of slums.[22]

In between, there is a global infrastructure of hotel chains, conference centers, VIP airport lounges, and limousines creating physical bridges between the nodes. Crucial for the smooth flow of people within these circuits, Castells argues, has also been the creation of a lifestyle and the design of "spatial forms aimed at unifying the symbolic environment of the elite around the world, thus superseding the historical specificity of each locale."[23] The dimension of a shared culture remains essential for the functioning of loosely coordinated yet highly interactive and complex networks. Ease of communication, personal trust, and the intimacy of face-to-face communication are still essential elements of interaction. The business lunch does not lose its role as a strategic site to initiate new relationships and close deals, nor does the bed. The ability of people from vastly different backgrounds to cooperate is based on a shared cosmopolitan culture. Leading universities, such as Boston's MIT, the London School of Economics, or the Singapore National University, are not only important producers of advanced knowledge, but also producers of the global elite's shared culture. Thus a cosmopolitan elite culture has emerged with its own trends, fashions, and codes, taking its inputs from nodes in the network rather than from the particular places where its members happen to reside.

The space of flows is the infrastructure of high-speed, high-volume, high-precision communication and transportation, spanning the globe but clustered in specific places based on their ability to provide the resources relevant to advancing the networks' particular programs. Through this infrastructure, elites produce and process vast amounts of information based on which decisions are made. The logic of these decisions cannot be understood by reference to the geographic location of the decision makers, or of those affected by the decisions. Rather, the relevant frame of reference is their position within the overall global networks organized in the pursuit of wealth and power. This placeless logic separates the space of flows, its physical nodes and the people operating them, from their geographic environment, the neighboring local population and their local cultures. In the mid 1980s, Castells summarized this trend as the growing "contradiction between placeless power and powerless places."[24]

It was from this initial observation that the theory of the space of flows was developed at the end of the 1980s. Its elaboration was based on an extensive analysis of the transformation of the spatial distribution of the most advanced industries: microelectronics, finance, and certain sectors of manufacturing.[25] At the time, access to the global communication infrastructure was, by and large, restricted to major organizations with significant financial and staffing resources. The internet was nowhere near a public communication medium. In fact, in Castells's empirical analysis which supported the first formulation of the concept, the distribution of fax machines played a far greater role than access to the internet. This situation of unequal access to communication and information processing infrastructure deepened during the first half of the 1990s. The restructuring continued at the centers of wealth and power, whereas smaller organizations, let alone individuals, still had neither the resources nor the skills to enter the space of flows. During the first half of the 1990s, the difference between the global organization of wealth and power and the local organization of people and cultures was, quite arguably, the most accentuated. Only the elites were able to act globally. In this context, it made sense to draw a sharp distinction between the space of flows, as the space of the elites and socially dominant processes, and the space of places, as the space of isolated and increasingly powerless local populations.

However, much has changed over the last decade. With the development of the internet into a mass medium, the range of people who can access the global communication infrastructure has grown exponentially. With several hundred million people online, it is not an elite space anymore, despite the continuing overrepresentation of the white, English-speaking North. In a way made possible by the lowering of the hurdles of access to the internet, small organizations and individuals have transformed some aspects of the social, technical, and spatial foundations of the space of flows. This has two important consequences in regard to Castells's model.

First, it is not only the dominant social processes managed by the elite that are organized in the space of flows, but an increasingly broad range of social activities, dominant and marginal, public and private, collective and individual, representing a much fuller range of human expressions, projects, and desires. Social movements, as we have seen, have found their way from the city to the space of flows at the end of the 1990s. Second, the dynamics of the space of flows no longer always supersede the dynamics of the space of places. On the contrary, from the Zapatistas to community networking and fully fledged digital cities, from the radical left to the radical right, social movements of all kinds are using the space of flows on behalf of locally rooted projects. Such initiatives are building linkages between flows and places. Using these linkages, people are finding ways to enter the space of flows without leaving the space of places, or to be more precise, to go back and forth easily. Furthermore, mobile technologies allow people to develop new spatial practices by coordinating each other, ad hoc, through the space of flows, congregating and dispersing in self-selected rhythms.[26] In short, in less than two decades, the space of flows has become a part of everyday life, not just influencing the lives of billions of people, but also providing resources which an ever growing number of people can draw upon creatively.

Does this require the theory of the space of flows to be revised? It seems clear today that the radical dichotomy of the space of flows and the space of places suggested in the late 1980s, and expanded in the first edition of *The Information Age* trilogy, has dissolved. Now the connections between the two types of space are much more complex and flexible. This, however, fits well into Castells's general theory of space. Space, of all types, is a resource that can be mobilized, to varying degrees, by a wide range of social actors in the pursuit of their particular agendas. After all, what Castells remarked in the early 1980s still applies: "Spatial forms will be produced by human action. . . . They will express and perform the interests of the dominant class. . . . At the same time, spatial forms will also be marked by resistance from exploited classes, oppressed subjects and abused women."[27] This is not fundamentally different in the space of flows. Thus Castells had little problem in revising his own theory by pointing out that "the geography of the new history will not be made, after all, of the separation between places and flows, but out of the interface between places and flows and between cultures and social interests, both in the space of flows and in the space of places."[28]

Apart from this necessary correction, the basic elements of the theory of the space of flows still seem supported by empirical reality. Nearly all the strategically dominant activities – generating most of the financial wealth and administering the most powerful institutions – operate through the space of flows, and their relative power, compared to activities organized on a purely local basis, has only increased. The global elite is still relatively cohesive, dominating fragmented local populations, even if the resistance and mutual interconnection of the latter have increased. Finally, the dominant activities are still highly clustered in a few central nodes. After all, the internet, with its relatively open access, is only a small aspect of the space of flows, which also includes private and closed networks, such as the financial markets or corporate intranets (which are global as well).

Today, the most powerful processes of resistance also operate through the space of flows.[29] This strengthens the hypothesis that the space of flows is the space of power, including, today, counter-power. For social movements this is not without risks. It could replicate the tension between flows and places, between the leaders who need to operate increasingly in the space of flows in pursuit of coalition building, and the communities, who build their resistance around places. However, it remains to be seen how this tension actually operates within the projects that utilize the space of flows on behalf of local identities. Given the extraordinary creativity of new social movements in building their own sociotechnical tools and strategies, this tension could turn out to be the source of important social innovation, leading to new models of representation and political articulation that invigorate the democratic processes currently under so much strain.

Yet the theory of the space of flows is not just about the growth of time-sharing practices across distances; otherwise we could still speak of time/space compression. On a more abstract level, Castells suggests that all these practices that are organized within this new space share certain characteristics which are particular to this space. This is another aspect of Castells's soft techno-determinism. Similarly to McLuhan, Castells argues that technologies have certain biases that shape the social organization built with them.[30] The space of flows is an integral part of the general transformation of the dominant pattern of social organization from fixed hierarchies to flexible networks. The connection between the new material basis of dominant social processes and their organizational form lies in the particular character of this new type of space, namely, its *binary spatial logic*.

As a material infrastructure, the space of flows is highly clustered in particular geographical places. Castells and many others have established this point empirically. There is no end of the city, and announcing the "death of distance" was premature.[31] Indeed, analyzing the spatial distribution of content production, which does not require the most sophisticated of infrastructures, Castells shows that even the internet is "overwhelmingly a metropolitan phenomenon . . . adapting to the preexisting metropolitan structure, rather than reversing it."[32]

However, from within the space of flows, particularly in respect to flows of information, the spatial distribution looks entirely different. Within the space of flows, there are, in principle, only two states of distance: "here" and "not here," presence and absence, no distance and infinite distance. It is this condition that allows nodes to flexibly connect within one another, no matter where they are located, because they are all "here" in the same time-sharing environment that is the space of flows. The connection between nodes, then, is dominated by functional considerations. Of course, organizations have always differentiated their components functionally, but conventionally the functional logic and the geographic logic overlapped and stabilized one another. Not anymore. Now they are being decoupled through the space of flows.

However, as Castells stresses, "the space of flows is not placeless, although its structural logic is."[33] The ability of a node to contribute to the program of a network is often directly related to its location, but seen from point of view of the network, nodes are differentiated functionally, not geographically. Seen from the point of view of places, we are witnessing the fragmentation of their ordering into a nonlinear pattern of locales which are increasingly disconnected from one another. Not because they are isolated – on the contrary, they are often hyperconnected – but because their integration no longer happens on the basis of their geography, but on the basis of their function in specific networks, coordinated through the space of flows. This enables two adjacent places to be part of completely different functional processes, shaped by dynamics that have no relation to one another. In other words, the functional integration of distant places through the space of flows, and the fragmentation of physical places into disconnected locales are complementary. Fragmentation is the effect imposed by the nonlinear logic of the space of flows on the organization of the space of places. In this sense, Castells's analysis from the late 1980s still remains valid:

> while organizations are located in places, and their components are place-dependent, the organizational logic is placeless, being fundamentally dependent on the space of flows that characterizes information networks. But such flows are structured, not undetermined. They possess directionality, conferred both by the hierarchical logic of the organization as reflected in instructions given, and by the material characteristics of the information systems infrastructure.[34]

This is the core of Castells's concept of the transformation of space. The space of flows is a material infrastructure that enables functional units to be organized into a single whole, operating in real time, independent of their geographical location. This applies as much to the global financial markets as to "virtual communities," as well as to those social movements which, as Castells puts it, "think local and act global," advocating local identities by mobilizing through the space of flows. The exact configuration between the nodes and their relation to the space of places depends on the program of the network. Yet, even for the Zapatista support network, the central organizational determinant is the ability of various nodes to support the indigenous struggle in Chiapas, rather than their proximity to it. It is not a contradiction to be a Zapatista in New York City. Such distant supporters are much more than a vague solidarity movement. They are key resources on which the struggle on the ground can draw directly and without delay. Their role is very different from that of the students marching against the Vietnam War, who had to rely on mass media as their (one-way) access to the nascent space of flows.

The Time of Flows

If Castells's current conception of space is implicitly Leibnizian, his conception of time is explicitly so. For Leibniz, in close analogy to space, there is no absolute, infinite time because "instants apart from things are nothing and they only consist in the successive order of things."[35] In other words, time is sequence. The sequence of events is what creates time, and the historically determined way of how this sequence is ordered constitutes the social character of time. This social character of time is always the result of a specific mix of multiple temporalities, but one tends to be dominant. It structures the most important processes of a given context, thus creating its characteristic type of time. For example, in the Middle Ages, the temporality was cyclical. It followed the rhythms of nature, which still dominated those of human culture. There was no sense of progress, and the past, present, and future were not clearly differentiated. This cyclical rhythm of human life took place on top of a linear flow of divine time, starting with the creation and ending with the day of the final judgment. However, this divine flow of time had little effect on the succession of things in everyday life. Only an elite group of priests was allowed to relate the two spheres together. Any unsanctioned announcement of the end of time and the imminent arrival of the final judgment was prosecuted as a severe act of heresy. Clearly, God's time was not for everyone to read.

A key element in the establishment of modernity was the secularization of linear time and the reordering of social relationships through the diffusion of mechanical clocks.[36] In Lewis Mumford's classic formulation, "the clock is not merely a means of keeping track of the hours, but of synchronizing the actions of men."[37] Clock time became the dominant social temporality, making possible notions such as punctuality, hourly wage, saving and wasting time, and the strict separation of past, present, and future. The British historian E. P. Thompson identified the new "time regime" as the central element in the transformation of peasants into workers.[38] Of course, cyclical temporalities continued to exist, but their relative importance decreased. The mechanical clock was a source, and a powerful symbol, of the growing dominance of man over nature. The establishment of daylight saving time in the twentieth century (1916 in the UK, 1966 in the US) can be seen as one of the most recent steps in a long process of the reordering of social rhythms through the clock. Due to an arbitrary decision, people across the world are

now moving their clocks forward and backward each year, highlighting the pure conventionality of modern time regimes. The only
people who had difficulty with this new invention in time were
those who lived closest to the rhythms of nature, fishermen and
farmers. Characteristically, their protests made no difference.

Castells argues that cyclical and linear temporalities have in
common that they establish relatively predictable sequences.
Indeed, it is this very ordering of events into sequences that establishes the relational notion of time in the first place. Under the influence of informationalism, the predictable sequence of events is
being disturbed in an increasing number of areas, from the natural
to the cultural, from the individual to the collective. If time is
sequence, and informationalism reorganizes events into instances
without meaningful sequence, then time itself is being called into
question. This is what Castells means by "timeless time," the "systemic perturbation in the sequential order of phenomena."[39]

In the current discussion on the transformation of time, many different concepts have been proposed. John Urry, for example, notes
a multiplicity of temporalities, ranging from the "computime" of
the financial networks to the "glacial time" of the environmental
movement, from the "biological time" of organic growth to the
"clock time" of industrial organization.[40] With the concept of "timeless time" Castells does not want to add yet another notion of temporality, but tries to account for the effect created by the interaction
of all of them. In the German discussion, the notion of *Verzeitlichung
der Zeit* has been proposed.[41] Usually, this is translated as "tempor-
alization," but it might be translated more adequately as "timing of
time." The idea is that the production of time, contrary to the classic
Newtonian concept, is itself a historical process. Time is constructed
in time. In the social sciences, this is not a particularly controversial
idea, but increasingly it is also accepted in the natural sciences.[42]
What *is* new, Castells suggests, is that there is no longer a dominant
temporality, neither traditional biological time, nor modern clock
time, nor any of the others. The cumulative effect of the interaction
of multiple temporalities, without reference to a dominant one, is a
chaotic fluctuation in the sequence of events. Society as a whole, so
runs Castells's thesis, has lost its ability to establish a reliable
pattern of sequence in relation to which individual and collective
actors can organize themselves; hence they are forced to embark on
the hazardous project of establishing their own temporality. As John
Urry's list indicates, some have been more successful than others in
this regard.

The formulation of "timeless time" itself may not be particularly helpful, as it defines time by what it no longer is, a sequence. Time that is not time, a paradox, and like many paradoxes this one feels a bit shallow. Timeless time is the only significant building block of his theory where Castells is forced to rely on a negative definition, post-time. Following the same logic, the space of flows would have to be called "placeless space," and thus would be much less convincing. It is perhaps best to think of the term "timeless time" as a place holder, waiting to be superseded by a more nuanced, forward-looking notion. However, a terminological weakness itself says little about the significance of the development it tries to make visible. A shattering of predictable sequences (rather than sequence itself, I suppose) into an order whose logic can only be established after the fact – in a wide range of areas, for a large number of people – would indeed be a different social experience, compared to time seen as an orderly succession of things. But is this so? Are we, as a society, becoming unable to (re)produce time reliably?

Castells presents a very uneven case in support of this strong claim. The financial markets are excessively timebound, but their time is manufactured and arbitrary, with the future defined by a range of contracts which are often specifically designed to affect the future on which they are speculating, with the past being discarded – unless it is reintroduced into what is essentially a never-ending real-time present. Time is measured in seconds or less, and the future is a commodity than can be traded like any other. The order of events, that is, time in the proposed relational sense, is a function of the environment itself, characterized by information turbulences, rather than a predictable sequence based on some inherent properties of the things themselves, or on a stable referent such as clock time. Perhaps such a collapsing of the future into the present is the case for all speculative social dynamics. But this is not Castells's concern. Rather, he argues that it is the *dominance* of this notion of time as a stochastic present, imposed by the financial markets on the global economy, which is historically new.

Similarly, Castells suggests, flexible work destroys the linearity of work time, in the sense that working hours and working time are no longer conforming to the regimented linear time of the factory, but also not returning to anything even loosely resembling a cycle. Time is no longer an objective category, but managed as a resource "with reference to the temporality of other firms, networks, processes and products."[43] Contrary to Harvey's notion of "time/space compression," time is not necessarily compressed. Time can also be selectively stretched. Events may only be recorded to be retrieved at a later date and then acted upon. The key point is that the instantaneous processing of information with the help of an advanced computing infrastructure allows a modulation of the temporal layout of processes according to shifting demands and strategies. Thus their sequence becomes strategic, and so unstable.

From the individual's point of view, Castells continues, the breaking down of reliable rhythms can be experienced on all timescales. For an increasing number of people, work is no longer nine to five. Rather, adapting to a dynamic global economy, it can shift through the day (and the night). Throughout the year, periods of excessive workload can be followed by periods of underemployment or unemployment. This is rendering traditional work patterns with stable employment and long-term career options – reflected in an employer's social responsibility and an employee's loyalty – less and less standard. "The key phenomenon seems to be the increasing diversification of working time and working schedules, reflecting the trend toward the disaggregation of labor in the work process. . . . Under such new arrangements, working time may lose its traditional centrality throughout the life cycle."[44]

Such unpredictability requires new types of organizations which are able to adapt to the fast changing environments, thus bringing further pressure on those that are still organized more inflexibly. For example, under such conditions, it makes sense to spread the family income over two wage earners: the uncertainty introduced by the new volatility is better managed when it is spread. Thus the new time regime is contributing to the transformation of the traditional, patriarchal family structure.

If we take time to be the sequence of events, and social organizations to be crucial in establishing their temporal patterning, a possible connection between the transformations of the social morphology and of time comes into view. Put simply, social institutions organized as flexible networks are less capable of stabilizing time than rigid hierarchies. Rigid hierarchies are too inflexible to deal with multiple temporalities; their historical rise to dominance, from the seventeenth century onward, was connected with the imposition of a dominant temporality, clock time, on everyone. Flexible networks, by their very flexibility, are not capable of doing this, and nor do they require it.

Unlike in traditional cultures organized as networks, nature plays at the most a subordinate role in structuring time in the information age. What we are witnessing, Castells seems to suggest, is the emergence of a temporality based on a form of organization – networks coordinated by instant flows of electronic data – unable to stabilize time because it is itself so dynamic and fluid. This new organization is operating in a completely artificial environment – the space of flows – which itself has no natural or otherwise fixed, or at least inherent, temporality. Similar to space, the characteristic logic of the new time is also binary: "now" or "not-now." As a consequence, each network has to create its own temporality, ranging from the microseconds of the financial markets to the millennia of the ecological movement. Yet none of these temporalities has become dominant. Rather, they are interacting in unpredictable ways, inducing systemic disturbances into the flow of social time.

Despite the ecological movement's attempts to anchor social time in the rhythms of nature again, the perturbations introduced by advanced technologies, Castells argues, reach deep into even the most fundamental biological processes: birth and death. In advanced societies, the norm today is birth control, and great efforts are undertaken to extend this control to women around the world, with varying degrees of success depending on economic and cultural conditions. As Castells notes, "in close interaction with the cultural and professional emancipation of women, the development of reproductive rights has altered the demographic structure and biological rhythms of our society in just two decades."[45]

But it is not just that women in advanced societies have fewer children and have them later. These are statistically well-established facts. Castells's argument goes beyond that. The development of reproductive technologies expands the time range during which women can have children and, most importantly in this context, it allows a differentiation between roles that have traditionally been inseparable. For example, the legal and the biological parents may not necessarily be one and the same anymore, and the biological mother may not necessarily be the mother giving birth. As a consequence, what were once stable, natural sequences of reproduction are now becoming mixed up. Children are born after the death of the mother, or conceived after the death of the father, and they can be orphaned before they are born, making for a rather strange succession of generations. Considering the still to be realized promises of genetic technologies, the range of interventions into the natural processes and rhythms of conception and birth are likely to grow. This leads Castells to the conclusion that we are headed toward "the final blurring of the biological foundation of the life-cycle concept

... [This] is another form of the annihilation of time, of human biological time, of the rhythms by which our species has been regulated since its origins."[46] To look to the annihilation of time might be a bit excessive, a consequence of the problematic negative concept of "timeless time": after all, people are still born, and they still die, in this sequence. Nevertheless, the rhythms at which they do so are certainly becoming more varied, and variable.

Through the concept of timeless time, Castells argues that informationalism, based on the "twin revolutions in microelectronics and genetic engineering," is introducing a new temporality that is characterized neither by natural rhythms, nor by a unifying abstract time ordering society along its fixed grid. Rather, the new temporality is characterized by an absence of a fixed sequence itself. How convincing is this assertion of a new temporality? For the moment, it is very intriguing but also very tentative. The argument is strongest in highlighting that in an increasing number of social processes the rhythms of the clock or those of nature are no longer dominant, or that they can at least be substantially distorted. They don't disappear completely as points of reference, but they interact with a different temporal patterning based on advanced computing and biological technologies. Established sequences of when things are done, throughout the day and throughout a person's life, are being mixed up for a growing number of people. Does this amount to an annihilation of time, any more than the space of flows annihilates space? The problem is that this assertion, which is a staple of postmodern theory, does not fit into Castells's basic framework according to which "space and time are the material, fundamental dimensions of human life."[47]

However, this still leaves the question of whether meaningful sequences are really disappearing from social life, thus suspending the network society in "eternal ephemerality," where everything is now and nothing is fixed. Here again, some hesitation seems warranted. Castells uses the example of "instant wars" as an indication of the nonlinearity that can be created by the most technologically advanced armies. However, the whole notion of "instant war" is dubious, particularly if we view the actual fighting on the ground (or in the air) not as an isolated instance, but as one moment in a long chain of events that is extremely structured and controlled. Taking Nato's war against Yugoslavia or the war against the Taliban in Afghanistan as examples, then all we can really say is that the duration of a war is directly related to the difference in power between the two armies. As Castells points out, if both armies are weak, wars can, and do, still grind on for years. However, that superior armies tend to win decisive, and rapid, victories is hardly new. It took Nazi Germany not much longer to occupy Poland in 1939 than it took the US to oust the Taliban in 2002, reminding us that in German "instant war" is best rendered as *Blitzkrieg*.

For now, the notion of a timeless time remains a promising speculation on a key topic. To move beyond that, two strategies could be pursued. One would be to anchor the new conception of time in a sustained and explicit theoretical argument.[48] Here, as elsewhere, this is not Castells's approach. Yet, in this case, he also fails to pursue the other possible strategy: empirical analysis of the temporal structure of a wide range of processes. Long-term social processes such as the transformation of time need to be studied over the appropriate timescale. However, Castells's analysis is primarily cross-cultural, rather than historical. For the study of time, this is problematic. Its transformation can only be grasped diachronically, yet Castells's analysis is by and large synchronic. However, one cannot study time in a snapshot. Yet he already claims that we "are decisively undermining the orderly life cycle *without* replacing it with an alternative sequence."[49]

Announcing the dissolution of one social pattern without any replacement is a tell-tale sign of a premature conclusion. There is no reason to believe that people will not be able to create meaning under such conditions, or find new ways to anchor the rhythms of their lives. There is anecdotal evidence that the cellphone-based cultures of teenagers are developing different notions of time, with plans constantly shifting around in relation to other events, thus undermining notions of punctuality and planning but replacing them with values such as connectivity and coordination, notions closely related to issues of timing.[50]

To move this argument beyond the anecdotal it would be necessary to include new temporality in the analysis of all social processes, rather than confine it to one brief section and never mention it again. By contrast with other underdeveloped concepts, such as Castells's notion of power, discussed in the previous chapter, there is nothing that suggests that the study of new temporalities, and the cumulative effect of their interaction, cannot be made into a substantial part of the theory of the network society as it stands now. This indicates both the strength and the centrality of this line of analysis. It just hasn't been done yet. Such a lack of development and integration becomes more striking considering the way Castells has made the space of flows into a central aspect of his analysis of production, experience, and power. The space of flows provides a key element not only in the transformation of all these processes, but also in the treatment of the space of places, that is, of cities in the space of flows.

Cities in the Space of Flows

Castells's analysis of the transformation of contemporary cities centers around three interrelated concepts: the "informational city," the "metropolitan region," and the "dual city." The first deals with the technical dimensions of this transformation, the second highlights new spatial forms, and the third focuses on changing social structures. These concepts differ from Castells's earlier theories about urban transformation. As discussed earlier, at the core of Castells's attempt to redefine urban sociology in the late 1960s was the search for a particular urban problem, that is, a social dynamic that was self-contained within a specific place, the city. Collective consumption, and the social movements built around it, provided a focus for the analysis of urban dynamics rooted in the particulars of places (say, struggles over an urban renewal program in Paris, or squatters at the edge of Santiago de Chile).

The new concepts are based on a radically revised perspective on the relationship between places and processes. With the emergence of the space of flows, translocal processes increased their influence on the development of local spatial forms. Social actors, such as urban social movements, which were operating exclusively on a local level, were losing whatever influence they had gained over the development of their neighborhoods and cities (which was probably never as extensive as Castells had assumed during the 1970s).[51] To keep up with this development, Castells shifted his perspective away from places to cross-border processes, which, of course, affect physical places but whose logic cannot be understood with reference to these places. This new focus has underlain the analysis of urban dynamics since *The Informational City* (1989a). A decade later, this new perspective has been taken up widely in urban research. Stephen Graham summarizes the consequences of this reorientation in the following way:

> When our analytical focus centres on how the wires, ducts, tunnels, streets, highways, and technical networks that interlace and diffuse are constructed and used, modern urbanism emerges as an extraor-

dinarily complex and dynamic sociotechnical process. . . . Cities and urban regions become, in a sense, staging posts in the perpetual infrastructurally mediated flow, movement, and exchange.[52]

The informational city is, quite literally, the material basis, the staging post, of incessant flows of information, goods, and people. It is built upon wires, highways, and airports which are connecting those places and activities that constitute nodes in the space of flows. Seen like this, it is evident that no city is ever entirely informational, and the real unit of the informational city is not geographic but functional. It is a process, Castells claims, not a place. From this perspective, he criticizes the concept of the global city, originally proposed by Saskia Sassen,[53] as "misleading," because it is

> a prisoner to a nineteenth-century, hierarchical conception of our society and space. What characterizes our society is its structure in networks and nodes, not in centrality and periphery. . . . In fact, hundreds and thousands of localities are connected in global networks of information-processing and decision-making. All large metropolitan areas . . . are thus global to some extent, with their relative nodal weight in the network varying depending upon time and issues.[54]

In other words, most cities have global components, and even in those cities where the largest number of global nodes are concentrated there are important places whose character is primarily local. After all, New York City is not just Manhattan, but also Queens and the Bronx.

In a seemingly paradoxical development, the clustering in cities of the information infrastructure (in Castells's view the key to reshaping all other infrastructures) creates processes that make the city obsolete, from an analytical point of view, as a frame of reference. Yet, as Castells stresses again and again, this is not the end of the city. There is no empirical evidence that telecommuting is replacing the journey to the workplace for a relevant number of people. Telework complements office work and so contributes to the flexibilization and individualization of working patterns. Yet, for Castells, even in this regard it is more an effect of economic restructuring than its cause. Thus the places of living and of working remain closely connected, contributing to the fact that for the vast majority of people everyday life, and the identity built through it, remain local.

In fact, the transformation of cities takes place amidst a trend of worldwide urbanization. For the first time ever, the majority of people on the globe now live in urban areas. Formerly rural areas are either integrated into the new informational mode of development (intensive high-tech agriculture, or alternatively, extensive "natural" parks and preserves), or marginalized, forcing people to migrate to the cities in the hope of finding better chances for survival. However, these urban areas are not cities in the traditional sense of distinct cultural and political constructions. The new urban unit is no longer the individual city, but the metropolitan region. In terms of the economy, Castells already argued this in the early 1970s, when he noticed that three intersecting dynamics were transforming the city into a "metropolitan region": public and private transport within the city, enabling its inhabitants to travel much longer distances; the introduction of new communication technologies into the processes of business; and the intensification of air transport linking regions to one another.[55]

Today, however, the metropolitan region no longer only characterizes the spatial distribution of advanced economic sectors: this new structure can be found in the configuration of virtually all its elements. Thus they are not simply very large cities; rather, they are "urban constellations scattered throughout huge territorial expanses, functionally integrated and socially differentiated, around a multi-center structure."[56] Most of these regions develop without deliberate planning. They emerge simply as an accumulated effect of many individual reorganizations whose aim was to take advantage of new infrastructural possibilities (which, in return, were expanded in the process). This lack of planning is indicated by the fact that most of these regions do not even have a name, an identity, or clear boundaries. In fact, the size of a metropolitan region, Castells suggests, is only limited by its ability to organize such flows efficiently, hence the central importance of communication and transportation infrastructures. They provide the key link between informationalism and the new spatial pattern characteristic of contemporary urbanism.

The emergence of the metropolitan region can be observed around the world, from the San Francisco Bay Area with almost 7 million people, to the Hong Kong–Guangzhou region with some 40–50 million inhabitants. Such huge constellations blur the distinctions between city and countryside, between center and periphery. Within the metropolitan region the social character of places is nonlinear, since their connection and integration are established through the space of flows, rather than through proximity. For example, advanced services centers link up across patches of intensive agriculture, bypassing underdeveloped areas and slums, creating functional units in a patchwork of areas, selectively connecting to some and disconnecting from other sections of the region. The spatial pattern is one of radical fragmentation rather than gradual transitions. Yet fragmentation does not mean disorganization, or disconnection. Rather, it is the spatial expression of a new logic of integration/exclusion realized through the space of flows. In many ways, the concept of the metropolitan region realizes to the full an observation Castells made in the early 1970s but could not integrate into his place-focused analysis, namely, that the real structures of cities are "flow patterns."[57]

The general pattern of selective integration and segregation finds its expression also at the level of social structure, captured in the image of the "dual city," that is,

> a system socially and spatially polarized between high value-making groups and functions on the one hand and devalued social groups and downgraded spaces on the other hand. This polarization induces increasing integration of the social and spatial core of the urban system, at the same time that it fragments devalued spaces and groups, and threatens them with social irrelevance.[58]

The key argument of the dual city is not just that of accentuated social inequality, because social inequality as such can have many causes. Rather, the dual city implies that the type of inequality, its social and spatial expression, is directly linked to the economic and political changes which accelerated during the 1980s. The economic restructuring, with its concentration of decision-making functions and its decentralization of execution, has relocated/downgraded many jobs in manufacturing on which the middle class depended. The dismantling of the welfare state aggravated this trend. It had provided not just assistance to many but also secure and well-paid jobs in its administration and in the programs it financed. At the same time, a significant number of jobs have been created in the information and knowledge intensive sectors, which in turn rely on an even more significant number of low-level service jobs to support the new professional lifestyle. Thus the economic restructuring reduced middle class jobs while expanding job opportunities at the high and at the low ends.

As Castells observed in 1989, "the differential reassignment of labor in the process of simultaneous growth and decline results in a sharply stratified, segmented social structure that differentiates between upgraded labor, downgraded labor and excluded people."[59] The exclusion, in turn, not only prompts the development of alternative, resistance identities, but also creates the spatial and social basis for the criminal economy to establish itself as the "perverse connection," taking over the lives of the local population. Around the world, slums and ghettos provide the operational basis for organized crime. It is often an important source of social services in areas that have been abandoned by the official city administration. In return, the local population is forced to accept its protection.

The "dual city" is not an entirely unproblematic concept, because it suggests that there is only one dualism, namely income. Castells is well aware of this shortcoming.[60] Nevertheless, he keeps returning to income stratification because it is the clearest link between the dual and the information city, even if the degree to which income stratification becomes a dominant characteristic of the social structure varies among the different metropolitan models.[61]

The three concepts – informational city, metropolitan region, dual city – are classic ideal types. They serve as entry points into an extraordinarily wide range of issues, allowing distinct and complex empirical realities to be integrated into a broad and general framework. Within this framework, the single most important, and the single most original, element is the theory of the space of flows. With it, Castells shows, convincingly in my view, that a new material basis has been created for the reorganization of social processes. This applies not just to the economy, for which the theory was originally developed, but it lends itself to the analysis of all social processes that involve, directly or indirectly, advanced telecommunications. The key aspect of the space of flows is not its separation from the space of places, but its ability to fragment localities and reintegrate some of the components into new functional units on the basis of their connection to the space of flows. On the ground, this creates an entirely new, nonlinear pattern of land use characteristic of contemporary urban development. The analytical clarification of this key point, the emergence of a new spatial logic, expressed in the space of flows and the fragmentation of physical space in a variable geography of hyperconnection and structurally induced "black holes," is one of the most substantial and original aspects of Castells's entire theory of the network society.

6

The Logic of Networks

So far, I have dealt mainly with the particulars of Castells's analysis of contemporary society, but little has been said about the underlying theory of networks. It is time to change this and assess the core of his argument. Networks have emerged as the primary form of organization for (dominant) social processes, driven by informational capitalism, managed through the reorganization of power and governance, and shaped by values advanced in, and challenges mounted by, social movements. The material of basis of this reorganization is the space of flows, fragmenting physical space by introducing a new organizational logic in which geography is but one of many variables, sometimes important, sometimes without consequence. The particulars of these processes, as they emerge from and across diverse, historically determined contexts, make up the bulk of Castells's empirical theory of the network society. It is on the pervasiveness of the new network form of organization, not just in the economy but in all domains of social life, that the claim rests that a new type of society has been created.

Highlighting the dominance of networks does not imply that other forms of organization have already disappeared, or will do so in the future. The industrial revolution also did not completely wipe out preindustrial forms of organization. Artisans and their crafts did not disappear with the rise of mass production, and the aristocracy still exists despite democracy and other forms of "rational" or "charismatic" government. However, then and now, the rise of a new organizational paradigm profoundly affects all others because it transforms the frame of reference in which people and organizations operate. Some of the players may remain the same, but the rules of the game change irreversibly.

As I have already argued, some of the conclusions developed from this general thesis, particularly in terms of information as property and the constitution of power, are wide open to critique. Nevertheless, Castells's argument concerning the transformation of social morphology is convincing and far-reaching. In the many reviews of, and debates on, the network society, the emergence of a new form of social organization, the network, has rarely been questioned as such. In this very general sense, a new consensus is emerging round Castells's most fundamental thesis.[1] What distinguishes Castells's thesis from that of others who reached the same conclusion is that tracing the emergence of networks as the dominant form of organization is the basis for a holistic, integrated social theory. Thus networks are not just an expedient way of organizing this or that process: they are the signature of a new era. It is the networking as such that is analytically most novel, rather than what people do with it, even if this is what the empirical research focuses on.

The immediate question, of course, is how meaningful an analysis can be derived from such a focus on the transformation of social forms. For political economists, particularly those in the Marxist tradition, changes in social morphology are much less important than the continuation of capitalism, and hence they voice strong doubts about any claims that we have entered a new historical epoch.[2] While certain aspects of their critique concerning Castells's economic analysis are well justified, the conclusion that we are witnessing simply a continuation and deepening of trends inherent in capitalism is nevertheless untenable in the light of the theory of the network society. For one thing, capitalism itself has been profoundly transformed by the informational mode of development and the associated changes in the structure of firms and the composition of labor. For Castells, this in itself is already historically significant. The depth of this transformation is brought into sharp focus by the comparison with statism, the other comprehensive sociopolitical system of the industrial mode of development, which was unable to manage its own restructuring (*perestroika*, in Russian). Yet economic restructuring is not the whole story. The rise of the network paradigm cannot be fully attributed to the economy. In fact, it is as much a consequence of new social values and institutions created outside the economy, as well as the relatively autonomous transformation of the state. Thus it makes no sense to attribute primacy to the mode of production and then argue that since there is still capitalism, all change must be subsumed under this one continuation.

Nevertheless, the question is valid: what is the relationship between a general social morphology and particular social dynamics? Castells is quite explicit on this point. He stresses the "pre-eminence of social morphology over social action."[3] The transformation of a basic, and pervasive, form of social organization is a development of historical dimensions, which affects in particular ways the individual events that constitute this process. Before rushing to the conclusion that here Althusserian structuralism or technological determinism raise their ugly heads,[4] it is worth examining in detail what Castells means by this "pre-eminence of social morphology." In order to do this, I will first examine Castells's notion of networks. Since he rarely discusses networks, or their properties, in general, I will have to make two brief detours, one through the field of complexity theory and network studies, the other through organizational theory, in order to develop a richer theoretical definition of networks than Castells has been willing to provide. The goal of this detour will be strictly limited to developing a perspective on Castells's notion of networks, rather than doing justice to the richness of the perspectives mentioned.

Making these detours does not imply that Castells derived his own notion of networks from these fields. Rather, by reviewing their explicit theoretical arguments and attempts to define networks, it will become easier to see Castells's implicit perspective on networks. I will show that the notion of networks that can be extracted from his empirical analysis is much more specific than what is suggested by the minimal, formal definition which he does provide. This will allow us to assess what Castells puts forward as the "network logic," and finally, the potential of the morphological approach, concentrating on the transformation of social forms.

What is a Network?

What is a network? Posed in this general way, the question yields very little. "A network," Castells writes repeatedly, "is a set of interconnected nodes. A node is the point at which a curve intersects itself."[5] This extremely formal and abstract definition can be applied to almost any form of organization, social or natural, animate or inanimate.[6] It is so broad that even a hierarchy can be seen as a specific type of network. This is not what Castells intends. For him, there are very definite differences between hierarchies and networks. If anything, he overemphasizes rather than conflates the distinction.[7] However, rather than clarifying his definition, he shifts gears and continues that "what a node is, concretely speaking, depends on the kind of concrete network of which we speak." As we have seen already several times, Castells tends to offer very broad and general definitions that shift much of the explanatory work to their empirical application. This is partly a result of his strategy of "communicating theory by analyzing practice," partly a consequence of the enormous scope of his claim: networks are becoming the preferred way of organizing in virtually all domains of social life. It would go against one of Castells's basic epistemological principles – theory has to be flexible enough to accommodate diverse empirical realities – to define more than most generally a concept that has to be applicable so widely.

This has the advantage that his notion of networks is, indeed, extremely flexible and easily stretches across the most diverse domains and scales, from "networked individualism," to the "network state," and the "network of networks," the internet. However, it has the disadvantage that the concept also becomes, as several critics have charged, "one-dimensional."[8] What do we gain when we find networks everywhere, and when anything can be a network? Not much. One critic goes so far as to call Castells's notion of the network an "empty signifier" because it is defined so broadly and abstractly.[9] This critique is understandable because Castells is not only extremely frugal with his definition of networks, but also does not use, or even refer to, any of the standard categories developed by network analysts over the last two decades. Castells does not analyze his networks in terms of "strength or number of links," "density of connections," or "symmetry of communication," or other classic network metrics.[10] Nor does he assess a network's topography, for example as "scale-free" or forming "small worlds," two key terms in the recent discussion on networks of various kinds.[11] Thus it could seem that Castells's networks are merely metaphorical.[12] However, they are not. Castells's approach to networks is much more precise and specific than his general definition indicates. Indeed, as the quasi-mathematical definition quoted above already suggests, there are important similarities between Castells's notion of the network and the one developed in the natural sciences.

Perhaps the most direct connection between Castells and the new science of complexity and self-organization is via Fritjof Capra. Not only was Capra for many years Castells's colleague at the University of California at Berkeley, but they have also engaged in "systematic discussions" (according to Capra) of each other's work. This is most explicit in Capra's *The Hidden Connections* (2003), where he bases much of his foray into social analysis on Castells's theory of the network society. But Castells also readily acknowledges the relevance of Capra for the development of a "non-linear perspective" which he sees as having relevance to his own work.[13] Both, of course, are original and independent thinkers and their influence on each other is far from straightforward. Nevertheless, Capra's "new unified framework for the understanding of natural and social phenomena" provides a good entry point into Castells's notion of the network, without suggesting any direct dependence.

Drawing on recent theories of biology and complexity, Capra distinguishes several dimensions on which a complex system can be analyzed. His goal is to define life, in a biological sense. The first level consists of the individual components that make up the system. In a cell, these are the molecular structures, such as the proteins of the DNA. Focusing on this level reveals the materiality of the components. However, as he argues, the analysis of molecular structures is insufficient to understand what makes a cell alive. The components in isolation, no matter how much we know about them, do not tell us enough about the system as a whole. For example, the DNA alone does not tell us whether the system is living or dead. It is possible to extract complete DNA from cells that have been dead for thousands of years. In other words, while any system is made up of material components, a complex system is much more than the sum of its parts.

The second level is what can be called a systemic level. The focus is not so much on the various components, but on the particular pattern of their interrelation. In a cell, a key component of the systemic analysis is the membrane which establishes a basic distinction between inside and outside. Based on this distinction, it is possible to determine the components that belong to the system and their relationship to one another. The particular relationship is what creates the "molecular identity," that is, a specific pattern of connection. Identity foregrounds the static aspects of the system: basic patterns of organization which remain stable over time. While this static, systemic approach already tells us more than the view of the components in isolation, it is still insufficient in the perspective proposed by Capra.

Complex systems are not static but are continually renewing themselves. Indeed, the notion of self-(re)creation, or "autopoiesis," lies at the heart of such a definition of life. It was first proposed by the Chilean biologists Humberto Maturana and Francisco Varela in the early 1970s. Life's distinguishing characteristic, they argued, is its ability to recreate itself. In other words, life is a process, rather than a system. It is not a material, or even a relational, characteristic, but an emergent property. Integrating the three levels, Capra writes, "living networks continually create, or recreate, themselves by transforming or replacing their components. In this way, they undergo continual structural changes, while preserving their weblike patterns of organization."[14] The term structure is used here in the tradition of the natural sciences, where it stands for "the material embodiment of [a] pattern of organization," rather than for the abstract pattern itself, as the term is used in the social sciences. What Capra suggests here is that living systems continually change their materiality while preserving their form. This, once could say, is "morphology over action," except that the form is here created by the materiality of action.

In this perspective, there are three basic levels of analysis – matter, form, and process. If we are interested in understanding complex systems, the key level is the third one. Their unique properties are emerging from dynamic processes. They cannot be reduced to the materiality of their constitutive parts, or even their particular configuration at any one time. Rather, they constitute a distinct level of analysis that unfolds over time. Biology cannot be reduced to chemistry, or chemistry to physics. Consequently, a property of a system, its life, is not determined by an individual component – for example, its DNA – but must be understood as an effect of the entire process of interaction. Of this process, all elements are constitutive, not just a few key ones. With this Capra argues against a "gene-centered" view of life which holds that biological forms and functions are determined by the cells' genetic blueprint. This view, popularized through notions such as "the selfish gene,"[15] reduces life to DNA, which is similar to arguing that computers are determined by their software.

Against such reductionism, Capra proposes a network-centric view of life. Life is understood as a property emerging from the particular interplay of heterogeneous components of which the DNA is but one. The emphasis on continuous recreation stresses also another aspect of this particular view on living systems. They are assumed to exist not as a stable equilibrium, but in an unstable state which complexity theory describes as "far from equilibrium" or at the "edge of chaos." The instability means that there are constant processes of decay at work, pulling the system toward equilibrium, that is, ultimately entropy or death. However, the process of recreation, the metabolism of a cell, continuously regenerates the structure as fast as its material components are decaying. This is how the materiality is constantly changed while the form is preserved, or transformed. Either way, continuous recreation prevents the disintegration of the patterns of interdependence which constitute the identity of the system. This replacement of decaying elements by the system itself is what defines life, according to the argument synthesized by Capra. It also points to the final level of analysis on which such systems can be understood: through their relation to the environment.

As Capra describes it:

> Living systems are organizationally closed – they are autopoietic networks – but materially and energetically open. They need to feed on continual flows of matter and energy from their environment to stay alive. Conversely [they] continually produce waste, and this flow-through of matter – food and waste – establishes their place in the food web.[16]

The relationship between the living system and its environment is complex. Two aspects are of particular interest in the present context. A living system takes from its environment the necessary raw materials to repair and maintain itself. However, the environment is not only a source of continuity, the system also receives from it stimuli which can trigger changes in its internal composition. How a system reacts to an external stimulus is not determined by the stimulus itself, but by the internal organization of the system. Capra uses the example of the difference between kicking a stone and kicking a dog. Both react to the laws of physics, but whereas the stone reacts to nothing but the laws of physics, the dog's reaction is not determined by these laws. The dog processes the input not mechanically, but based on its particular internal state at the time of kicking. By contrast with the stone, whose mechanical reaction is easy to predict, the dog's internal processes are too complex to be predictable. The dog might run away, or bite.

Duncan Watts, one of the leading sociologists working on a (mathematically based) science of networks, arrives at the same point. "The trick is," he concludes his analysis of causation in networks, "*not* to focus on the stimulus, but on the structure of the network that the stimulus hits."[17] The ramifications of this shift in

perspective are very substantial. Most directly, it inverts the relationship between cause and effect. It is only through analyzing the
effect that we can determine the cause. Analysis of the initial trigger
does not allow us to predict the effect. What we take as the stimulus (the kick) plays only a small part in creating the effect (the dog's
reaction). Thus one of the core tenets of complexity theory is that
small causes can have large effects, and large causes may have very
small effects. Contrary to classic physics, there is no proportional-
ity between cause and effect.

The second aspect in the relationship between a living system
and its environment arises because it is not only a recipient of input,
but also produces changes in the environment. First, by creating
an output, waste and other materials that are continuously put
back into the environment. They are the raw materials for other
living systems, thus establishing the principle of interdependence
between organisms ("structural coupling") and continuous recy-
cling of material. Nothing is ever wasted and energy is never lost.
This is the core of any ecological perspective. The network-centric
view on life that Capra develops builds on this, but contains also
another, more intriguing element in the relationship between the
living system and the environment. He draws again on the foundational work of Humberto Maturana and Francisco Varela. They
argue that a living system not only reacts unpredictably to an external influence, but also specifies to which influence it reacts. Through
the particular ways in which it is coupled to the environment,
certain events are perceived, while others remain unnoticed, or less
anthropomorphically, are structurally unnoticeable. Some events
the system simply cannot detect, in the way that we cannot see in
the dark or hear ultrasonic sounds.

Through this act of noticing/reacting to selective aspects of the
environment, a living system creates its own environment. This is
key. What constitutes the environment is specific to each living
entity, determined by its internal organization, rather than by the
environment as such. Why, Maturana and Varela ask, does an
orange keep its color when we carry it from the fluorescent light of
the kitchen into the sunlight of the garden? Assuming that color is
an objective function of the wave length reflected by the object, the
color of the orange should not remain the same. The physical properties of the light reflected by the orange change along with the
source of light. To make a long argument short, they conclude that
the perception of color is not solely determined by the light that is
reflected from an object, but also by the reaction of the system (the

brain, following its internal configuration) to select aspects of input (light waves within certain frequency bands).

This argument has profound and complex implications for our understanding of cognition, which Maturana and Varela see as a property of all living systems. Cognition, in their view, is not about creating (more or less accurate) representations of the outside world inside a brain across the gap that separates inside and outside, the brain from the world, or the subject from the object. Rather, it is processes of "bringing forth a world" through the process of life itself, which is always coupled with others. In other words, there is a profound connection between the knowing subject and the object of knowledge. In fact, they are mutually constitutive. Since all subjects are part of larger ecologies, they are related to other subjects, of the same species and of other species.[18] This radical notion of cognition is far from universally agreed upon, but this does not need to concern us here. All that is important is that according to this school of thought, the selective sensitivity of a living system to environmental influences is itself an essential part of what constitutes the environment.

The purpose of this simplified rush through Capra's and Maturana/Varela's already highly condensed syntheses of vast and dynamic fields was not to represent them in their own right, and even less to assess the possibility or validity of such a unified approach. That is not necessary in this context. All it has provided us with are elements for formulating a more fleshed-out definition of a network relevant to Castells's analysis. These elements are the importance of emergent properties for characterizing a complex system; the continuous self-(re)creation and transformation of a network as a function of internal processes, influenced but not determined by input from the environment; the selectivity of input recognition as an influence on the environment; and the principle of identity to characterize a network.[19]

This, however, is only one strand that can help us work out Castells's particular notion of networks. Contrary to Capra, for whom all complex systems are networks, Castells's entire argument is premised on the difference between networks and other forms of social organization. After all, why bother calling something a network society if hierarchies are networks as well? Again, Castells does not really elaborate much on this point, so, unfortunately, the second detour is necessary.

Sociological theory knows of four basic patterns of organization by which it characterizes social entities, providing the ideal types of social morphology: hierarchies, markets, networks, and communes. Organization theory has been the branch that dealt with the different types most intensively. Owing to its affiliation with economics departments and business schools, organization theory has concentrated for a long time on the relationship between the first two forms: firms – thought of as vertically integrated hierarchies – and markets – thought of as episodic exchange relations between independent entities. Depending on the kind of task, either firms or markets were assumed to be more efficient. In fact, one of the key tasks of management, in this view, is to determine which resources are better produced internally, and which are better bought on the market.

The critical variable, according to the school of thought pioneered by Roland H. Coase in the late 1930s, is "transaction costs."[20] Firms exist, he argued, because it is cheaper to organize particular processes internally than buying them on the market. Acquiring resources on the market includes additional expenditure related to finding the right item, negotiating a price, setting up a contract, and enforcing it in case of difficulties, and so on. All of these costs are in addition to the actual price of the good or service. Stripped of its subtleties, Coase's argument was that if markets were perfect, there would be no transaction costs and no need for firms. But because real markets are imperfect, certain things are more efficiently organized outside the market, that is, within the firm. The firm reaches the limits of its expansion when the costs associated with organizing production inhouse exceed those of acquiring the necessary resources externally.

As firms were simply assumed to be vertically integrated corporations, a strict dichotomy was drawn up between centralized hierarchies and decentralized markets as the two main organizational principles of capitalist economies. However, in the mid 1980s, several theorists began to argue that a third form of organization was emerging that is neither the vertically integrated firm nor the decentralized markets of autonomous agents: the business network. Since then, mountains of evidence have been compiled to support their central observation (and debate the conclusions they drew from it). As a consequence, organization theory now recognizes three basic patterns of organization: firms, markets, and networks.[21] The latter is differentiated from the initial pair in the following way:

> From a structural perspective, every form of organization is a network, and markets and hierarchies are simply two manifestations of

the broader type. However, when considered as a form of governance, the network form can be distinctly characterized. We define a network form of organization as any collection of [two or more] actors that pursue repeated, enduring exchange relations with one another and, at the same time, lack a legitimate organizational authority to arbitrate and resolve disputes that may arise during the exchange. In a pure market, relations are not enduring, but episodic, formed only for the purpose of a well-specified transfer of goods and resources and ending after the transfer. In hierarchies, relations may endure for longer than a brief episode, but a clearly recognized, legitimate authority exists to resolve disputes that arise among actors.[22]

While this definition is clearly geared toward an economic analysis, several points of the underlying argument can be generalized. Networks are enduring forms of organization. It is precisely the formation of distinct patterns of interaction over time ("exchange relations" in the broad sense) that gives networks their identity. This is the aspect that most sociological definitions concentrate on. For John Urry, for example, a network is characterized as "relational constancy between components."[23] Sporadic or short-term interaction is not enough to form a distinct entity, that is, a network. In this process of pattern- or identity-building, a network is defined simultaneously by its nodes and the relationships among them. The whole makes the parts and the parts make the whole. This is different in a market. It is modeled on a clear distinction between individual entities (say, consumers, firms) and the whole, which is an aggregate of individual actions (say, the market for consumer goods). In his model, there is first the actor and then the market. The actors are not primarily defined by their interaction in the market. Rather, they are defined by their individual strategies which are external to the market. One school of thought, rational choice theory, assumes these strategies to be characterized by resource maximization ("homo economicus"), or in a less idealized version, that individual strategies are shaped by "bounded rationality," that is resource maximization limited (or bounded) by factors such as incomplete information, prejudice, or "competing values." Consequently, an economic actor can enter and leave a market without much effort.

In a network, on the other hand, it makes no sense to argue that nodes come first and then they begin to create connections. Rather, it is through the connections that nodes create and define one another. Nodes are created by connections, and without nodes there can be no connections. Compared to markets, it is much more consequential to enter or leave a network, because so much of what constitutes an actor (or node) is bound up with the particulars of the network of which he, or she, or it, is a constitutive part. Markets, ideal-typically, are impersonal; networks, equally ideal-typically, personal (for better or worse). However, compared to hierarchies, the individual components in a network are much more autonomous. In a vertically integrated hierarchy, it is the whole that defines its parts and they have no independent identity. In a network, the process of interdefinition is bidirectional. In short, the patterns of interaction within a network are more enduring than in a market, but more flexible than in a hierarchy. This is the first important distinction.

Despite the long-term nature of the interaction, there is no formalized procedure by which one node within the network would be able to resolve conflicts which arise from this interaction. Rather, conflicts are settled by negotiations among network participants, or by reference to commonly accepted external authorities (say, commercial arbitration). Internally, within the network, there is no single point that has the formal authority to impose its will on other network participants in the same way that decisions can be imposed by a chief executive thanks to her unique position within the organization. If such a node did exist, the organization could no longer be characterized as a network; rather, it would be a centralized hierarchy. Put more generally, while hierarchies are characterized by command-and-control structures, networks are shaped by the continuous interdefinition of network participants, or even more generally, mutual adjustment among its elements. This mutual adjustment is not random, or entirely open, but determined by the overall pattern of interaction, created in the course of the network's existence. This provides the identity of the network – from which the identity of the network participants is often hard to separate. A node is where the curve intersects itself.

This aspect of the network form is stressed in a definition offered by the French sociologist Pierre Musso. For him, a network is "an unstable structure of connections, composed of interacting elements, whose variability follows certain functional rules."[24] Instability points to the need for continual, internal readjustment because all elements are inter*acting*, rather than one determining the others. This allows for much greater flexibility – instability in a positive sense. Nodes are added and dropped with relative ease. Yet the transformations a network undergoes are not random, but follow the network's own internal logic. The way a network changes is directly related to the network's internal patterns, its identity, which Musso calls its "functional rules." In other words, the way a network changes over time reflects its own history, that is, the history of all its components, rather than the will of a single node. This is very similar to what complexity theorists call "path dependence," that is, the past prefigures the future, though not in a deterministic way.

Largely ignored in organization theory is the fourth basic form of social organization – collectives or communes – because they are regarded as primitive, or, in the light of twentieth century experience, as not belonging to a market economy. Yet their difference from networks is instructive. Communes, in one way or another, center round shared, egalitarian living and/or working relationships. They constitute themselves by minimizing their internal differentiation and establishing distinct differences from their environment. Ideal-typically, they operate by consensus among all their members. The focus of the organization is on the equality, or sameness, of its constituent parts on some deep and inclusive level. Collectives offer strong identity, and the hurdles of entering or leaving are substantial. Collectives tend to be so comprehensive that an individual can usually belong to only one. Indeed, the whole notion of individuality is problematic in the context of a collective, which is assumed to subsume or even override it.

In this aspect, the dominance of the whole over its parts, communes share certain similarities with hierarchies. A network, on the other hand, is not based on the idea of sameness, but on the idea of difference among its constituent parts. As much as nodes are defined by a network, they still retain a crucial degree of autonomy that prevents the network from collapsing into one big mega-node, that is, a collective. Networks are fundamentally asymmetrical, which may, or may not, amount to some kind of informal hierarchy. More generally speaking, the asymmetry can be understood as complementarity, that is, the differing nodes require each other, for their own identity and for the functioning of the network as a whole. What holds the heterogeneous elements of a network together, then, is neither a well-defined hierarchy, nor a deep similarity of its members, but a more or less explicit purpose. The purpose – producing goods for the global markets, distributing drugs, fighting corporate globalization, developing new sexual identities, organizing higher learning – provides the network as a whole with some fundamental values in relation to which internal negotiations can take place. In general terms, networks operate on the basis of a common protocol and a shared set of goals. Both can change over time, but without them the network disintegrates. In fact, it is in relation to the shared protocols, goals, or culture that nodes are linked to, or disconnected from, the network.

This second short detour has provided us with another, partially overlapping set of characteristics through which to define networks. In this perspective, networks are an enduring form of social organization; composed of asymmetrical, interacting elements; held together by a shared set of values, standards, or functional rules; coordinated through ongoing negotiation by which the elements (re)define not only the network's identity, but also their respective positions within it; and the process of continual redefinition creates, at the same time, flexibility and path dependence. Combining the two perspectives, we can draw up the following, interim definition of a network, as implicit in Castells's analysis. A network is an enduring pattern of interaction among heterogeneous actors that define one another (identity). They coordinate themselves on the basis of common protocols, values, and goals (process). A network reacts nondeterministically to self-selected external influences, thus not simply representing the environment but actively creating it (interdependence). Key properties of a network are emergent from these processes unfolding over time, rather than determined by any of its elements (emergence).

However, one element, central in Castells's view, is still missing. While complexity theory does not differentiate between networks and other forms of organization (they are all networks), organization theory only partially addresses the question of why networks have suddenly become so important. The usual answer to this question is that networks are more flexible than vertically integrated hierarchies and thus operate more efficiently in a fast-changing environment. So far, so good. However, this does not address what differentiates networks today from networks that have always been around. Post-Fordism, owing to its initial formulation, has taken the new type of business to be an artisanal enterprise, highly specialized and flexible at the same time. From this, it draws a picture of small, adaptive firms organized in networks, competing successfully against large, vertically integrated, inflexible corporations. In the words of Piore and Sabel, who contributed much to this perspective, business networks thrive on "economies of scope," that is, the ability to produce a wide range of things in reaction to fluctuating demand. Traditional corporations, on the other hand, focus on "economies of scale," that is, the ability to produce very large numbers of the same thing. The faster and the more unpredictable the markets become, the more decisive the advantage of scope over scale.[25]

This dichotomy of small and flexible versus large and inflexible, Castells argues, has always been problematic as a general analysis, but certainly today, in the light of empirical evidence, it can no longer be maintained. From the mid 1980s onward, we have seen the rise of giant global corporations which are themselves organized as networks, thus combining economies of scope and scale.[26] This indicates that there must be something that distinguishes the network form of organization today from traditional types of social networks.

Informational Networks

What makes today's networks so profoundly different from traditional social networks is that, for the first time, they scale well. Their growth, and the tasks which can be organized through them, are no longer strictly limited by the complexities of their internal coordination. Castells writes,

> to be sure, networks have always existed in human organization. But only now have they become the most powerful form for organizing instrumentality, rather than expressiveness. The reason is fundamentally technological. The strength of networks is their flexibility, their decentralizing capacity, their variable geometry. . . . Their fundamental weakness, throughout history, has been the difficulty of co-ordination toward a common objective, toward a focused purpose, that requires concentration of resources in space and time within large organizations, like armies, bureaucracies, large factories, vertically organized corporations. With new information and communication technology, the network is, at the same time, centralized and decentralized. It can be co-ordinated without a centre.[27]

Networks are complex forms of organization. Held together by communication, their elements are constantly negotiating their relative positions within an unstable overall network. Thus Scott Lash argues for replacing the concept of the information society with that of the "communications society."[28] The resulting relationships among the different nodes are rich and specific. Affective, or informal, social relationships have traditionally been organized as networks because they rely on this richness of communication and the ability to accommodate continuous fluctuations easily. The downside of this richness in communication has been that beyond a certain level of complexity the process of interdefinition has become unmanageable. It involved just too much communication, resulting in a cacophony of voices and a lack of coordination.

In a formal hierarchy, on the other hand, communication is simplified because the definition of the elements is no longer a matter of internal coordination but has been externalized into the architecture of the organization itself. This is, in fact, what makes the hierarchy formal. Vertically integrated hierarchies can be adequately represented in organizational charts, while networks can only be mapped. Communication within a hierarchy of this sort is relatively sparse and the relationship between its elements restricted and formal. The hierarchy, ideally, it is not affected by the people who make it up, because their main task is to execute orders or follow formal rules as precisely as possible. The whole defines all its parts, which have no identity outside the hierarchy. According to Max Weber, what distinguishes modern bureaucracy from premodern forms of administration is that authority is rendered impersonal, vested in a position and not in a person, the person being seen as occupying a position only temporarily.

If we take networks as communication-rich and formal hierarchies as communication-poor forms of organization, it is not surprising that one of the factors deciding which form of organization is best suited to a particular task has always been communication technologies. In what McLuhan called the "Gutenberg Galaxy" – characterized by reliance on the printed alphabet as the dominant means of communication – hierarchies based on documents and written, impersonal rules became the preferred way of organizing large-scale social processes.[29] They offered a reduction in communicative complexity which enabled an increase in their scale. Thanks to print, the documents through which bureaucracies operated could be created uniformly and cheaply, and thus be easily passed around, but not changed. Thus these organizations have been able to span time and space in a way that organizations based on verbal agreements and implicit traditions could not. As local societies became integrated into large nation-states, the realm of bureaucracies continuously increased. Relationships among people were rendered more formal and less personal. Analyzing this process has been one of the core themes of modern sociology, most notably in Germany. Ferdinand Tönnies (1855–1936) offered the classic distinction between "Gemeinschaft" (community, based on shared culture) and "Gesellschaft" (society, based on contracts). Max Weber feared the cold rationality of bureaucracies, and Jürgen Habermas warned that the "lifeworld" was being subjected to colonization through the "system world." For Habermas, in particular, diverging styles of communication – one leading to communicative action, the other to instrumental action – are what differentiate these worlds from one another, though he makes no connection to particular forms of organization.[30]

The introduction of new communication technologies has fundamentally affected the balance between hierarchies and networks. Quantitatively speaking, computer-based technologies enable the processing of more communication (purposeful flows of information), in less time, across larger distances. The traditional trade-off between richness of communication, enabling flexibility and involvement, and reduction of communication, enabling scale and focus, has virtually vanished. What used to be the key advantage of integrated hierarchies – their ability to increase coordination through formal and rigid rules – has turned into a terminal disadvantage, because new technologies facilitate coordination without requiring rigidity. Consequently, networks are suddenly able to operate on the same scale and with the same degree of coordination as hierarchies, while preserving flexibility. "This results," Castells concludes, "in an unprecedented combination of flexibility and task performance, of coordinated decision-making and decentralized execution, of individualized expression and global, horizontal communication, which provide a superior organizational form for human action."[31]

In Castells's theory of the network society, a network is always an informational network. It is an enduring pattern of large-scale interaction among heterogeneous social actors coordinating themselves through electronic information flows. It combines organizational flexibility with coordination. It is held together by a common frame of reference, constituted by shared protocols, values, and goals. Its most important effects emerge from the interaction of all elements, rather than being imposed, or determined, by a single one. Through continuous interdefinition of its elements, selective sensitivity to inputs, and emergent effects, networks bring forth their own world, rather than merely reacting to, or acting upon, an environment shared by everyone.

With such a conceptualization of networks, Castells shares considerable ground with recent attempts to renew the social sciences through incorporating models and ideas formulated in what is now called "complexity theory."[32] This renewal is undertaken from two directions. On one side, there has been a steady import of metaphors such as "self-organization," "emergence," "attractor," "dissipative structures," and the like in recent formulations of sociological metatheories.[33] What they share is an interest in replacing linear cause–effect relationships with nonlinear feedback systems. In one way or another, they are all trying to overcome dichotomies that have plagued social theory since the beginning, most importantly, the structure/agency pair. For Scott Lash, for example, what is characteristic about the present, which he calls "second modernity," is the "emergent demise of the distinction between agency and structure altogether"[34] as an effect of the shift toward networked forms of organization.

At the other end of the scale, what is being integrated from complexity theory is less the metaphors than the methods. There is a rise in what one might call "mathematical sociology," trying to find patterns, and to analyze them through computer models, in a large variety of network dynamics, social and natural.[35] While one could imagine a fruitful point of convergence between the two approaches, for now they remain separate and limited. The new breed of metatheories remains, perhaps not surprisingly, excessively metaphorical and vague. Suddenly, everything seems to be an emergent system, and butterfly effects abound. On the other hand, the new science of networks is still in its infancy, dealing with extremely basic questions, content to find patterns in fluctuating dynamics, and replacing the contingency of individual agency with statistical probabilities that can be found in large populations.

This is not to belittle the two attempts to renew social theory: they are, I am convinced, pointing in the right direction. All that it is necessary to note right now is that Castells takes a very different approach to theory building, even if he arrives, in terms of his notion of network, at surprisingly similar conclusions. Also here, Castells remains resolutely empirical. Rather than importing metaphors, or constructing computational simulation models, he sticks to the standard toolkit of social research. Methodologically speaking, he remains much closer to more conservative approaches such as social network analysis. Yet the conclusions he draws from this research are much more radical and far-reaching. For example, Barry Wellman, one of the leading scholars of (online) social networks, sees the influence of new technology primarily as enabling loose social networks to be stretched across time and space. He puts great emphasis on traditional questions of community building, and more generally, argues that "computer networks are social networks."[36] For Castells, on the other hand, informational networks, as we have seen, are not just informal social networks stretched translocally; rather, the practice of informational networking constitutes a social transformation of the greatest importance. Indeed, it is on the practice of informational networking, and the resulting effects, that the claim for a new social epoch is based. Thus Castells substantiates, by way of standard empirical research methods and a rather traditionalist terminology, some of the core arguments advanced speculatively by the new complexity-oriented social theory. This is not without it problems – as we have seen in the questions of power, conventional terminology and definitions can be inadequate – yet the advantage is that Castells is able to avoid excessively vague metaphors and simplistic computational simulations.

The Network Logic

The networks of Castells's network society are not simply malleable "sets of interconnected nodes." Rather, they have very specific characteristics and their effects are ubiquitous in his analysis of the network society. These characteristics provide the core of what he calls "the networking logic" which permeates all domains of contemporary life. "Coordination through electronic information flows," the first element in the definition provided above, is reflected in the importance of computer-based communication for all networks analyzed. In the network society, all dominant social processes, including their counterprocesses, rely on advanced communication technologies to coordinate their actions globally, and increasingly, locally as well.[37] Over less than 30 years, the material basis of human communication has been radically transformed. Indeed, for Castells, there is a close affinity between the characteristics of advanced information technologies and networking. It is resting on these technologies that networking has emerged as the dominant strategy for economic restructuring, renewing the institutions of governance, and building new social movements. In turn, the demands from these sectors greatly accelerated the development of new technologies. These two dynamics, initially independent but soon feeding on each other, established the network society over the course of just three decades. The technological aspect of the definition of networks links the networking logic with two of the cornerstones of Castells's theory: informationalism and the space of flows.

Informationalism is the material configuration of processes centering round the "augmentation of the human capacity in information processing" through advanced technologies. It is precisely this augmentation which enables social actors to (re)organize their efforts in networks of unprecedented size and manage the high degrees of organizational complexity that come with them. Informationalism and networking are two different levels of the same empirical phenomenon, one focusing on its technological aspects, the other on its morphological ones. In terms of Castells's network society, their coupling is a matter of history, not of necessity. Networking is much older than informationalism, and advanced digital technologies did not determine that the pattern of their use had to be a network. It could have been different. But it was not, and this is no coincidence either. On the one hand, informational networking served as a way of advancing numerous powerful economic, political, and social agendas. On the other hand, many of the creators of the foundational technologies were inspired by the (nontechnical) "networking values" of the 1960s counterculture, and built technologies to support them. The relationship between informationalism and networking is one of positive feedback loops, rather than of cause and effect chains.

If informationalism is the technological expression of the contemporary networking logic, then the space of flows is its spatial expression. Indeed, what Bruno Latour notes about technological networks in general can be applied specifically to the space of flows. Networks, Latour writes,

> are composed of particular places, aligned by a series of branchings that cross other places and require other branchings in order to spread. Between the lines of the network there is, strictly speaking, nothing at all: no train, no telephone, no intake pipe, no television sets. Technological networks, as the name suggests, are networks thrown over spaces, and they retain only a few scattered elements of those spaces. They are connected lines, not surfaces. They are by no means comprehensive, global or systematic, even though they embrace surfaces without covering them, and extend a very long way.[38]

While Latour downplays the importance of surfaces in order to focus on connections, for Castells the analysis of surfaces, that is of physical space, remains a critical part of the theory of the network society. Informational networks reorganize geographical space by creating a new "material foundation of time-sharing." Through the space of flows locales can be connected to and disconnected from one another easily and selectively without regard to their proximity. The relationship between the two types of space is a key element of the networking logic so very prominent in Castells's analysis. Networks have surfaces, but these are fractured and discontinuous. In metropolitan regions, patches of high-intensity agriculture are located right next to high-tech development centers; the ghettos of the poor spring up in the immediate vicinity of gated communities of the rich; and production facilities are distributed throughout the area and across different regions, but still function as units in real time, their connections reflecting the requirements of short-term business projects. The fragmentation of physical space, and its new, nonlinear organization, are a direct consequence of the fact that dominant social processes are organized as networks of unprecedented scale through information technologies.

The theme of the "combination of flexibility and coordination" is ubiquitous as well in Castells's account of the new social organizations, in business, government, and social movements. While his economic analysis builds on ideas of post-Fordist, or flexible, production, his distinct notion of networks is reflected in two important modifications to those theories. First, the emphasis on informationalism enables him to overcome the dichotomy of small and flexible versus large and inflexible. Focusing on the restructuring of major global enterprises, he notes that flexibility and coordination now characterize organizations at all scales. Indeed, they find their most powerful expression at the largest scale, where the effects of successful coordination are the most significant. Second, the efficiency gains of this combination are not only to be realized in business organizations: they drive restructuring in virtually all domains of social life.

In terms of Castells's analysis of governance, the focus on "flexibility and coordination" creates the most useful aspects of the theory of the otherwise problematic notion of the network state. They are developed in reference to the notion of "neo-medievalism," that is, the flexible negotiation of overlapping and competing claims of governing authorities so characteristic of the European Union. Rather than forging a single, integrated hierarchy of power within the EU, the various nodes rearrange themselves all the time in order to address specific issues more efficiently (that is, in order to be able to address them at all). Many of the key projects of the EU unfold through unique networks: the countries participating in the common currency, the euro, are not the same as those belonging to the common market, and the euro and the market do not map on to the EU's external borders, to list just the most obvious examples. The new combination of flexibility and coordination also underlies Castells's notion of instant war, characterized by the speed, flexibility, and extreme focus typical of war waged by high-tech armies. It also informs Castells's analysis of those social movements that are organized as networks (rather than as communes). The prime example is the antiglobalization movement. Only by being extremely flexible can it accommodate the heterogeneity of its members while achieving coordination to such a degree that the movement has been able to influence the terms of global policy debates, if not the content of global policies themselves.

Expressed spatially, the "coordination and flexibility" combination corresponds to the simultaneous processes of centralization and decentralization. Cities, Castells has been arguing for a long time, are deeply affected by the centralization of decision-making and the decentralization of execution. Owing to his early focus on cities as the places of "collective consumption," this aspect of what would later become the networking logic was the one to be worked out first. Reflecting on the novel spatial configuration of the high-tech industry in Paris, he noted in the early 1970s that in this industry the existence of a "decision-making center is not the spatial expression of bureaucratization, but, on the contrary, the logical consequence . . . of the process of technocratization of highly industrialized societies."[39] This observation was confirmed and extended in various ways by virtually all of Castells's studies over the following three decades.

Besides focusing on the importance of electronic information flows, and the novel combination of flexibility and coordination, the third element of Castells's notion of networks is its constitution around a shared "project." Indeed, it is the ability of each node to contribute to this shared project that determines its fate within the network and the configuration of the network as whole. "Nodes increase their importance for the network," Castells writes, "by absorbing more information and processing it more efficiently. The relative importance of nodes does not stem from its specific features but from its ability to contribute valuable information to the network."[40] The more a node contributes, the more importance it assumes; the less it contributes, the smaller its role in the network. If it contributes nothing, the network reconstitutes itself without that node; if its contribution is negative it will be actively expelled from the network. In online communities, expelling troublemakers from the community is the most radical, and effective, step taken to reduce friction.[41] The value of each node is not intrinsic to the node, but stems from its relation to the overall project, which, in turn, is shaped by the actions of the various nodes. By contrast with a hierarchy, where the whole defines the parts, or the markets, where the parts define the whole, in the network the node and the network define one another.

The shared project provides the frame of reference against which the internal negotiations of the network take place. The project can change over time, but without a project the network has no orientation. The range of the actual project reflects the range of social agendas shaping the network society. However, a common project is not enough. Because networks are constituted by communication, common "protocols and values," in short, a shared culture, is necessary to facilitate this communication. Without a shared culture – "systems of values and beliefs informing codes of behavior" – communication breaks down and the network disintegrates. A common fate of corporate mergers and restructuring. Castells concludes:

> The performance of a given network depend[s] on two fundamental attributes of the network: its *connectedness*, that is, its structural ability to facilitate noise-free communication between its components; and its *consistency*, that is, the extent to which there is a sharing of interests between the network's goal and the goals of its components.[42]

The level of noise, that is the difference between what is sent and what is received, depends on two aspects. One is the state of communication media. Computer networks have improved communication, in terms of accuracy, speed, and volume of transmission. However, as linguists and semioticians know, while communication may be noise-free in its technical aspects, in its human dimensions it never is. Here the difference between what is sent and what is received is a matter of interpretation, rather than static. In order to keep noise at this level to a productive minimum, it is necessary that the members of the network share a common cultural framework that facilitates the coding and decoding of the messages sent so crisply through the digital channels. Thus the connectedness of a network is a cultural as well as a technical function. Consistency, on the other hand, is a function of the interdefinition of the network and the nodes. If it is too low, if the various nodes do not see their being part of the network as advancing their individual goals, then either the network goals or the composition of the network needs to be readjusted, or the network falls apart. After all, the network is constituted around the shared project.

The importance of a shared culture for the performance of the network contributes to what Castells sees as the renaissance of social movements, after their crisis in the late 1970s and early 1980s, when he saw them as operating at the wrong scale (local urban movements in a world of globalizing economies). Thanks to access to the space of flows, scale is no longer a real hurdle. The power of social movements stems from the fact that their most native domain is precisely the innovation of shared culture. Yet the sharing of culture should not be understood as something intrinsically harmonious. On the contrary. The sharing occurs primarily, if not exclusively, within a single network, rather than across the various networks that constitute society as a whole. Consequently, the emphasis on common culture is not contradicted by the observation of a fragmentation of culture to a degree that social communication becomes seriously affected. Indeed, these are two sides of the same coin. To mitigate this effect, Castells argues, bridges between these cultures, facilitating communication across rather than within cultures, are essential for the reconstitution of civic democracy.[43]

Perhaps the most controversial aspect of Castells's notion of networks is the idea that its most important characteristics emerge from the interaction of all elements and cannot be reduced to the actions of a few. Emergent effects, it is important to stress, are not the same as unintended consequences, that old classic of sociological analysis. Rather, they are "higher level phenomena [which] appear to exhibit properties that are not revealed at lower levels,"[44] whereas unintended consequences occur at the same level. In Capra's example, life, constituting the higher level of biology, emerges from the interactions of molecules, constituting the lower level of chemistry. A car accident, on the other hand, might be an unintended consequence of speeding. Because such effects emerge at a higher level of systemic integration, they are largely out of the control of the agents at the lower level that constitutes them. Chemistry does not determine biology.

The emphasis on emergent effects is most pronounced in Castells's analysis of the financial markets. They are characterized by action that cannot be controlled by the actors. It is reflected in the image of the "faceless collective capitalist" that dominates all the individual capitalists. If we take this faceless capitalist to be an emergent effect, a "mighty whirlwind" as Castells also likes to call it, then it is also not necessary to assume a need for a capitalist class to constitute it. In fact, from such a perspective the notion of a class, as Peter Marcuse notes, appears as something akin to a conspiracy.[45] Castells does not use the concept of a global class because it would attribute agency to a group of actors who do not control the actions ascribed to them. This is why he is only comfortable talking about a global elite, with a focus on the shared culture facilitating communication in the global networks of power and wealth.

At one point, Castells speaks about "the behavior of living systems, both in society and nature,"[46] though he leaves open which social systems he characterizes as living. I doubt that Castells would go as far as Capra, who argues that social organizations are actually, and not just metaphorically, living entities. Yet the notion of the financial markets as an "automaton," as a "material reality [which] imposes itself as a natural phenomenon that cannot be controlled," shows some strong affinities.

The notion of emergence is also reflected in Castells's analysis of global governance, which he sees as a temporary convergence of interest formulated at the lower, that is, national level. The primary actors of international relations are still nation-states, even if they are no longer the only ones. Their interaction creates phenomena which sometimes take on a life of their own, for example the global bureaucracy of international institutions. Their inner workings, though, remain opaque. Similarly, the network state can be understood as an effect of endless, shifting negotiations carried out by actors (such as national or regional governments, or interest groups) who remain anchored at a lower level. The supranational components of the network state are an emergent effect in the sense that the actors who constitute it follow strategies developed within a different frame of reference. The actions of national governments reflect fundamentally national interests, even if they are part of global governing bodies. Those of regional governments have to be understood within a regional horizon. The mayor of Barcelona represents the point of view of his city, even when he is networking internationally. The success or failure of his actions will be assessed locally, and he remains accountable only to the local population. Thus the new actors constituting the highest level of integration – the European Commission, the UN, or the IMF – appear as comparatively ephemeral, to judge from the scant attention they receive in Castells's theory of the network society.

The notion of emergent effects is powerful because it suggests that there can be order without planning, or more generally, order that is nondeterministic. To understand self-organizing networks, this is absolutely essential.[47] However, the transfer of concepts from the natural to the social sciences is always problematic. Systems theory has long struggled to adapt the notion of a boundary, so central to cell biology, to social organizations. An issue which Giddens has shown, convincingly in my view, to be unresolvable.[48] What, after all, is the border of a family? Also problematic, though for very different reasons, is the transfer of the notion of emergence. What differentiates human societies from natural systems is their ability to affect, more or less deliberately, the rules of the game. This "reflexivity" is a central feature in theories of "high" or "late" modernity, and relates as much to our ability to change course politically as to our ability to affect the course of nature.[49] Thus the question of intentionality (what should the new rules look like?) and power (who gets to decide them?) enters into the processes in ways that the concept of emergence makes it difficult to see. And, indeed, Castells's analysis of power is the weakest part of the theory of the network society, both theoretically, where he uses a classic but ill-fitting definition, and empirically, where he does not specify sufficiently who holds it or how it operates. Yet this is not an irresolvable problem, as I tried to point out earlier. What we need is an adapted notion of power that integrates notions of design and of emergence.[50]

In my view the most profound, original and far-reaching aspect of Castells's notion of networks is the suggestion that a network does not represent the environment, but that each brings forth its own world. Networks are not just "autopoietic," in the sense that they create and reproduce themselves, but they also create their own couplings with the environment. In short, the environment is constituted by the network, rather than the other way round. Again, this is most obvious in the global financial markets. They do not represent global production or trade, but follow their own internal dynamics. In this sense, they are divorced from the "real" economy. On the other hand, they incorporate selectively, and unpredictably, information from the outside, and this linking has extraordinarily powerful effects. This is why they are also the core of the "real" economy. Put simply, the financial markets are coupled with their environment, and this coupling is indirect and goes both ways.

Castells, as already mentioned, uses the example of the financial crisis of the 1997–8, which started in South East Asia, but spread to

Brazil and Russia. On the one hand, there were standard macro-economic factors relating to the banking sector of several Asian countries that precipitated the devaluation of local currencies. These factors, however, cannot explain why Russia and Brazil were affected as well. This relationship was established by the way the financial markets interpreted geography through the category of "emerging markets," which lumped all these economies together. Given the power of the financial markets, this turned out to be a self-fulfilling prophecy. The "objective" connection between Thailand, Brazil, and Russia was constituted by the "subjective" interpretation of the financial markets. Another example of how the selective sensitivity to environmental inputs creates the environment is the way the structural blindness of the financial markets to anything other than the bottom line and its anticipated rise or fall creates new realities in the workplace. The deterioration of working conditions and the reliance on exploited labor even by highly profitable corporations are a direct effect of the particular way in which financial markets are coupled to their environment.

This aspect of the network logic is even more pronounced in Castells's analysis of social movements. As he stresses again and again, they are not about taking over power, by revolution or by marching through the institutions. Rather their main field is the development of new practices among their members. Their way of transforming society is by relating only to specific, self-selected aspects of the social totality. This is entirely different from traditional political parties, be they revolutionary, progressive, or conservative. These claim to represent a significant part of society (say, the working class), or even society as whole (say, the nation), and advocate a comprehensive program for society at large. Indeed, electoral politics assumes that influence should stand in direct relation to the proportion of the population represented by each party. Those with the most votes get to rule. Major social movements, on the other hand, do not really represent anyone. Their claim for influence is not proportional to the number of people they represent. Rather, they constitute a practice, and it is from this practice that their (moral) authority derives. This practice is determined both by the internal constitution of the various elements of the movement (in the sense of a mutual interdefinition of individual and collective goals), and by their autonomous reaction to select events in the environment. Indeed, politically speaking, the influence of social movements comes from their ability to focus significant resources on a few issues, while ignoring others altogether. It is a source of strength for Amnesty International not to have to say much about global trade, or environmental degradation.

Put simply, networks constitute not only themselves, but also their own, specific context. They don't operate in reference to an objective reality, or in reliance on an external context. This idea is most radicalized in Castells's analysis of time in the network society. Modernity was organized in relation to the stable referent of linear clock time. By definition, it was external to all (social and natural) processes, and thus able to provide a common frame of reference to all of them, no matter how quickly or slowly they unfolded. Before modernity, cyclical time was inherent in the most dominant rhythms (those of nature), which imposed themselves on social processes without being influenced by them. Thus, in very different ways, linear time and cyclical time established stable references against which all social processes could be ordered. With the concept of timeless time, Castells suggests, this common framework has been broken. Now, each network establishes its own temporal framework. This echoes an observation made by Bruno Latour a long time ago. Developing a network-centric view of agency, he observed that

> most of the difficulties we have in understanding science and technology proceed from our belief that time and space exist independently in an unshakable frame of reference inside which events and place would occur. This belief makes it impossible to understand how different spaces and different times may be produced inside the networks built to mobilize, cumulate and recombine the world.[51]

This malleability of time is an integral part of Castells's network logic. The resulting notions of time range from the microseconds which constitute the eternal present of the financial markets, to the millennia which constitute the horizon of the "deep ecology" movement. In other words, time is no longer produced by society as a whole, or forced upon society by nature. Rather, each network according to its own internal constitution produces its own temporal space. A particular timeframe is literally, not just metaphorically, one of the aspects of the unique world that each of them brings forth. The effect on society as a whole, which is constituted by a myriad of networks, is a destabilization of time through the interaction and collision of distinct temporal frameworks. In short, "time and space are contingent categories . . . relative to their context and practice."[52]

This is one of the reasons why the question of inclusion/ exclusion is the most fundamental in the network society. Each network constitutes its own, self-centered world, characterized by a particular temporal, spatial, and cultural horizon. It is the existence of such a framework, understood as a set of resources, which makes action possible. Outside of it, action becomes very difficult because of the lack of resources and, since many of these resources are cultural, because of the lack of communication. In this sense, Castells writes, "networks also act as gatekeepers. Inside networks, new possibilities are relentlessly created. Outside the networks, survival is increasingly difficult. . . . Once such a network is constituted, any node that [is not connected] is simply bypassed, and resources continue to flow in the rest of the network."[53] Because of the ability to bypass areas that are of no value to the project that constitutes the network, global capitalism is characterized by its ability to exclude large portions of humanity. They literally don't exist in the world brought forth by these networks. That is, unless they force themselves back in and thus transform the network, as the antiglobalization movement is trying to do. Quite fittingly, their slogan is "another world is possible." Or unless the networks fall apart and the social devastation that exists on the outside is suddenly exposed and people who were rendered mute suddenly begin to speak. This is what happened in Argentina in late 2001.

Thus, for Castells, the real message of networking is not superior efficiency. That is what makes it socially dominant, but if that were all there was, we would just have modernity-on-speed. This is not the case. Analytically speaking, the most important aspects of networks are that they induce a decisive break with fundamental practices and categories of modernity. The uniform, stable horizons of space and time on which the clear hierarchies were built that made up the project of modernity, both institutionally and conceptually, have been shattered. The space of flows – but also, under its influence, the space of places – is of flexible dimensions, and rather than uniform, it is fragmented. The predictability of time, in terms of social as well as biological processes, has been called into question and is being challenged by a multiplicity of context-dependent timeframes. The arrow of time still flies, there is no end of history, but it seems there are many arrows, each with a different length and velocity. This leads to a decentering of previously vertically integrated institutions at all levels. The nation-state, built over several hundred years into the pinnacle of power, has lost its sovereignty and is subsumed into various networked forms of governance. At the other end of the scale, individualism – haunted by the specter of atomism, and frightened by the prospect of being left alone in the cold after the retreat of the welfare state – is being redefined. People, individually and collectively, are reconstituting their sense of self into a form of "networked individualism," as first proposed by Wellman and immediately taken up by Castells.[54]

Of course, not everything that belonged to modernity has disappeared and many institutions are in the middle of a contradictory process of transformation, but, as the theory of the network society convincingly asserts, there is a directionality to this transition and, given its interlocking character, it is irreversible.

Preeminence of Morphology over Action

If the networks that make up the network society were understood simply as any set of connections among social actors, insisting on the importance of a new social morphology would be rather meaningless. However, Castells's particular notion of networks is characterized by a distinct logic. It is because of the pervasiveness of this logic, affecting all processes organized as informational networks, that he can argue for the preeminence of social morphology over action. This does not imply that self-determined action is not possible, or that networks determine the content of social activity. Far from that. The notion of a network is very actor oriented; after all, networks are constituted around projects which reflect the particular agendas of their constituent actors. Networks are not structures working somewhere below the surface of the visible. Rather, they are a practice. They are what reconstitutes the surface in new, fragmented patterns.

Most of the projects around which networks are being built are not specific to the network society. Accumulation by the owners of capital is characteristic of capitalism in all its forms, mercantile, industrial, or informational. The search for dignity, justice, and meaning in reference to diverse cultural frameworks is also not specific to the network society. In this sense, not everything is new. What is specific to the network society, and thus historically new, is how these projects are carried out. The configuration of material and immaterial resources on which actors can draw at specific historical junctures is crucial to how they go about realizing their aspirations, independent of what their projects are. Since social organization is a communicative process, the means of communication play a very important role. But they are not everything. Putting emphasis on the influence of social forms and arguing that they are affected by the means of communication is not technological determinism. Rather, Castells argues, they are a necessary, but not a sufficient condition in the transformation of social morphology. With the spread of new communication technologies since the 1970s, it has become possible to organize social processes more efficiently than before, in the sense that the new organizational paradigm gradually replaced the old organizational pattern of the dominant social processes. What happened was a collective, if uneven, upgrading of capacities which translated into a downgrading for those who were excluded from this transformation. But this process should not be attributed to technology itself.

To frame the difference between technological and organizational change, Keohane and Nye, two eminent theorists of international relations, distinguish between "message velocity" and "institutional velocity."[55] The former is directly related to the state of technology. A telegraph carries a message faster than the pony express. However, message velocity reached its maximum (real time) with the advent of the radio and telephone some hundred years ago. Institutional velocity, on the other hand, indicates how fast organizations can operate. This is a function of the organizational model and as such only loosely coupled to the means of communication. Flexible organizations can be built on relatively slow means of communication. This is what Castells highlights when he argues that networking, for example in the Toyota production system, is older than digital communication. On the other hand, a higher message velocity enables limitations inherent in slow means of communication to be overcome. Both elements need to come together: the ability to communicate quickly, and the desire/need for institutions to operate at high speeds. Once they come together, both trends tend to reinforce one another.

The main advantage of the morphological approach is its ability to support a holistic analysis. Focusing on form, Castells is able to draw out not just similarities, but the interdependence of a vast array of issues. The main problem of the focus on form is that conflicts and politics virtually disappear. Not totally – Castells is too empirically oriented for this to happen. But they remain hard to integrate and appear mainly as a leftover from earlier times. In terms of his economic analysis this leads to a managerial bias, as many critics have noted. This is not because Castells has suddenly turned into an apologist for capital, as Bob Jessop has suspected.[56]

This is clear from his indignation at the downgrading of labor and the rise of exploitation at the core of the most advanced processes of production. Rather, the focus on form, on new management techniques and efficient forms of organization, is also characteristic of management literature and so the focus and style become similar. This makes Castells insensitive to new forms of conflict, particularly, as I have argued, around issues of intellectual property, which is not an issue of form but of content. Thus, perhaps not surprisingly, Castells's enormous expansion of scale, creating the precondition for developing a holistic analysis, comes at a price, namely an inadequate distinguishing of the different characters of similar forms. For Castells, this is to nobly restrain from politics, in the tradition of Weber's attempt to separate facts from opinions. For most of his critics, and I include myself in this group on this matter, it makes the theory of the network society, for all its scope, incomplete.

Conclusion

Overall, the theory of the network society is both highly ambitious and comparatively modest. It is ambitious in the sense that it strives to provide an integrated sociological framework through which to analyze the key dynamics constituting the present. It does so by resolutely refocusing the analysis away from places and structures to flows and networks. This reorientation makes it possible to revive the project of sociological macrotheory after several decades in which such grand narratives were deemed either undesirable or impossible. This, in itself, can serve as an indication that the time of transition is coming to an end and that new social configurations are beginning to take shape, even if highly unevenly and far from being fully developed. The many backward-oriented definitions – "postindustrialism," "postmodernism," "post-Fordism," "postnationalism," "risk society," "disorganized capitalism" – which have dominated social theory since the 1970s are being replaced by new forward-looking concepts centering around networks and their particular dynamics of continuity and change, fragmentation and integration, unpredictability and repetitiveness. As Scott Lash writes, "the network society is what comes after the risk society. It puts order into the previous disorder of disorganized capitalism. It imparts a new systemacity to the previously fragmented world system."[1] Of course, the deepening understanding of emerging network patterns and their constitutive logic cannot be attributed to one person or even one approach. It is the result of a collective endeavor of many sociologists developing varied analyses around notions of networks, mobility, complexity, and nonlinearity that are very much "in the air." Yet, so far, Castells's theory of the network society is the most coherent and comprehensive account of this new order and systemacity.

Yet the theory of the network society is also modest. Castells has learned from his generation's, and his personal, flirtation with intellectual dogmatism and theoretical hubris. The analytical framework he proposes now is extraordinarily open. Rather than a single, unified perspective, the theory of the network society is best thought of as a set of interrelated propositions whose relations with one another can be (re)arranged according to the practical analytical task at hand. Instead of postulating a new hierarchy of causes and effects, the theory points to the continuous interdefinition of self-conscious and creative actors, constituting three irreducible yet highly interdependent sources of dynamism: the capitalist economy, politics, and culture. In this sense, Castells applies the logic of networking to his own theory: it is flexible, without fixed hierarchy, with no clear beginning or end, contains not one but many points of view, and is easily reconfigurable, with elements to be dropped or added ("disposable theory"), yet it is still integrated and comprehensive. The theory as a whole is larger than the sum of its parts because it manages to identify, empirically and theoretically, a unifying trend across the many domains it covers: the emergence of a new type of social organization, informational networks, superseding vertically integrated hierarchies as the carrier of dominant social processes. This new morphology provides the signature of the new era, hence the network society.

In the economy, the financial markets have become the beginning and end of all major economic activity. Equally important is the rise of the network enterprise driving the globalization of production, management, and consumption, and thus creating a new and flexible international division of labor. It transforms the realities in the workplace, introducing a new cleavage between those providing "informational" and those providing "generic" labor. In the process, capital has been strengthened while labor has been weakened, to such a degree that their conflict, constitutive for twentieth century politics, is no longer dominant, despite increasing income inequality. The Soviet Union, unable to initiate a similar process of restructuring to keep its own economy afloat, collapsed, bringing to an end the "short twentieth century."[2] The sovereignty of the nation-state is eroding, breaking up a political constellation whose foundations were laid in the mid seventeenth century. The nation-state as a sovereign power has been replaced by the "network state," a system of governance created by flexible collaboration and competition between various state and nonstate actors, who (re)gain influence by continuously negotiating competing claims of authority. In the wake of this development, the institutions of representative democracy are thrown into crisis; the distance between politicians and their constituency increases, while the trust between the two suffers one blow after another from media-centered politics. Culture, in the sense of codes of behavior and embedded values, is being transformed by a resurgence of social movements, many of them skillfully linking local concerns with global flows of information and people. They shape the network society by developing new social values and institutions as self-defined interpretations of overall social development (of which they are a part).

In all of this technology plays an important, enabling role. Put simply, without information and communication technology, none of these developments would have followed the present path of development. Not least because the coordination of networks is a much more complex affair than the management of hierarchies. The sheer amount of communication necessary to accomplish this task could not have been managed with the means of communication that existed prior to the development of microelectronics. Yet the technologies did not cause the transformation. Networking as such preceded new technologies, both as a ubiquitous way of organizing small-scale social interaction, and as a specific strategy to increase flexibility in advanced production processes (pioneered by Toyota). Thus the network society did not emerge out of historical or structural necessity, but was sparked by a coincidence or simultaneity of economic crises, technological innovations, and the formulation of new social values. Initially independent, these developments soon began to interact, and those who were able to manage this interaction creatively, for their own ends, soon came to occupy many of the central positions in their fields. Thus the networks that make up the network society are informational networks.

Created by scientific researchers and economic actors, but now populated by a wide range of social actors, a new type of space has emerged, one which has no historical precedence: the space of flows. It provides the material basis for the particular new form of social organization – flexible networks coordinating themselves in real time across distances, large and small. The interaction between the space of flows and the space of places transforms, literally, the surface of the world. It is fragmenting places, connecting some across distances into new functional units, while disconnecting and isolating others. The people who inhabit those disconnected places are condemned to poverty, their marginalization hardened by growing structural disadvantages. This new form of exclusion amidst hyperconnectivity provides the ground for organized crime, operating globally, extending all the way to the core of economic and political processes. The space of flows is the material basis on which the twin developments of centralization and decentralization can take place, enabling the new combination of coordination and flexibility, or, what amounts to the same thing, endurance and instability. The space of flows is cause and effect of fast-changing opportunities and challenges, which can arise from anywhere on the globe (depending on the network under consideration). By facilitating the exploitation of such opportunities, the space of flows is the foundation on which instability is institutionalized. The volatility of the financial markets and the power of organized crime operating in the shadows of the new regime are highly visible indicators of this normalized volatility.

Apart from the far-reaching concept of the space of flows, the theory of the network society raises the most profound questions in its (still embryonic) analysis of time as being transformed by the disappearance of integrative rhythms, whether the cycles of nature or the uniform linearity of clock time. In their place multiple new time regimes are being created within specific networks, and their interaction with one another, as well as with clock time and biological time outside the networks, is profoundly affecting rhythms of everyday life around the globe.

From all of this emerges a very particular notion of the network characterizing the new type of social organization: flexible entities which coordinate themselves through extensive communication among their constitutive members. Such networks are not a representation of their environment, but are creating their own world through the practice of continuous interaction. These worlds are extremely differentiated, based on particular communication codes, extending all the way down to definitions (and practices) of time and space. At the extreme, this could create a world in which – not despite, but because of the abundance of communication – the various networks could no longer communicate with one another. The worlds constituted by each of them might have fewer and fewer points of contact, and the codes might become mutually unintelligible.

It seems safe to predict that the theory of the space of flows and the concept of timeless time (with the latter most likely under a different name) will be among the most enduring contributions of the theory of the network society to our understanding of the new historical period. These two provide, empirically and theoretically, the basis for all the other elements, from the network enterprise to the network state, from the rise of new social movements to the transformation of the criminal economy. Indeed, a new sense (and practice) of time and space, challenging, if not already replacing, even the most foundational categories of modernity, substantiated empirically and integrated centrally in the theory, is what makes the claim for a new era ultimately convincing.

Yet the theory also has substantial problems, directly related to Castells's focus on the transformation of forms, and the relatively traditional vocabulary through which he tries to account for this new condition. The two most important challenges that arise from the particular construction of the theory of the network society are the inadequate treatment of the transformation of power, and the lack of attention to the creation of new property claims – copyrights, patents, and trademarks – and the contradictions they introduce into the heart of informational capitalism and the network society.

These are not sins of omission, blanks that could easily be filled in, like Castells's complete lack of attention to major countries, such as India. Rather, there is no real place for them in the theory of the network society. Power, the theory seems to suggest, has diffused into something omnipresent yet impossible to pin down. The nation-state, as the pinnacle of power, is no longer able to impose its will, internally or externally, as it used to. Powerful global economic processes – from the financial markets, to trade and production – seem to run on autopilot, driven by blind competition among flexible networks centering around multinational corporations. Its main effects are emerging at a higher level and are, by and large, not understood, perhaps not even understandable, at the lower level where the actors operate. Thus international institutions, despite the enormous rise in their number, are not just virtually ignored in the empirical elaboration; more importantly, they have no real place in the theory.

This is because Castells sticks to a definition of power which is based on coercion, while the new form of power characteristic of the network society operates through exclusion. Castells does little to analyze this transformation of power. He remains focused on how one form of power, as defined by Weber, is weakening. As I have proposed, this needs to be complemented with an analysis of the new forms of power, operating at the level of network protocols, be they technical, legal, financial, or cultural. It is at this level that we can combine an analysis of deliberate design with an analysis of emergent effects. As it stands now, the theory of the network society falls short on one of the key analytical questions native to the new historical period: how to account for processes that are controlled and chaotic at the same time? While this is a substantial shortcoming of the theory, it seems that the framework does contain the seeds that can be developed into a robust analysis of such questions. I suspect this would require an overhaul of the concept of the network state, which is unconvincing as it stands, in a way that puts more emphasis on the coordination function of international institutions and their practice of protocol definition. It might turn out to be difficult to maintain the deliberately apolitical flavor of the theory, but it would probably not challenge it fundamentally.

The second major gap, the lack of attention to the emerging global regime of intellectual property (IP), is more fundamental. Apart from a few disjointed remarks here and there, this issue receives no attention at all. The theory of informational capitalism is squarely focused on process innovation – networked forms of production, management, and consumption – and ignores product innovation, that is, the rise of a new class of immaterial commodities. Thus it is no coincidence that the industries most dependent on IP, such as entertainment and pharmaceuticals, are virtually absent from Castells's analysis of the transformation of the economy. Additionally, for the reasons indicated above, the arenas in which these new regimes are developed and implemented, international organizations and more traditional bilateral treaties, remain outside of the analysis. Hence Castells's treatment of informational capitalism, so focused on form, offers no hooks on which to attach an analysis of IP.

If this were just an economic question, it would belong to the same class of problems as the underdeveloped notion of power, creating a substantial but not a fundamental theoretical problem. But it is not just an economic problem. Rather, since the network society is constituted round the incessant creation and transformation of cultural codes, or knowledge-based information, through informational networks, attempts to increase control over these codes introduce a fundamental tension into the very foundation of the network society. This contradiction is being articulated in virtually all its domains. We can find it in battles over patents relating to organisms, and in struggles between framers and multinational agrobusinesses. It lies at the heart of the controversy over access to drugs for developing countries, and is visible in the prosecution of thousands of people in the US and Europe over what is alleged to be a multi-billion dollar criminal operation but is seen by the perpetrators as, at worst, a minor offense: the unauthorized sharing of music files. Issues of free versus proprietary software affect the very infra-structure of informational networking, and rising pressures to com-mercialize knowledge shape the evolution of higher education. The tight control of IP creates new opportunities for organized crime (commercial piracy) and is rising to a prominent issue in inter-national relations. The US and Europe are using their political weight to force upon less powerful countries legislation that will deepen their structural disadvantages, and the developing nations, led by Brazil and India, are organizing themselves in response. A new geopolitical constellation is emerging. An argument could be made that this is *the* defining contradiction of the network society, replacing the increasingly disarticulated conflict between capital and labor.

Castells is clearly aware of all of these battles, but the theory does not manage to integrate and analyze them in any substantial way. Arguably, the two issues, the transformation of power and the rise of new informational commodities, are related. Physical property is based on the right of exclusive exploitation and consumption. Intel-lectual property cannot be consumed. Rather, it rests on the right, and ability, to prevent others from using a resource, even though it cannot be used up. In other words, for both, the practice of exclu-sion is characteristic. Accounting for these transformations will be the most significant challenge to the evolution of the theory of the network society. If it does not manage to integrate these issues, the theory will fall short of its own goal: to provide a coherent frame-work for analyzing the key dynamics constituting the network society.

Yet even in the light of these challenges, the theory of the network society represents an outstanding achievement. Castells has con-vincingly demonstrated that it is possible to develop a holistic analysis of the present, that the very fracturing of reality can be made into one of the unifying themes and related back to develop-ments of historical dimensions, encompassing the full range of human experience.

While it is futile to speculate whether Castells's trilogy, *The Infor-mation Age*, will still be read in 80 years or more, the comparison to Max Weber's *Economy and Society*, published posthumously in 1921, is not too fanciful. There are many connections between the two, not just the broad range of their vision, and the empirical style and rigor of elaboration: they also share a sense of modesty about the possibilities of their, or anyone's, knowledge building. Adhering to a comparable epistemology that restricts the building of theory to what can be observed empirically, which I have characterized as neo-Kantian positivism, both resist the temptation of trying to predict the future. Their analysis does not aim at uncovering historical laws or ahistorical structures, but rather at extracting conceptual models, often formulated as ideal types, from observation. Like Weber's major work, Castells's theory of the network society represents a turning point in social theory. It closes old controversies and opens new lines of research by offering an integrative framework. But this is not the early twentieth century; it is the beginning of the twenty-first. The difference is manifest in the lines of approach taken by these major theorists. Where Weber felt the need to anchor his analysis in history, Castells aims to anchor it in the present, preferring cross-cultural scope to historical depth. Whether this is already an effect of the disordering of time, which features so prominently in the theory, and how this affects its long-term relevance, remain to be seen.

One way or the other, the theory of the network society sets the benchmark against which future macrotheory will be measured. It seems safe to predict that this benchmark will stand for some time. And even when it is superseded – as all social theory, bound to its time, eventually will be – it will remain as the single most advanced testimony of our imperfect understanding of a world entering a new era.

Notes

Introduction

1 Bell, *The Coming of Postindustrial Society*.
2 See Webster and Dimitriou, *Manuel Castells*, for a three volume collection of debates of Castells's work over the last three decades.

Chapter 1 Transformation of Baselines

1 Castells, "Les Politiques d'implantation des entreprises industrielles" (1967a); Touraine, Ahtik, Ostrowetsky-Zygel, and Castells, "The Mobility of the Firm and Urban Structures" (Castells 1972a).
2 Castells and Himanen, *The Information Society and the Welfare State* (2002a).
3 Castells, *The Urban Question* (1977a), pp. 437–71; Castells, *The City and the Grassroots* (1983a), pp. xv–xxi.
4 Giddens, *The Third Way*.
5 Castells, "Is There an Urban Sociology?" (1976a).
6 See, for example, Walton, "Urban Sociology."
7 For a thorough, yet still readable, critique of Althusser's epistemology in the context of urban sociology, see Saunders, *Social Theory and Urban Questions*, pp. 152–82.
8 Castells, "Theory and Ideology in Urban Sociology" (1976b), p. 60. Besides the particulars of Althusser's argument, the label "ideological" was a standard catch-all method to dismiss a theory. For Castells the approach of Henri Lefebvre was ideological (in the sense of non-scientific), because Lefebvre stressed utopian, revolutionary aspects. For Lefebvre, Castells's work was ideological (in the sense of

conservative) because its excessive focus on structures made the room for spontaneous social action disappear.

9 This was a project with the greatest of ambitions. For Althusser, only Marx had succeeded in creating a science (historical materialism) for a field (political economy) that hitherto had been entirely ideological, that is nonscientific. At the time, Castells aimed to do the same for the field of urban sociology.

10 Castells, *City, Class, and Power* (1978a), p. 182.

11 Castells, *The Urban Question* (1977a), p. 263.

12 Ibid., p. 21.

13 Ibid., pp. 454–6.

14 Castells's notion of consumption is not connected to later notions of consumer culture focusing on individual consumption.

15 Castells, *The Urban Question* (1977a), p. 237.

16 Castells, *City, Class, and Power* (1978a), p. 3.

17 Castells, *The Economic Crisis and American Society* (1980a).

18 Castells, "Theoretical Proposition for an Experimental Study of Urban Social Movements" (1976c).

19 Althusser remained vague on the precise extent of this autonomy. He held on to the core tenet of historical materialism that the economy determines all other levels, but only in the "last instance." Yet, as he put it in a most poetic formulation, "from the first moment to the last, the lonely hour of the 'last instance' never comes" (Althusser, *For Marx*, p. 113), quoted in Saunders, *Social Theory and Urban Questions*, p. 186.

20 Castells, *City, Class, and Power* (1978a), pp. 93–125.

21 Castells, *The City and the Grassroots* (1983a), pp. 73–96.

22 Castells, *Monopolville. L'entreprise, l'état, l'urbain* (1974a).

23 Castells, *The City and the Grassroots* (1983a), pp. 213–88.

24 Castells, *City, Class, and Power* (1978a), pp. 152–66.

25 The other main perspectives were provided by Henri Lefebvre, *The Production of Space* and David Harvey, *Social Justice and the City*. A contemporary version is Tajbakhsh, *The Promise of the City*; for an assessment, see Milicevic, "Radical Intellectuals."

26 Walton, "Urban Sociology," p. 299.

27 Pickvance, "La Contribution de la sociologie urbaine," p. 54 (my translation).

28 Saunders, *Social Theory and Urban Questions*, p. 204.

29 Castells, *Monopolville. L'entreprise, l'état, l'urbain* (1974a).

30 Althusser argued for a theoretical "anti-humanism," because he saw history as a "process without a subject." Deliberate human agency counted for little in relation to the determining "structural practices." He went as far as substituting the concept of the social actor by that of the "support-agent." At the height of his commitment to Althusser's approach in the early 1970s, Castells followed this, arguing that actors were merely "expressing particular combinations of the social structure through their practices" (Castells, *City, Class, and Power* (1978a),

p. 78). The idea of human agency as an autonomous force was summarily dismissed as "ideology."

31 Castells, *The Urban Question* (1977a), p. 370.
32 Ibid., p. 437.
33 Castells, *The City and the Grassroots* (1983a), p. xvi.
34 For an assessment by one of the major protagonists, see Latour, "When Things Strike Back."
35 Latour, *Pandora's Hope*.
36 For an overview of and an important contribution to this debate, see Hacking, *The Social Construction of What?* For a sustained polemic, against all attempts to rethink this problem, see Sokal and Bricmont, *Fashionable Nonsense*.
37 Castells, *The Informational City* (1989a), p. 10.
38 Ibid., p. 11.
39 Webster, "Information and Urban Change," pp. 20–1.
40 Webster, *Theories of the Information Society*, p. 272.
41 Castells, *The Internet Galaxy* (2001a), pp. 9–63.
42 A similar argument, though with much more pessimistic implications, is made by Lessig, *Code and Other Laws of Cyberspace*.
43 Castells, *The Informational City* (1989a), pp. 11–12.
44 Ibid., p. 4.
45 Castells, *The Rise of the Network Society*, 2nd edn (2000a), p. 17.
46 Here Castells introduces the concept of the "informational mode of production" for the first time, but characteristically, only at the end, when attempting to locate the social movements within the broader social transformation (*The City and the Grassroots* (1983a), p. 307).
47 The fact that many of these values, for example, being gay, claim to be beyond history does not mean that they are. Rather, as Castells shows (*The Power of Identity*, 2nd edn (2004a)), to claim to be beyond history is a particular strategy of creating alternatives to fast paced change.
48 Castells, "Materials for an Exploratory Theory of the Network Society" (2000c), pp. 8–9.
49 Ellul, *The Technological Society*, p. 97.
50 McLuhan, *The Gutenberg Galaxy*.
51 Innis, *The Bias of Communication*; for a very good discussion of McLuhan and Innis, see Kroker, *Technology and the Canadian Mind*.
52 Castells, *The Rise of the Network Society*, 2nd edn (2000a), p. 495 n80.
53 Castells, *The Internet Galaxy* (2001a), p. 3.
54 The transition is visible when he suddenly defines the mode of development as "the technological arrangements through which humans act upon matter (nature), *upon themselves, and upon other humans*" (Castells, "Materials for an Exploratory Theory of the Network Society" (2000c), p. 9, emphasis added). Here the mode of development, quite contrary to its original meaning, is extended to experience and power, that is, all aspects of society. Yet this creates very awkward theoretical constructions, such as the mode of development of the

social relations of experience. Consequently, in his later writing, Castells no longer uses the concept (see Castells, "Informationalism and the Network Society" (2001b)).

55 Castells, "Informationalism and the Network Society" (2001b), pp. 155–6, paraphrasing Kuhn, *The Structures of Scientific Revolutions*.

56 Castells, "Informationalism and the Network Society" (2001b), p. 159.

57 Increasingly, advanced computing power is becoming essential even to the social sciences, particularly in areas such as complexity studies or the new "network science." Duncan Watts, a leading sociologist in this area, writes: "indeed, in many ways networking dynamics problems are ideal grist for the mill of computer simulation . . . Pencil-and-paper math rarely works on its own. . . . In the same way that physicists do experiments in the lab, computers have enabled mathematicians to become experimentalists, testing their theories in a multitude of imaginary laboratories where the rules of reality can be manipulated at will" (Watts, *Six Degrees*, p. 77).

58 Moore's Law, named after the cofounder of Intel Corp., Gordon Moore, states that computing power doubles every 18 months in relation to its price. Over the last 30 years, this has turned out to be rather accurate, and, for now, it looks as if it might continue to be so.

59 See Braudel, *The Wheels of Commerce* and *History of Civilizations*.

60 Castells, "Informationalism and the Network Society" (2001b), p. 158.

61 See, for example, Gilder, *Microcosm*.

62 Guéhenno, *The End of the Nation-State*.

63 Webster, "Information and Urban Change," p. 17.

64 Touraine, "Global Thinking for the Information Age," p. 128.

65 Castells, "Globalization and Identity in the Network Society" (2000d), p. 137.

66 Castells, *The Rise of the Network Society*, 2nd edn (2000a), p. 5.

67 Calhoun, "Resisting Globalization or Shaping it?" p. 101.

68 Levinson, *The Soft Edge*, p. 4.

69 Castells, *The City and the Grassroots* (1983a), p. 297–8.

70 In Castells and Ince, *Conversations with Manuel Castells* (2003a), he recalls Poulantzas, rather than Althusser, being his major Marxist influence (p. 15). However, in publications during the 1970s, the references to Poulantzas are few and far between.

71 Castells, *The Urban Question* (1977a), p. 438.

72 Castells, *The City and the Grassroots* (1983a), pp. xvi–xvii.

73 Castells, "Materials for an Exploratory Theory of the Network Society" (2000c), p. 6.

74 First formulated in Glaser and Strauss, T*he Discovery of Grounded Theory: Strategies for Qualitative Research*. Castells uses the term "grounded theory" occasionally but he does so in a colloquial sense – a theory grounded (anchored) in empirical research – and not as a reference to an established methodology.

75 Quoted in Hekman, *Weber, the Ideal Type, and Contemporary Social Theory*, p. 31.

76 Castells, *The City and the Grassroots* (1983a), p. xx.
77 Castells, *The Urban Question* (1977a), p. 6.
78 Castells, *End of Millennium*, 1st edn (1998a), p. 359.
79 Castells, *The Internet Galaxy* (2001a), p. 4.
80 Interview with the author, June 18, 2003.
81 Castells, "Globalization and Identity in the Network Society" (2000d), pp. 148–9.
82 Borja and Castells, *Local and Global* (Castells 1997b).

Chapter 2 Production

1 Castells, "Flows, Networks, and Identity" (1999c), p. 39.
2 Among economists there is still a debate about the "productivity paradox." Conventional indicators do not show a steady increase in productivity since the 1970s, yet firms that did not restructure lost the competition against those that did. Castells, like many economists, argues that this primarily reflects the inadequacy of conventional indicators for measuring an economy that has been profoundly transformed (Castells, *The Rise of the Network Society*, 2nd edn (2000a), pp. 78–99; Stehr, "Deciphering Information Technologies").
3 Bell, *The Coming of Postindustrial Society*, pp. 126–7.
4 Castells, "The Service Economy and the Post-industrial Society" (1976d).
5 Machlup, *The Production and Distribution of Knowledge in the United States*; Porat, *The Information Economy*.
6 Castells, *The Rise of the Network Society*, 2nd edn (2000a), p. 220.
7 Ibid., p. 220.
8 For Bell's own reflections on the fate of postindustrialism as a concept, see Bell, *The Coming of Postindustrial Society*, 2nd edn (1999). For a critique of Bell, see Webster, *Theories of the Information Society*, pp. 30–58.
9 Castells, *The Urban Question* (1977a), p. 21.
10 Castells, *The Economic Crisis and American Society* (1980a).
11 Castells, *The Rise of the Network Society*, 2nd edn (2000a), p. 95.
12 Marxist approaches spoke of the latter. For an early such analysis of the information society, see Schiller, *Who Knows*.
13 Castells, *The Informational City* (1989a), p. 3. "Logic" is perhaps a misleading word here, as what is really preserved is the *primary purpose* of the system – creation of profit to be appropriated by the owners of capital – by changing the *modus operandi* through which this purpose is realized.
14 Ibid., p. 307.
15 Castells, "Technological Change, Economic Restructuring and the Spatial Division of Labor" (1986b); Castells, "High Technology and the New International Division of Labour" (1989b).
16 Castells, *End of Millennium*, 2nd edn (2000b), p. 170.
17 Ibid., p. 134.

18 Castells, *The Informational City* (1989a), pp. 140–1.
19 Eichengreen, *Globalizing Capital*, p. 136.
20 For many observers, particularly those of postmodernist inclinations, this "dematerialization" of money was taken to be the beginning of the new era. See, for example, Harvey, *The Condition of Postmodernity*.
21 Hamelink, *Finance and Information*.
22 Michael Milken rose to fame as an executive at Drexel Burnham Lambert, Inc., a New York City investment firm, where he transformed corporate takeovers and financing by the use of high-yield "junk bonds." He was indicted for insider trading in 1989 and subsequently sent to jail.
23 Castells, "Information Technology and Global Capitalism" (2000e), p. 53.
24 Castells, *End of Millennium*, 2nd edn (2000b), p. 206.
25 Castells, "Information Technology and Global Capitalism" (2000e), pp. 56–7.
26 Castells, *The Internet Galaxy* (2001a), p. 87.
27 Castells, *The Economic Crisis and American Society* (1980a).
28 Castells, *The Rise of the Network Society*, 2nd edn (2000a), p. 166.
29 The classic formulation of this thesis is Piore and Sabel, *The Second Industrial Divide*. For a review, see Webster, *Theories of the Information Society*, pp. 59–96.
30 For the most significant elaboration of this approach to the information society in the US context, see H. Schiller, *Information and the Crisis Economy*; D. Schiller, *Digital Capitalism*.
31 Castells, *The Rise of the Network Society*, 2nd edn (2000a), p. 185. Castells uses as an example the Japanese "kan-ban" (just in time) system, which was pioneered by Toyota in 1948, and new flexible production methods, experimented with by Volvo, among others, which "required a change in mentality, rather than a change in machinery" (ibid., p. 184).
32 Ibid., p. 176.
33 Castells, "Informationalism and the Network Society" (2001b), p. 168.
34 Castells, *The Rise of the Network Society*, 2nd edn (2000a), pp. 121–2.
35 Ibid., pp. 180–4.
36 Ibid., p. 184.
37 Castells, *The Internet Galaxy* (2001a), p. 67.
38 Mulgan, *Communication and Control*, p. 241.
39 Castells, *The Rise of the Network Society*, 2nd edn (2000a), pp. 188–95.
40 Castells and Himanen, *The Information Society and the Welfare State* (2002a).
41 This is somewhat contradictory to Castells's assertion that Cisco is the "archetypical" network enterprise. However, rather than revealing a fundamental problem in the analysis, it is another example of his often rather imprecise vocabulary.

42 See, for example, Smart, "A Political Economy of New Times?"; Jessop, "Informational Capitalism and Empire"; Van Dijk, "The One-Dimensional Network Society of Manuel Castells."

43 Boston Consulting Group, quoted in Podolny and Page, "Network Forms of Organization," p. 71.

44 Heiskala, "Informational Revolution, the Net and Cultural Identity," p. 240.

45 Castells, *The Rise of the Network Society*, 2nd edn (2000a), p. 170.

46 Ibid., p. 175.

47 Ibid., pp. 201–2.

48 Ibid., p. 208, emphasis added.

49 Confusingly, Castells attributes this argument to theories of "post-industrialism and informationalism," only to say immediately afterwards that he takes another approach (ibid., p. 217). This leaves one wondering to whose theory of informationalism he is referring, if not his own.

50 Ibid., p. 246.

51 See, for example, Rifkin, *The End of Work*, whom Castells calls a "demagogue." High unemployment, Castells contends, is not a direct consequence of the transformation of the economy, but of the inflexibility of social institutions in coping with it.

52 Castells, *The Rise of the Network Society*, 2nd edn (2000a), p. 290.

53 Ibid., p. 255.

54 This distinction follows one proposed by Reich, *The Work of Nations*. For Reich, the new occupational structure was divided into "symbolic analysts," "in-person services," and "routine production services."

55 Castells, *The Internet Galaxy* (2001a), p. 94.

56 Ross, *No Sweat*.

57 See Sassen, *Cities in a World Economy* and Leyshon and Thrift, *Money/Space* for the role of advanced service infrastructures in cementing the dominant position of "global cities" in the informational economy.

58 Castells, *The Internet Galaxy* (2001a), p. 92.

59 Ibid., p. 169.

60 Ibid., p. 507.

61 Castells and Himanen, *The Information Society and the Welfare State* (2002a).

62 Castells, *The Informational City* (1989a), p. 17.

63 Castells, "Information Technology and Global Capitalism" (2000e), p. 52.

64 Castells, *The Rise of the Network Society*, 2nd edn (2000a), p. 77.

65 Kelly, *Out of Control*; Castells, *The Rise of the Network Society*, 2nd edn (2000a) quotes Kelly several times approvingly.

66 Castells, *The Rise of the Network Society*, 2nd edn (2000a), p. 504.

67 Mulgan, *Communication and Control*, pp. 28–9.

68 Castells, *The Rise of the Network Society*, 2nd edn (2000a), p. 505.

69 Halcli and Webster, "Inequality and Mobilization in *The Information Age*."
70 Mollenkopf and Castells, *Dual City* (Castells 1991a), p. 415.
71 Ibid., p. 417.
72 Ibid., p. 410.
73 Castells, *The Rise of the Network Society*, 2nd edn (2000a), p. 140.
74 Sklair, *The Transnational Capitalist Class*.
75 See, for example Bateson, *Steps to an Ecology of Mind*.
76 See Mosco, *The Political Economy of Communication* for an overview of the discipline, and D. Schiller, *Digital Capitalism* for an extensive study.
77 Jessop, "Informational Capitalism and Empire," quoted after the manuscript.
78 Drahos with Braithwaite, *Information Feudalism*, ch. 3.

Chapter 3 Experience

1   Sennett, *The Hidden Injuries of Class* and *The Corrosion of Character*.
2   The exception is his treatment of the "reproduction of mothering," but this foray into psychology is derived from a single source and sits oddly in his work. Why, after all, should psychology matter only in this one area? Castells, *The Power of Identity*, 2nd edn (2004a), pp. 288–91.
3   Castells, *The Rise of the Network Society*, 2nd edn (2000a), pp. 14–15.
4   Touraine, *Return of the Actor*.
5   Klandermans, "Social Movements."
6   Castells, *Luttes urbaines* (1973a); Castells, *The City and the Grassroots* (1983a).
7   Castells, *The Power of Identity*, 2nd edn (2004a), p. 3.
8   Snow, "Collective Identity and Expressive Forms," points out the relationship of the theory of "collective identity" to that of "class consciousness" (Marx) and "collective conscience" (Durkheim), all of which center around the idea of collective agency.
9   Castells, *The City and the Grassroots* (1983a), p. 276.
10 Castells, *The Power of Identity*, 2nd edn (2004a), p. 114.
11 Ibid., p. 73.
12 Castells, *The City and the Grassroots* (1983a), p. 10.
13 He continues by defining organizations as "specific systems of means oriented to the performance of specific goals," and institutions as "organizations vested with the necessary authority to perform some specific tasks on behalf of society as a whole" (Castells, *The Rise of the Network Society*, 2nd edn (2000a), p. 164).
14 Castells, *The City and the Grassroots* (1983a), p. 278, emphasis added.
15 Castells, *The Urban Question* (1977a), p. 305.
16 Castells, *The City and the Grassroots* (1983a), p. 331.
17 After all, reactionary social movements are not such a recent phenomenon. The Islamic fundamentalist movement captured the

world's headlines in 1979 when it succeeded in overthrowing the Western-oriented Shah of Persia.

18 Etzioni, *The Spirit of Community*.
19 Castells, *The City and the Grassroots* (1983a), p. xviii.
20 Castells, "Urban Social Movements and the Struggle for Democracy" (1978b).
21 This was also the basis for limiting the research to the male aspects of the movements, because, as he put it, "lesbians, unlike gay men, tend not to concentrate in a given territory, but establish social and interpersonal networks. . . . Thus they are 'placeless' and much more radical in their struggle" (Castells, *The City and the Grassroots* (1983a)).
22 See, for example, Stack, *Ethnic Identities in a Transnational World*.
23 Castells, *The Power of Identity*, 2nd edn (2004a), pp. 6–7.
24 Giddens, *Modernity and Self-Identity*.
25 Lash and Urry, *Economies of Signs and Space*.
26 Giddens, "Living in a Post-traditional Society."
27 Castells also has no interest in questions of the construction of personal identities that relate specifically to new information technologies and the resulting notions of experimentation and fluidity. See Turkle, *Life on the Screen*.
28 Castells, *The Power of Identity*, 2nd edn (2004a), p. 8.
29 Castells here explicitly follows Antonio Gramsci, for whom civil society was a set of institutions through which society organized and represented itself autonomously from the state and the economy. As he put it, "between the economic structure and the state with its legislation and coercion stands civil society" (Gramsci, *Selections from the Prison Notebooks*).
30 Castells, *The Internet Galaxy* (2001a), p. 140.
31 Castells, *The Power of Identity*, 2nd edn (2004a), p. 8.
32 Ibid., p. 8.
33 Castells, "L'École française de sociologie urbaine vingt ans après" (1994b), p. 58, my translation.
34 Castells, *The Power of Identity*, 2nd edn (2004a), p. 194. The patriarchal family is defined as a married couple living together with their children.
35 Ibid., p. 228.
36 A classic example is Bennett, *The Broken Hearth*, who paints an apocalyptic picture because of the decline of the "nuclear family, defined as a monogamous married couple living with their children, [which] is vital to civilization's success."
37 Castells borrows this formulation from Jane Mansbridge, "What is the Feminist Movement?"
38 Castells, "Frauen in der Netzwerkgesellschaft: Fragen an den Feminismus" (2002b), p. 152, my translation. Feminists famously asked their male comrades: "who will carry out the trash in the morning after the revolution?"
39 Castells, *The City and the Grassroots* (1983a), pp. 97–172.

40   Castells, *The Power of Identity*, 2nd edn (2004a), pp. 266–71.
41   Thayer, "Transnational Feminism."
42   Castells, *The Power of Identity*, 2nd edn (2004a), p. 286.
43   Fukuyama, *The Great Disruption*.
44   Castells, *The Power of Identity*, 2nd edn (2004a), p. 13.
45   Berlin, *Against the Current*, pp. 1–23.
46   Castells, *The Power of Identity*, 2nd edn (2004a), p. 29.
47   Friedman, *The Lexus and the Olive Tree*; Barber, *Jihad vs McWorld*; Huntington, *The Clash of Civilizations and the Remaking of World Order*.
48   Of course, not all did. In the West as well, particularly in the US, a fundamentalist movement emerged waging "culture war" against the progressive social movements.
49   Castells, *The Power of Identity*, 2nd edn (2004a), p. 22.
50   See the following chapter.
51   Castells, *The Power of Identity*, 2nd edn (2004a), p. 143.
52   Castells refers here to Edward Said's analysis in *Orientalism*.
53   Margalit and Buruma, "Occidentalism."
54   Castells, *The Power of Identity*, 2nd edn (2004a), p. 22.
55   A young Afghan fighter, quoted in Margalit and Buruma, "Occidentalism."
56   Castells, *The Internet Galaxy* (2001a), p. 164.
57   Castells, *The Rise of the Network Society*, 2nd edn (2000a), p. 404.
58   Castells, *The Internet Galaxy* (2001a), p. 202.
59   Castells, *The Rise of the Network Society*, 2nd edn (2000a), p. 402.
60   Castells, "Informationalism and the Network Society" (2001b), pp. 169–70.
61   For a similar, though narrower, analysis of cultural fragmentation through interactive media, see Shapiro, *The Control Revolution*.
62   Castells, *The Internet Galaxy* (2001a), p. 204.
63   Castells, *The Power of Identity*, 2nd edn (2004a), pp. 340–55.
64   Castells, *The Economic Crisis and American Society* (1980a), ch. 4.

Chapter 4   The Network State and Informational Politics

1   Castells, *The Rise of the Network Society*, 2nd edn (2000a), p. 15. Weber's original definition of power: "the possibility of imposing one's will upon the behavior of other persons" (*Max Weber on Law in Economy and Society*, p. 323).
2   Castells, *The Rise of the Network Society*, 2nd edn (2000a), p. 8.
3   Giddens, *The Nation-State and Violence*.
4   For a useful overview, see Held and McGrew, *The Global Transformations Reader*; Keohane, *Power and Governance in a Partially Globalized World*.
5   Guéhenno, *The End of the Nation-State*; Omae, *The End of the Nation State*; Wriston, *The Twilight of Sovereignty*.

6 Castells, *The Power of Identity*, 2nd edn (2004a), p. 303.
7 In a reply to three critics pointing out his lack of clarity in this matter, Castells comes up with an informal definition of influence as "the process by which a social actor frames others' choices, in the sense of its interests, while not being able to impose these interests by sheer force" (Castells, "A Rejoinder" (1998c), p. 170).
8 Castells, *The Power of Identity*, 2nd edn (2004a), p. 361.
9 If Castells were to state one cross-cultural historical law, it would be "where there is domination, there is resistance."
10 Castells, *The Power of Identity*, 2nd edn (2004a), pp. 356–64.
11 Gramsci, *Selections from the Prison Notebooks*.
12 See Giddens, *The Third Way*.
13 This integration of new values and new actors has not always been successful. Some states did lose legitimacy and collapsed, for example, East Germany or Yugoslavia.
14 Castells, *The Power of Identity*, 2nd edn (2004a), p. 305.
15 Ibid., pp. 306–7.
16 Ferguson, *The Cash Nexus*.
17 This process, however, is somewhat more uneven than Castells makes it out to be. For example, he fails to mention that important areas, such as agriculture in the G8 countries, are still managed as predominantly national domains, protected by tariffs and subsidies.
18 The case is different for internal conflicts, which is why Castells writes that "low tech armies are not armies at all, but disguised police forces" (Castells, *The Power of Identity*, 2nd edn (2004a), p. 325).
19 Ibid., p. 318.
20 Herman and McChesney, *The Global Media*.
21 Garnham, *Capitalism and Communication*; Smith, *The Age of Behemoths*; D. Schiller, *Digital Capitalism*.
22 Frank, *One Market under God*.
23 Castells, *The Power of Identity*, 2nd edn (2004a), p. 319.
24 Kalathil and Boas, *Open Networks, Closed Regimes*.
25 Castells, *The Power of Identity*, 2nd edn (2004a), p. 366.
26 Ibid., p. 375.
27 Ibid., p. 396.
28 For example, *Spin City*, a TV sitcom produced by ABC, which originally ran from 1996 to 2002 and has been in rerun ever since.
29 Castells, *The Power of Identity*, 2nd edn (2004a), p. 375.
30 Castells, *The Rise of the Network Society*, 2nd edn (2000a), p. 365.
31 Habermas, *The Structural Transformation of the Public Sphere*; McLuhan, *Understanding Media*.
32 See, for example, McChesney, *Rich Media, Poor Democracy*; Bagdikian, *The New Media Monopoly*.
33 Martin, *Framed!*
34 Herman and Chomsky, *Manufacturing Consent*.
35 Castells, *The Rise of the Network Society*, 2nd edn (2000a), p. 363.

36   Castells, *The Informational City* (1989a), p. 349.
37   Carnoy, Castells et al., *The New Global Economy in the Information Age* (Castells 1993a).
38   Habermas, *Die postnationale Konstellation*.
39   Castells, "Four Asian Tigers with a Dragon Head" (1992a), p. 56.
40   Castells, *End of Millennium*, 2nd edn (2000b), pp. 333–4.
41   Castells, "Four Asian Tigers with a Dragon Head" (1992a), p. 58. He also stresses that it was this nationalist project that created the conditions of social peace which many observers misread as an expression of a docile "Asian mentality." A nationalist project also plays a role in the rise of the Catalan network society (Castells, *The Network Society in Catalonia* (2002c)).
42   Castells and Himanen, *The Information Society and the Welfare State* (2002a). Though it remains unclear if Finland can continue to escape pressure to cut the taxes which are necessary for financing the welfare state (see, Patomäki, "An Optical Illusion").
43   Castells, *The Power of Identity*, 2nd edn (2004a), p. 316.
44   Castells and Himanen, *The Information Society and the Welfare State* (2002a), p. 164.
45   Marcuse, *One-Dimensional Man*.
46   Castells, *The Informational City* (1989a), p. 233.
47   This argument is made only implicitly by Castells. It is made explicitly by theorists such as Georgio Agamben, *State of Exception* and Hardt and Negri, *Multitude*.
48   Keohane and Nye, "Globalization."
49   Castells, *The Power of Identity*, 2nd edn (2004a), p. 356.
50   Ibid., p. 361.
51   Borja and Castells, *Local and Global* (Castells 1997b), p. 3.
52   Castells, "Global Governance and Global Politics" (2005a).
53   Castells, *The Power of Identity*, 2nd edn (2004a), p. 356. It remains unclear how Castells's conception of shared sovereignty is compatible with the notion, which he also advocates, that sovereignty is either absolute or not at all.
54   Held and McGrew, *The Global Transformations Reader*.
55   Castells, *The Power of Identity*, 2nd edn (2004a), p. 351.
56   Ibid., p. 330.
57   Ibid., p. 331.
58   Castells, *The Rise of the Network Society*, 2nd edn (2000a), p. 141.
59   Castells, *The Power of Identity*, 2nd edn (2004a), p. 332.
60   Castells, "Informationalism, Networks, and the Network Society" (2004c); Castells, "Global Governance and Global Politics" (2005a).
61   Castells, *The Power of Identity*, 2nd edn (2004a), p. 329.
62   Castells, *End of Millennium*, 2nd edn (2000b), p. 363.
63   Bull, *The Anarchical Society*.
64   Hirst and Thompson, "Globalization and the Future of the Nation State," pp. 422–3.

65 Kobrin, "Back to the Future."
66 Castells, *End of Millennium*, 2nd edn (2000b), p. 364.
67 Urry, *Global Complexity*, p. 47.
68 Castells, *The Rise of the Network Society*, 2nd edn (2000a), p. 7.
69 Castells and Ince, *Conversations with Manuel Castells* (2003a), p. 79.
70 Castells, *The Power of Identity*, 2nd edn (2004a), pp. 424–5, emphasis in the original.
71 Lyon, *Surveillance after September 11*; Schlosser, "The Prison Industrial Complex"; Urry, *Sociology beyond Societies*.
72 See, for example, Held and McGrew, *The Global Transformations Reader*; Lash, "Reflectivity as Non-linearity."
73 P. Marcuse, "Depoliticizing Globalization."
74 For a useful overview, see Beeson, "Governance Goes Global"; see also Held and McGrew, *The Global Transformations Reader*.
75 Sassen, *Losing Control?* p. 52.
76 Castells, "Informationalism and the Network Society" (2001b), p. 167, emphasis added.
77 Galloway, *Protocol*, p. 75.
78 Ibid., p. 12.
79 Castells, "Informationalism, Networks, and the Network Society" (2004c), p. 32.
80 Ibid., p. 33.
81 Not one of the 19 essays in Castells, *The Network Society* (2004b) contains material relevant to this question.
82 Lessig, *Code and Other Laws of Cyberspace* and *The Future of Ideas*.
83 See chapter 1.
84 Drahos with Braithwaite, *Information Feudalism*, p. 197.
85 Castells, *The Rise of the Network Society*, 2nd edn (2000a), p. 137.
86 Castells, *The Internet Galaxy* (2001a).
87 Castells, *The Power of Identity*, 2nd edn (2004a), p. 425, emphasis in the original (in the original the previous sentence is also in italics).
88 Ibid.
89 Castells, "Materials for an Exploratory Theory of the Network Society" (2000c), p. 8.
90 Galtung, "Violence, Peace and Peace Research."
91 Agre, "Peer-to-Peer and the Promise of Internet Equality," p. 42.
92 P. Marcuse, "Depoliticizing Globalization."

Chapter 5 Flows and Places

1 Castells, *The Urban Question* (1977a), p. 115.
2 Leibniz's argument, like that of Newton, was ultimately theological. He argued that space was created by the things, which in turn were created by God. Space could not be absolute because God could always intervene in the constitution of space.

3   Ong, *Orality and Literacy*, p. 3.
4   Sandbothe, *Die Verzeitlichung der Zeit*; Capra, *The Web of Life*.
5   McLuhan, *The Gutenberg Galaxy*; Castells, *The Internet Galaxy* (2001a).
6   Castells, *The Urban Question* (1977a), p. 430. What Castells then called "the ideological" is similar to what today he would call "the cultural."
7   Castells, *The Rise of the Network Society*, 2nd edn (2000a), p. 441.
8   Ibid., p. 453.
9   Castells, *The Informational City* (1989a).
10 Innis, *Empire and Communications*.
11 Braudel, *The Wheels of Commerce*; for an account of this stretching of social relations across time and space in the seventeenth century, see Wills, *1688*.
12 Chandler, *The Visibile Hand*. If we follow James Beniger, *The Control Revolution*, the growth of administrative units of commerce and government in the wake of the integration of national territory also constitutes the origin of the information society. In order to manage these units, new techniques, and new technologies, were needed to process unprecedented amounts of information and avert what he calls the "control crisis."
13 Giddens, *The Constitution of Society*.
14 Harvey, *The Condition of Postmodernity*.
15 Virilio, "Speed and Information."
16 Castells, *The Rise of the Network Society*, 2nd edn (2000a), p. 442.
17 de Sola Pool, *Forecasting the Telephone*.
18 Eichengreen, *Globalizing Capital*.
19 Leyshon and Thrift, *Money/Space*.
20 Sassen, *The Global City* and *Cities in a World Economy*.
21 Castells and Hall, *Technopoles of the World* (1994a).
22 Davis, "Planet of Slums."
23 Castells, *The Rise of the Network Society*, 2nd edn (2000a), p. 447.
24 Henderson and Castells, *Global Restructuring and Territorial Development* (Castells 1986a), p. 7.
25 Castells, *The Informational City* (1989a), pp. 126–71.
26 Castells et al., *The Mobile Communication Society* (2004e).
27 Castells, *The City and the Grassroots* (1983a), pp. 311–12.
28 Castells, "Grassrooting the Space of Flows" (1999a), p. 27.
29 Castells, "Global Governance and Global Politics" (2005a); Juris, "Networked Social Movements."
30 See chapter 1.
31 Cairncross, *The Death of Distance*.
32 Castells, *The Internet Galaxy* (2001a), p. 220.
33 Castells, *The Rise of the Network Society*, 2nd edn (2000a), p. 443.
34 Castells, *The Informational City* (1989a), pp. 169–70.
35 Quoted after Castells, *The Rise of the Network Society*, 2nd edn (2000a), p. 494 n78.
36 Landes, *Revolution in Time*.

37 Mumford, *Technics and Civilization*, p. 14.
38 Thompson, *The Making of the English Working Class.*
39 Castells, *The Rise of the Network Society*, 2nd edn (2000a), p. 494.
40 Urry, *Global Complexity.*
41 Sandbothe, *Die Verzeitlichung der Zeit.*
42 Capra, *The Web of Life* and *The Hidden Connections*; Coveney and High-field, *Frontiers of Complexity*; Hawkins, *A Brief History of Time.*
43 Castells, *The Rise of the Network Society*, 2nd edn (2000a), p. 468.
44 Ibid., pp. 470, 473.
45 Ibid., p. 479.
46 Ibid., p. 480.
47 Ibid., p. 407.
48 Sandbothe, *Die Verzeitlichung der Zeit.*
49 Castells, *The Rise of the Network Society*, 2nd edn (2000a), pp. 476, emphasis added.
50 See, for example, Plant, "On the Mobile"; Rheingold, *Smart Mobs*; Castells et al., *The Mobile Communication Society* (2004e), pp. 232–6.
51 Castells now acknowledged that "urban social movements had more success as a theoretical construction than as a social practice" ("L'École française de sociologie urbaine vingt ans après" (1994b), p. 58, my translation.
52 Graham, "Introduction: Cities and Infrastructure Networks," p. 114.
53 Sassen, *The Global City* and *Cities in a World Economy.*
54 Castells, "The Culture of Cities in the Information Age" (2001c), p. 372. Characteristically, he nevertheless uses the concept, sometimes inter-changeably with informational city.
55 Castells, *The Urban Question* (1977a), pp. 21–4.
56 Castells, "Urban Sociology in the Twenty-First Century" (2001d), p. 394.
57 Castells, *The Urban Question* (1977a), p. 191.
58 Castells, "The Informational City is a Dual City" (1998b), p. 26.
59 Castells, *The Informational City* (1989a), p. 225.
60 Mollenkopf and Castells, *Dual City* (Castells 1991a).
61 Castells, "Space of Flows, Space of Places" (2004d).

Chapter 6   The Logic of Networks

1 For a compilation of some of these debates, see Webster and Dimitriou, *Manuel Castells*, vols 2 and 3.
2 Hirst and Thompson, *Globalization in Question*; focusing on Castells, see Jessop, "Informational Capitalism and Empire"; P. Marcuse, "Depoliti-cizing Globalization"; Smart, "A Political Economy of New Times?"
3 Castells, *The Rise of the Network Society*, 2nd edn (2000a), p. 500.
4 Van Dijk, "The One-Dimensional Network Society of Manuel Castells"; Webster, *Theories of the Information Society.*

5   Castells, *The Rise of the Network Society*, 2nd edn (2000a), p. 501; see also Castells, *End of Millennium*, 2nd edn (2000b); Castells, "Informationalism and the Network Society" (2001b); Castells, "Informationalism, Networks, and the Network Society" (2004c).

6   Such a notion of networks is used as the basis for attempts to reconnect biology and physics, the social and the natural sciences. For general introductions to the science of networks, see Holland, *Emergence*; Johnson, *Emergence*; Strogatz, *Sync*.

7   Heiskala, "Informational Revolution, the Net and Cultural Identity."

8   Van Dijk, "The One-Dimensional Network Society of Manuel Castells"; Wolf, "Das Netzwerk als Signatur der Epoche?"

9   Perkmann, "The Two Network Societies," p. 263.

10 See Barnes, *Social Networks*, Wasserman and Faust, *Social Network Analysis* and Monge and Contractor, *Theories of Communication Networks*, for a good overview of the field's development.

11 See Barabási, *Linked*; Watts, *Six Degrees*; Urry, *Global Complexity*.

12 This is the main critique of Nas and Houweling, "The Network Metaphor."

13 This affinity has been there for some time but has grown recently, as evidenced by the deepening of the relevant section in the 2nd edition of *The Rise of the Network Society* (2000a), p. 75 (see Castells, *The Rise of the Network Society*, 1st edn (1996a), p. 65), and in Castells's most recent attempts to formalize his own theory, Castells, "Informationalism, Networks, and the Network Society" (2004c).

14 Capra, *The Hidden Connections*, p. 9.

15 Dawkins, *The Selfish Gene*.

16 Capra, *The Hidden Connections*, p. 11.

17 Watts, *Six Degrees*, p. 249.

18 Maturana and Varela, *The Tree of Knowledge* (quoted after the German translation).

19 Other aspects of biological theories that have influenced the social sciences, such as the concept of the border, find no correspondence in Castells's work, which after all is *not* modeled after these theories. This is a distinct difference in terms of theory-building from, say, systems theory, both in its original formulation (Parsons, *Societies*) and in the most influential recent formulation (Luhmann, *Ecological Communication*), which draws explicitly on Maturana and Varela, *The Tree of Knowledge*.

20 Coase, "The Nature of the Firm."

21 Powell, "Neither Market nor Hierarchy"; Monge and Contractor, *Theories of Communication Networks*.

22 Podolny and Page, "Network Forms of Organization," p. 59.

23 Urry, *Global Complexity*, p. 41.

24 Musso, *Critique des réseaux*, p. 320 (my translation).

25 Piore and Sabel, *The Second Industrial Divide*.

26 For a discussion of Castells's critique of post-Fordism, see chapter 2, "Production."

27 Castells, "Information Technology, Globalization and Social Development" (1999b), p. 6.
28 Lash, *Critique of Information.*
29 McLuhan, *The Gutenberg Galaxy*; Eisenstein, *The Printing Revolution in Early Modern Europe.*
30 Habermas, *Lifeworld and Systemworld.*
31 Castells, *The Internet Galaxy* (2001a), pp. 1–2.
32 Waldrop, *Complexity*; Coveney and Highfield, *Frontiers of Complexity*; Kauffman, *At Home in the Universe.*
33 Emirbayer, "Manifesto for a Relational Sociology"; Kelly, *Out of Control*; Lash, *Critique of Information*; Urry, *Global Complexity.*
34 Lash, "Reflectivity as Non-linearity," p. 49.
35 Johnson, *Emergence*; Barabási, *Linked*; Watts, *Six Degrees.*
36 Wellman, "Computer Networks as Social Networks."
37 Castells et al., *The Mobile Communication Society* (2004e).
38 Latour, *We Have Never Been Modern*, pp. 117–18.
39 Castells, *The Urban Question* (1977a), p. 231.
40 Castells, "Informationalism and the Network Society" (2001b), p. 167.
41 Lovink, *My First Recession.*
42 Castells, *The Rise of the Network Society*, 2nd edn (2000a), p. 187.
43 Castells, "Global Governance and Global Politics" (2005a).
44 Monge and Contractor, *Theories of Communication Networks*, p. 11.
45 P. Marcuse, "Depoliticizing Globalization."
46 Castells, *The Rise of the Network Society*, 2nd edn (2000a), p. 75.
47 Urry, *Global Complexity.*
48 Giddens, *The Constitution of Society.*
49 For an overview by three of the main protagonists of this approach, see Beck, Giddens, and Lash, *Reflexive Modernization.*
50 By pointing to the importance of "programming" for the constitution of networks ("Informationalism, Networks, and the Network Society" (2004c) and "Global Governance and Global Politics" (2005a)) Castells has taken the first steps in this direction.
51 Latour, *Science in Action*, p. 288.
52 Castells, "The Culture of Cities in the Information Age" (2001c), p. 381.
53 Castells, *The Rise of the Network Society*, 2nd edn (2000a), pp. 187, 147.
54 Wellman, "Physical Place and Cyber Place"; Castells, *The Internet Galaxy* (2001a).
55 Keohane and Nye, "Globalization."
56 Jessop, "Informational Capitalism and Empire."

Conclusion

1 Lash, *Critique of Information*, p. 127.
2 Hobsbawm, *Age of Extremes.*

Bibliography of Manuel Castells

Dates appear in each section with the most recent first. Works which have been translated into English are listed according to the year of their English publication, together with details of their original publication. If no English translation is available, the language of original publication is listed. The letters in [square brackets] indicate the citation in the main text or notes; where there are two letters they refer to the successive editions.

Books: author or main author
2005
Globalización, Desarrollo y Democracia: Chile en el Contexto Mundial. Santiago de Chile: Fondo de Cultura Económica.
1996–2004
The Information Age: Economy, Society, and Culture. Oxford and Cambridge, Mass.: Blackwell.
[a],[a] Volume 1: *The Rise of the Network Society* (1996; 2nd edn 2000).
[a],[a] Volume 2: *The Power of Identity* (1997; 2nd edn 2004).
[a],[b] Volume 3: *End of Millennium* (1998; 2nd edn 2000).
(The trilogy is published in Spanish by Alianza Editorial, Madrid and Siglo XXI, Mexico; in French by Fayard; in Chinese by Academy of Social Sciences, Beijing, and by Tonsan, Taipei; in Portuguese by Paz e Terra, São Paulo, and by Gulbenkian, Lisbon; in Russian by Higher School of Economics Press; in Swedish by Daidalus; in Korean by Hansul; in Japanese by Toshindo; in German by Leske & Budrich; in Italian by Edizioni

Bocconi; in Catalan by Edicions UOC; additional translations in Parsi, Croatian, Bulgarian, Romanian, Lithuanian, Danish. Translations currently in progress in Macedonian, Serbian, Arabic, Indonesian.)

2001

[a] *The Internet Galaxy: Reflections on the Internet, Business, and Society.* Oxford: Oxford University Press.

(Published in Spanish by Plaza & Janes; in French by Fayard; in Catalan by Rosa dels Vents; in Italian by Feltrinelli; in German by Leske & Budrich; in Russian by U-Factoria; in Swedish by Daidalos; in Korean by Hansul. Being translated in Polish, Dutch, Portuguese, Hungarian, Danish, Chinese.)

1999

[Global Economy, Information Society, Cities, and Regions.] Tokyo: Aoki Shoten.

(Published only in Japanese.)

1990

The Shek Kip Mei Syndrome: Economic Development and Public Housing in Hong Kong and Singapore. London: Pion.

1989

[a] *The Informational City: Information Technology, Economic Restructuring and the Urban-Regional Process.* Oxford and Cambridge, Mass.: Blackwell.

(Published in Spanish by Alianza Editorial, Madrid; translated in Chinese.)

1986

Nuevas tecnologías, economía y sociedad en España, 2 vols. Madrid: Alianza Editorial.

1983

[a] *The City and the Grassroots: A Cross-Cultural Theory of Urban Social Movements.* Berkeley: University of California Press and London: Edward Arnold.

(Published in Spanish by Alianza Editorial, Madrid; in Japanese by Honsei University Press; partially translated in Korean.)

1982

Capital multinacional, estados nacionales y comunidades locales. Mexico: Siglo XXI.

1981

Crisis urbana y cambio social. Madrid and Mexico: Siglo XXI.

1980

[a] *The Economic Crisis and American Society.* Princeton, N.J.: Princeton University Press.

(Published in French by Presses Universitaires de France; in Spanish by Laia, Barcelona; in Chinese in Shanghai and Taipeh.)

1978

[a] *City, Class, and Power:* London: Macmillan and New York: St Martin's Press.

(Translated in Japanese.)

Crise du logement et mouvements sociaux urbains. Enquête sur la région parisienne. Paris: Mouton.

(Partially translated in Italian.)

1977

[a] *The Urban Question: A Marxist Approach* (trans. Alan Sheridan). London: Edward Arnold.

Originally published as *La Question urbaine.* Paris: François Maspéro, 1972; revised edn, Paris: La Découverte, 1980.

(Also translated in Spanish, Italian, German, Portuguese, Greek, Polish, and Japanese.)

1975

Sociologie de l'espace industriel. Paris: Anthropos.

(Translated in Spanish.)

1974

[a] *Monopolville. L'entreprise, l'état, l'urbain.* Paris: Mouton.

1973

[a] *Luttes urbaines.* Paris: François Maspéro.

(Translated in Spanish, Italian, German, Portuguese, Greek.)

1971

Problemas de investigación en sociología urbana. Madrid and Mexico: Siglo XXI.

(Translated in Portuguese.)

Books: coauthored

2003

La Societat Xarxa a Catalunya (with Imma Tubella, Teresa Sancho, Isabel Díaz de Isla, Barry Wellman). Barcelona: Plaza & Janes Editores.

2002

[a] *The Information Society and the Welfare State: The Finnish Model* (with Pekka Himanen). Oxford: Oxford University Press.

(Translated in Finnish, Spanish, Catalan, Russian.)

1997

[b] *Local and Global: The Management of Cities in the Information Age* (by Jordi Borja and Manuel Castells in collaboration with Mireia Belil and Chris Benner). London: Earthscan.

(Also published in Spanish; translated in Italian.)

1995

The Collapse of Soviet Communism: A View from the Information Society (with Emma Kiselyova). International and Area Studies Book Series. Berkeley: University of California Press.
(Republished by Figueroa Press, Los Angeles, 2003.)

1994

[a] *Technopoles of the World: The Making of Twenty-First Century Industrial Complexes* (with Peter Hall). London and New York: Routledge.
(Published in Spanish by Alianza; translated in Chinese, Korean.)

1993

[a] *The New Global Economy in the Information Age* (by Martin Carnoy, Manuel Castells, Stephen Cohen, and Fernando Cardoso). University Park, Pa.: Penn State University Press.

1992

Spain beyond Myth (with C. A. Zaldívar). Madrid: Alianza Editorial.
(Also published as *España, fin de siglo*. Madrid: Alianza Editorial.)

1975

Metodología y epistemología de las ciencias sociales (with Emilio de Ipola). Madrid: Ayuso.
Participación y cambio social en la problemática contemporánea. Buenos Aires: Sociedad Interamericana de Planificación.

1973

La Rénovation urbaine à Paris. Paris: Mouton.

Books: edited or coedited

2004

[b] *The Network Society: A Cross-Cultural Perspective.* London: Edward Elgar.

2002

Muslim Europe or Euro-Islam (coedited with Nezar Al-Sayyad). Washington DC: Lexington Books.

1994

Estrategias para la reindustrialización de Asturias. Madrid: Editorial Civitas.

1992

Andalucía: Innovación tecnologíca y desarrollo económico. Madrid: Espasa-Calpe.

1991

[a] *Dual City: Restructuring New York* (ed. John Hull Mollenkopf and Manuel Castells). New York: Russell Sage.

La industria de las tecnologías de información: España en el contexto mundial (1985–1990). Madrid: Fundesco.

Las grandes ciudades en La década de los noventa. Madrid: Sistema.

1989

The Informal Economy: Studies in Advanced and Less Developed Countries (coedited with Alejandro Portes and Lauren A. Benton). Baltimore: Johns Hopkins University Press.

1986

[a] *Global Restructuring and Territorial Development* (ed. Jeffrey Henderson and Manuel Castells). London: Sage.

1985

High Technology, Space, and Society. Beverly Hills: Sage.

1974

Estructura de clase y política urbana en América Latina. Buenos Aires: Sociedad Interamericana de Planificación.

1973

Imperialismo y urbanización en América Latina. Barcelona: Gustavo Gili.

Articles, essays, book chapters and theses

2005

[a] "Global Governance and Global Politics," *PS, Bulletin of the American Political Science Association* (Jan.).

2004

[c] "Informationalism, Networks, and the Network Society: A Theoretical Blueprint." In Manuel Castells (ed.), *The Network Society: A Cross-Cultural Perspective.* London: Edward Elgar, pp. 3–45.

[d] "Space of Flows, Space of Places: Elements for a Theory of Urbanism in the Information Age." In Stephen Graham (ed.), *The Cybercities Reader,* London: Routledge, pp. 82–93.

"Estado y sociedad en la democracia chilena," *Política Exterior,* 100 (July–Aug.).

2003

"La interaccio entre les tecnologies de la informacio i la comunicacio i la societat xarxa: un proces de canvi historic," *Coneixement i Societat* (Barcelona), 1: 8–21.

2002

[b] "Frauen in der Netzwerkgesellschaft: Fragen an den Feminismus" (trans. Jochen Schimmang). In Heinrich-Boell-Stiftung, Feministisches Institut (eds), *feminist_spaces. Frauen im Netz:*

Diskurse, Communities, Visionen, Koenigstein/Ts: Ulrike Helmer Verlag, pp. 147–52.

"An Empirical Assessment of the Information Society: Employment of Occupational Structures of G7 Countries, 1990–2000"(with Yuko Aoyama), *International Labour Review*, 141 (1–2): 123–59.

2001

[b] "Informationalism and the Network Society." Epilogue to Pekka Himanen, *The Hacker Ethic and the Spirit of Informationalism*, New York: Random House, pp. 155–78.

[c] "The Culture of Cities in the Information Age." In Ida Susser (ed.), *Castells Reader on Cities and Social Theory*, Oxford and Malden, Mass.: Blackwell, pp. 367–89.

[d] "Urban Sociology in the Twenty-First Century." In Ida Susser (ed.), *The Castells Reader on Cities and Social Theory*, Oxford and Malden, Mass.: Blackwell, pp. 390–406.

"Globalization, the Knowledge Society and the Network State: Poulantzas at the Millennium" (with Martin Carnoy), *Global Networks*, 1 (1) (Jan.): 1–18.

2000

[c] "Materials for an Exploratory Theory of the Network Society," *British Journal of Sociology*, 51 (1) (Jan.–Mar.): 5–24.

[d] "Globalization and Identity in the Network Society: A Rejoinder to Calhoun, Lyon, and Touraine," *Prometheus*, 4: 108–23.
(Reprinted in Webster and Dimitriou, *Manuel Castells*, vol. 2, pp. 135–51.)

[e] "Information Technology and Global Capitalism." In Will Hutton and Anthony Giddens (eds), *On the Edge: Living with Global Capitalism*, London: Jonathan Cape and New York: New Press, pp. 52–74.

"Globalización, estado y sociedad civil: el nuevo contexto histórico de los derechos humanos," *Isegoria*, 22: 5–17.

"Russia in the Information Age" (with E. Kiselyova). In Victoria Bonnell and George Breslauer (eds), *Russia in the New Century: Stability or Disorder?* Boulder, Colo.: Westview, pp. 126–57.

"Russian Federalism and Siberian Regionalism, 1990–2000" (with E. Kiselyova), *City* (June).

1999

[a] "Grassrooting the Space of Flows," *Urban Geography*, 20 (4) (May–June): 294–302.

(Reprinted in James O. Wheeler, Yuko Aoyama and Barney Warf (eds), *Cities in the Telecommunication Age: The Fracturing of Geographies*, London: Routledge, 2000, pp. 18–27.)

[b] "Information Technology, Globalization and Social Development." United Nations Research Institute for Social Development, Geneva.

[c] "Flows, Networks, and Identity: A Critical Theory of the Informational Society." In Manuel Castells, Ramon Flecha, Paolo Freire, Henry A. Giroux, Donaldo Macedo, and P. Willis (eds), *Critical Education in the New Information Age*, New York: Rowman & Littlefield, pp. 37–64.

"The Social Implications of Information and Communication Technologies." In *World Social Science Report*, Paris: Unesco, pp. 236–46.

1998

[b] "The Informational City is a Dual City: Can It Be Reversed?" In Don Schon et al. (eds), *Information Technology and Low-Income Communities*, Cambridge, Mass.: MIT Press, pp. 25–42.

[c] "A Rejoinder: On Power, Identities and Culture in the Network Society," *New Political Economy*, 3 (3): 473–83.

(Reprinted in Webster and Dimitriou, *Manuel Castells*, vol. 2, pp. 169–79.)

"The Real Crisis of Silicon Valley: A Retrospective Perspective." *Competition and Change*, 2.

1997

"Globalization, Flows, and Identity: The New Challenges of Design." In William Satinders (ed.), *Architectural Practices in the Nineties*, Princeton, N.J.: Princeton Architectural Press in New York City.

1996

"The Net and the Self: Working Notes for a Critical Theory of the Informational Society," *Critique of Anthropology*, 16 (1): 9–38.

"Insurgents against the New Global Order: A Comparative Analysis of Mexico's Zapatistas, the American Militia, and Japan's Atim Shinrikyo" (with S. Yazawa and E. Kiselyova), *Berkeley Journal of Sociology* (Fall).

1995

"Les flux, les réseaux et les identités. Ou sont les sujets dans la société informationnelle?" In François Dubet and Michel Wieviorka (eds), *Penser le sujet*, Paris: Fayard.

1994

[b] "L'École française de sociologie urbaine vingt ans après: retour au futur?" *Les Annales de la Recherche Urbaine*, special issue (Oct.).

"Paths towards the Informational Society: Employment Structure in G-7 Countries, 1920–1990" (with Yuko Aoyama), *International Labour Review*, 133 (1): 1–33.

"Flujos, redes e identidades." In *Nuevas perspectivas criticas en educación*, Barcelona: Paidos, pp. 15–53.

1993

"Sociología de la crisis política rusa," *Política Exterior*, 7 (32): 55–80.

"European Cities, the Informational Society, and the Global Economy," *Journal of Economic and Social Geography*, 84 (4): 247–57.

1992

[a] "Four Asian Tigers with a Dragon Head: State Intervention and Economic Development in the Asian Pacific Rim." In Richard Appelbaum and Jeffrey Henderson (eds), *State and Society in the Pacific Rim*, London: Sage, pp. 33–70.

"Rusia, Año I: el Presidente en su laberinto," *Política Exterior* (Spring).

1991

"Las tecnologías de la información (1985–1990): España en el contexto mundial" (with M. Gamella). In Roberto Dorado et al. (eds), *Ciencia, tecnología e industria en España*, Madrid: Fundesco.

"La nueva revolución rusa," *Claves* (Oct.).

"Estrategias de desarrollo metropolitano: la articulación entre crecimiento económico y calidad de vida." In Jordi Borja et al. (eds), *Las grandes ciudades en la década de los noventa*, Madrid: Sistema.

"Die zweigeteilte Stadt – Arm und Reich in den Städten Lateinamerikas, der USA und Europas." In Tilo Schabert (ed.), *Die Welt der Stadt*, Munich and Zurich: Piper, pp. 199–216.

"Informatisierte Stadt und soziale Bewegungen." In Martin Wentz (ed.), *Stadt-Räume*, Frankfurt: Campus Verlag, pp. 137–48.

"Sotsiologicheskie ocherki." In *Yezhegodnik*, Moscow: Vyshie Sotsiologicheskie Kursi, pp. 7–27.

"Sotsiologiya modernizatsii i ekonomicheskogo razvitia." In *Kurs Lektsii*, Moscow: Vyshie Sotsiologicheskie Kursi, pp. 3–8.

"Modernizatsiya: ekonomika i sotsialnie structuri." In *Materiali Kruglogo Stola*, Moscow: Vyshie Sotsiologicheskie Kursi.

1990

"El fin del communismo." *Claves*, 1.

"V ysokie tekhnologii i obschestvo." In *Lektsiya: Vlianie novoi tekhnologii na rabotu i zdanyatost*, Moscow: Vyshie Sotsiologicheskie Kursi.

1989

[b] "High Technology and the New International Division of Labour," *Labour Studies* (Oct.).

"The New Dependency: Technological Change and Socio-economic Restructuring in Latin America" (with Roberto Laserna), *Sociological Forum*, (Fall). (Reprinted in A. D. Kincaid and A. Portes (eds), *Comparative National Development*, Chapel Hill: University of North Carolina Press, 1994.)

"Ntievas tecnologías y desarrollo regional." *Economía y Sociedad*, 2: 23–40.

"World Underneath: The Origins, Dynamics and Effects of the Informal Economy" (with Alejandro Portes). In A. Portes, M. Castells and L. Benton (eds), *The Informal Economy*, Baltimore: Johns Hopkins University Press.

"Social Movements and the Informational City," *Hitotsubashi Journal of Social Studies*, 21: 197–206.

"High Technology and the Changing International Division of Production: Implications for the US Economy" (with Laura Tyson). In Randall B. Purcell (ed.), *The Newly Industrializing Countries in the World Economy: Challenges for US Policy*, Boulder, Colo.: Lynne Rienner, pp. 13–50.

1988

"Innovation technologique et centralité urbaine," *Cahiers de la Recherche Sociologique*, 6 (2): 27–36.

"The New Industrial Space: Information Technology Manufacturing and Spatial Structure in the United States." In George Sternlieb and James W. Hughes (eds), *America's Market Geography*, New Brunswick, N.J.: Center for Urban Policy Research, Rutgers University.

"Nuevas tecnologías, economía y sociedad." In *Lección inaugural del curso académico 1988–89*, Madrid: Universidad Autónoma de Madrid.

"Crisis urbana, Estado y participación popular." In *Lectures*, Cochabamba, Bolivia: Colegio de Arquitectos de Cochabamba.

"High Technology Choices Ahead: Restructuring Interdependence" (with Laura Tyson). In John W. Sewell and Stuart K. Tucker (eds), *Growth, Exports and Jobs in a Changing World*, Washington DC: Overseas Development Council and Transaction Books, pp. 55–95.

1987

"Competitività internazionale, innovazione tecnologica e trasferimento di tecnologia in un'economia aperta: l'esperienza della Spagna degli anni ottanta" (with Javier Nadal). In Patrizio Bianchi (ed.), *Crescita e Competitività: Strategie Nazionali*, Bologna: Nomisma, Laboratorio di Politica Industriale.

"Revolución tecnológica y reestructuración económicopolitica del sistema mundial." In Manuel Castells et al., *Impacto de las tecnologías avanzadas sobre el concepto de seguridad*, Madrid: Fundación de Estudios sobre la Paz y las Relaciones Internacionales.

"Ocho modelos de desarrollo tecnológico," *Nuevo Siglo*, 1: 5–13.

1986

[b] "Technological Change, Economic Restructuring and the Spatial Division of Labor." In Walter Stohr (ed.), *International Economic Restructuring and the Territorial Community*, Vienna: United Nations Industrial Development Organization.

"High Technology and Urban Dynamics in the United States." In Mattei Dogan and John D. Kasarda (eds), *The Metropolis Era*, vol. 1, Beverly Hills: Sage.

"High Technology, World Development and Structural Transformation," *Alternatives*, 11 (3).

"The New Urban Crisis." In Dieter Friek (ed.), *The Quality of Urban Life*, Berlin and New York: Walter de Gruyter.

1985

"Urbanization and Social Change: The New Frontier." In Orlando Fals Borda (ed.), *The Challenge of Social Change*, London: Sage Studies in International Sociology, pp. 93–106.

"El impacto de las nuevas tecnologías sobre los cambios urbanos y regionales." In Peter Hall et al., *Metropolis, Territorio y Crisis*, Madrid: H. Blume, pp. 37–62.

"Estado, cultura y sociedad: las nuevas tendencias históricas." In *Cultura y Sociedad*, Madrid: Ministerio de Cultura.

1984

"Class and Power in American Cities" (review essay), *Contemporary Sociology*, 13 (3): 270–3.

"Madrid: planeamiento urbano y gestión municipal," *Ciudad y Territorio* (Jan.–June): 13–40.

"Participation, Politics, and Spatial Innovation: Commentary on Bologna, Orcasitas, and SAAL." In Richard Hatch (ed.), *The Scope of Social Architecture*, New Jersey Institute of Technology and Van Nostrand.

"After the Crisis?" (with Martin Carnoy), *World Policy Journal* (Spring): 495–516.

1983

"Crisis, Planning, and the Quality of Life." In *Environment and Planning* D, 1 (1): 3–21.

1982

"Squatters and Politics in Latin America." In Helen J. Safa (ed.), *Towards a Political Economy of Urbanization in Third World Countries*, New Delhi: Oxford University Press, pp. 242–62. (Reprinted in Josef Gugler (ed.), *The Urbanization of the Third World*, Oxford: Oxford University Press, 1988.)

"Cultural Identity and Urban Structure: The Spatial Organization of San Francisco's Gay Community" (with Karen Murphy). In *Urban Affairs Annual Reviews*, 22, Beverly Hills: Sage, pp. 237–60.

1981

"Local Government, Urban Crisis, and Political Change." In *Political Power and Social Theory*, Research Annual, 2, Greenwich, CT, 1–20.

1979

"Revisar a Engels," *Argumentos* (July).

"La intervención administrativa en los centros urbanos de las grandes ciudades," *Revista de Sociología*, 11: 227–50.

1978

[b] "Urban Social Movements and the Struggle for Democracy: The Citizen Movement in Madrid," *International Journal of Urban and Regional Research*, 2 (1): 133–46.

"Mouvements sociaux urbains et changement politique." In Alain Touraine (ed.), *Mouvements sociaux d'aujourd'hui*, Paris: Éditions Ouvrières.

1977

"Towards a Political Urban Sociology." In Michael Harloe (ed.), *Captive Cities*, London: John Wiley, pp. 61–78.

"Marginalité urbaine et mouvements sociaux au Mexique: le mouvement des posesionarios dans la ville de Monterrey," *International Journal of Urban and Regional Research*, 1 (2): 145–50.

"Les conditions sociales d'émergence des mouvements sociaux urbains," *International Journal of Urban and Regional Research*, 1 (1).

"Apuntes para un análisis de clase de la política urbana del Estado mexicano," *Revista Mexicana de Sociología,* 4.

1976

[a] "Is There an Urban Sociology?" In Christopher Pickvance (ed.), *Urban Sociology: Critical Essays,* London: Tavistock, pp. 33–59.
(Originally published as "Y a-t-il une sociologie urbaine?" *Sociologie du Travail,* 1 (1968): 72–90.)

[b] "Theory and Ideology in Urban Sociology". In Christopher Pickvance (ed.), *Urban Sociology: Critical Essays,* London: Tavistock, pp. 60–85.
(Originally published as "Theorie et ideologie en sociologie urbaine," *Sociologie et sociétés,* 2 (1969): 171–91.)

[c] "Theoretical Proposition for an Experimental Study of Urban Social Movements." In Christopher Pickvance (ed.), *Urban Sociology: Critical Essays,* London: Tavistock, pp. 147–73.

[d] "The Service Economy and the Post-industrial Society: A Sociological Critique," *International Journal of Health Services,* 6 (4): 596–607.

"Crise de l'État, consommation collective et contradictions urbaines." In Nicos Poulantzas (ed.), *La Crise de l'État,* Paris: Presses Universitaires de France, pp. 179–208.

"The Wild City," *Kapital-State,* 4–5 (Summer): 1–30.
(Reprinted in Joe R. Feagin (ed.), *The Urban Scene,* New York: Random House, 1979.)

"La crise urbaine aux États-Unis: vers la barbarie?" *Les Temps modernes* (Feb.): 1178–240.

1975

"Advanced Capitalism, Collective Consumption and Urban Contradictions." In Leo Lindberg et al. (eds), *Stress and Contradiction in Modern Capitalism,* Lexington, Mass.: Heath, pp. 175–98.

"Urban Sociology and Urban Politics: From a Critique to New Trends of Research," *Comparative Urban Research,* 3 (1).
(Reprinted in John Walton (ed.), *The City in Comparative Perspective,* Beverly Hills: Sage, 1976.)

"La fonction sociale de la planification urbaine: le cas de la region de Dunkerque," *Recherches Sociologiques,* 3.

"Immigrant Workers and Class Struggle: The Western European Experience," *Politics and Society,* 1.

1974

"Contradizione e desiguaglianza nella citta," *Il Mulino,* 1.

"Consommation collective, intérêts de classe et processus

politique dans le capitalisme avancé," *Revista de Sociologia,* special issue: 63–90.

"Remarques sur le pouvoir local" (review essay), *Revue Française de Sociologie* (June).

1973

"Epistemologia y ciencias sociales," *Revista Latinoamericana de Ciencias Sociales,* 1.

"Il rinovo urbano di Parigi: aspetti economici e politici," *Archivio di Studi Urbani e Regionali,* 2.

"Movimiento de pobladores y lucha de clases en Chile," *Revista Latinoamericana de Estudios Urbanos,* 3.

"Tesi sulla questione urbana," *Archivio di Studi Urbani e Regionali,* 1.

"La teoría marxista de las clases sociales y la lucha de clases en América Latina." In *Las clases sociales en América Latina,* Mexico: Siglo XXI.

1972

[a] "The Mobility of the Firm and Urban Structures" (by Alain Touraine, Vitomir Ahtik, Sylvia Ostrowetsky-Zygel, and Manuel Castells), *International Studies of Management and Organization,* 2 (3): 75–296.

(Originally published as "Mobilité des entreprises et structure urbaine," *Sociologie du Travail,* 4 (1967): 369–405.)

"Luttes de classes et contradictions urbaines," *Espaces et sociétés,* 6–7 (Oct.)

"Symbolique urbaine et mouvements sociaux," *Versus: Studi Semiotici.*

1971

"La sociologie et la question urbaine," *L'Architecture d'aujourd'hui* (Sept.): 91–100.

"El mito de la cultura urbana," *Revista Latinoamericana de Estudios Urbanos,* 3: 27–42.

"La détermination des pratiques sociales en situation de retraite" (with Anne-Marie Guillemard), *Sociologie du Travail,* 3.

"L'urbanisation dépendante en Amérique Latine," *Espaces et sociétés,* 3: 5–23.

1970

"Structures sociales et processus d'urbanisation," *Annales* (Aug.): 1155–99.

"Reconquête urbaine et rénovation-déportation à Paris" (co-author), *Sociologie du travail,* 4: 488–514.

"La rénovation urbaine aux Etats-Unis." *Espaces et sociétés,* 1: 107–37.

"Les nouvelles frontières de la méthodologie sociologique," *Information sur les sciences sociales*, 79–108.

1969

"Le centre urbain," *Cahiers internationaux de sociologie* (May): 83–106.

"Entreprise industrielle et développement urbain," *Synopsis* (Sept.): 69–79.

"Vers une théorie sociologique de la planification urbaine," *Sociologie du travail*, 4: 130–43.

1968

"La mobilité des entreprises industrielles dans la region parisienne" (co-author), *Cahiers de l'Institut d'Amenagement et d'Urbanisme de la Region Parisienne*, 11.

1967

[a] "Les Politiques d'implantation des entreprises industrielles dans la région de Paris." Doctoral thesis, University of Paris.

Main research monographs, 1984–2004
2004

[e] *The Mobile Communication Society* (with Mireia Fernandez, Jack Lin Chuan Qiu, and Araba Sey). Los Angeles, University of Southern California, Annenberg Research Network on International Communication.

2002

[c] *La societat xarxa a Catalunya/La sociedad red en Cataluña/The Network Society in Catalonia* (with Imma Tubella, Teresa Sancho, Isabel Díaz de Isla, and Barry Wellman). Research monograph, Project Internet Catalonia (PIC), Universitat Oberta de Catalunya, Barcelona, published online, July (full text available in Catalan, Spanish and English).

La era de la información en América Latina: ¿es sostenible la globalización? Ponencia al Seminario sobre la Era de la Información en América Latina, Programa de Naciones Unidas para el Desarrollo, Santa Cruz, Bolivia, Mar.

2001

Diffusion and Uses of Internet in Catalonia and in Spain: A Commented Summary of Available Evidence. Barcelona, Universitat Oberta de Catalunya, Internet Interdisciplinary Institute, working paper, Dec.

The Finnish Model of Information Society (with Pekka Himanen). Helsinki: Finnish National Fund for Research and Development (SITRA).

1999

> *Russia in the Information Age* (with Emma Kiselyova). Berkeley: University of California, Center for Slavic Studies, and Carnegie Foundation.
>
> *Globalización, identidad y Estado en América Latina.* Santiago de Chile: Programa de Naciones Unidas para el Desarrollo.

1998

> *Russia as a Network Society* (with Emma Kiselyova). Stanford, Calif.: Stanford University Conference on Russia, conference proceedings.

1996

> *The Missing Link: Siberian Oil and Gas and the Pacific Economy* (with Emma Kiselyova and Alexander Granberg). Berkeley: University of California, Institute of Urban and Regional Development.

1994

> *La reindustrialización de Asturias; problemas, perspectivas yestrategias.* Oviedo: Presidencia del Principado de Asturias. (Director.)
>
> *La modernización tecnológica de las empresas industriales de electrónica y telecomunicaciones en Rusia.* Madrid: Universidad Autónoma, Instituto de Sociología de Nuevas Tecnologías, Programa de Estudios Rusos. (Director.)
>
> *El proceso de cambio político y social en la Rusia postcomunista.* Madrid: Universidad Autónoma, Instituto de Sociologísa de las Nuevas Tecnologías, Programa de Estudios Rusos. (Director.)

1993

> *Paths toward the Informational Society: The Transformation of Employment Structure in the* G-7 *Countries*, 1920–2005 (with Yoko Aoyama). Berkeley: University of California, Berkeley Roundtable on the International Economy.

1992

> *Informe sobre la formación del medio de innovación tecnológica "Cartuja 93"* (Sevilla, Spain) (with Clara Garcia and Isabel Ramos). Seville: Sociedad Estatal Expo '92.
>
> *Informe-Dictamen sobre el desarrollo sostenible del entorno del Parque Nacional de Donana* (Andalusia, Spain). Seville: Junta de Andalucia. (Coordinator.)

1991

> *The University as Engine of Development in the New World Economy*, report prepared for the World Bank. Washington, DC: World Bank.

1989

El impacto de las nuevas tecnologías en la economía mundial. Implicaciones para la economía espanola. Informe para el Ministerio de Economia, Madrid.

The State and Technological Policy: A Comparative Analysis of the US Strategic Defense Initiative, Informatics Policy in Brazil, and Electronic Policy in China. Berkeley: University of California, Berkeley Roundtable on the International Economy. (Director.)

1988

Economic Modernization and Technology Transfer in the People's Republic of China (with Martin Carnoy and Patrizio Bianchi). Stanford, Calif.: Stanford University, School of Education, CERAS.

Desarrollo tecnológico, cooperación internacional y espacios de innovación. Report prepared for Sociedad Estatal Expo '92. Seville.

The Developmental City State in an Open World Economy: The Singapore Experience. Berkeley: University of California, Berkeley Roundtable on the International Economy.

Economic Development and Public Housing in the Asian Pacific Rim: A Comparative Analysis of Hong Kong, Singapore, and Shenzhen Special Economic Zone (with Reg W. Kwok and Lee Goh). Berkeley: University of California, Institute of Urban and Regional Development.

1987

The Real Crisis of Silicon Valley. Santa Cruz: University of California, Silicon Valley Research Group.

1986

Public Housing and Economic Development in Hong Kong. Hong Kong: University of Hong Kong, Centre of Urban Studies and Planning.

High Technology, Economic Policies, and World Development, report prepared for the Committee for a Just World Peace. Berkeley, Calif.: Berkeley Roundtable on the International Economy, University of California.

1985

El impacto de las nuevas tecnologías sobre la economía y la sociedad en Espana. Madrid: Informe para la Presidencia del Gobierno. (Director.)

1984

Towards the Informational City? High Technology, Economic Change, and Spatial Structure. Berkeley: University of California, Institute of Urban and Regional Development.

Books on Manuel Castells
2006
Pffiegler, Geraldine, *Sociologie de la sociologie de Manuel Castells*. Paris, Fayard.

Hsia, Chu-Joe [The Theories of Manuel Castells and their Relevance for China]. Beijing: Academy of Social Sciences (in Chinese).

2005
Pascual, Mayte, *Entender el mundo. Manuel Castells y su obra*. Madrid, Alianza Editorial.

2004
Webster, Frank and Dimitriou, Basil (eds), *Manuel Castells*, 3 vols. London: Sage.

2003
[a] Castells, Manuel and Ince, Martin, *Conversations with Manuel Castells*. Cambridge: Polity.
(Translated in Portuguese and Korean.)

Calderón, Fernando (ed.), *¿Es sostenible la globalización en América Latina? Debates con Manuel Castells*, 2 vols. Mexico: Fondo de Cultura Económica.

2001
Cloete, Nico and Muller, Johan (eds), *Challenges of Globalisation: South African Debates with Manuel Castells*. Cape Town: Longman.

Susser, Ida (ed.), *The Castells Reader on Cities and Social Theory*. Oxford and Malden, Mass.: Blackwell.

Steinbicker, Jochen, *Zur Theorie der Informationgesellschaft. Ein Vergleich der Ansätze von Peter Drucker, Daniel Bell und Manuel Castells*. Opladen: Leske & Budrich.

Other References

Agamben, Giorgio, *State of Exception*, trans. Kevin Attell. Chicago: University of Chicago Press, 2005.

Agre, Philip E., "Peer-to-Peer and the Promise of Internet Equality," *Communications of the ACM*, 46, no. 2 (2003): 39–42.

Althusser, Louis, *For Marx* (1965), trans. Ben Brewster. London: Allen Lane, 1969.

Bagdikian, Ben, *The New Media Monopoly* (1983). Boston: Beacon Press, 2004.

Barabási, Albert-László, *Linked: The New Science of Networks*. Cambridge, Mass.: Perseus Books, 2002.

Barber, Benjamin, *Jihad vs McWorld: How Globalism and Tribalism Are Reshaping the World*. New York: Ballantine Books, 1996.

Barnes, James Allen, *Social Networks*. Reading, Mass.: Addison-Wesley, 1972.

Bateson, Gregory, *Steps to an Ecology of Mind*. New York: Ballantine Books, 1972.

Beck, Ulrich, Giddens, Anthony, and Lash, Scott (eds), *Reflexive Modernization: Politics, Tradition and Aesthetics in the Modern Social Order*. Cambridge: Polity, 1972.

Beeson, Mark, "Governance Goes Global: Power, Authority and Order in the Twenty-first Century," *Australian Journal of International Affairs*, 58, no. 4 (2004): 511–21.

Bell, Daniel, *The Coming of Postindustrial Society: A Venture in Social Forecasting*. New York: Basic Books, 1973. Second edition, with a new foreword, 1999.

Beniger, James R., *The Control Revolution: Technological and Economic Origins of the Information Society*. Cambridge, Mass.: Harvard University Press, 1986.

Bennett, William J., *The Broken Hearth: Reversing the Moral Collapse of the American Family*. New York: Doubleday, 2001.

Berlin, Isaiah, *Against the Current: Essays in the History of Ideas*. London: Pimlico, 1997.

Braudel, Fernand, *The Wheels of Commerce* (1979), vol. 2 of *Civilization and Capitalism 15–18th Century*, trans. Sian Reynolds. London: Collins, 1982.

——*History of Civilizations* (1987), trans. Richard Mayne. New York: Penguin, 1993.

Bull, Hedley, *The Anarchical Society: A Study of Order in World Politics*. London: Macmillan, 1977.

Cairncross, Frances, *The Death of Distance: How the Communications Revolution will Change our Lives*. Boston: Harvard Business School Press, 1997.

Calhoun, Craig, "Resisting Globalization or Shaping it?" *Prometheus*, 3 (2000): 29–67; reprinted in Webster and Dimitriou, *Manuel Castells* (2004), vol. 2, pp. 93–114.

Capra, Fritjof, *The Web of Life*. London: HarperCollins, 1996.

——*The Hidden Connections*. London: Flamingo, 2003.

Chandler, Alfred D. Jr, *The Visibile Hand: The Managerial Revolution in American Business*. Cambridge, Mass.: Harvard University Press, 1977.

Coase, Roland H., "The Nature of the Firm," *Economica*, no. 4 (Nov. 1937).

Coveney, Peter and Highfield, Roger, *Frontiers of Complexity: The Search for Order in a Chaotic World*. New York: Ballantine, 1995.

Davis, Mike, "Planet of Slums: Urban Involution and the Informal Proletariat," *New Left Review*, no. 26 (Mar.–Apr. 2004): 5–34.

Dawkins, Richard, *The Selfish Gene*. New York: Oxford University Press, 1976.

de Sola Pool, Ithiel, *Forecasting the Telephone: A Retrospective Technology Assessment of the Telephone*. Norwood, N.J.: Ablex, 1982.

Drahos, Peter with Braithwaite, John, *Information Feudalism: Who Owns the Knowledge Economy?* London: Earthscan, 2002.

Eichengreen, Barry, *Globalizing Capital: A History of the International Monetary System*. Princeton: Princeton University Press, 1996.

Eisenstein, Elisabeth, L., *The Printing Revolution in Early Modern Europe*. Cambridge: Cambridge University Press, 1983.

Ellul, Jacques, *The Technological Society* (1954), trans. J. Wilkinson. New York: Knopf, 1967.

Emirbayer, Mustafa, "Manifesto for a Relational Sociology," *American Journal of Sociology*, 103, no. 2 (1997): 281–317.

Etzioni, Amitai, *The Spirit of Community: Rights, Responsibilities, and the Communitarian Agenda*. New York: Crown, 1993.

Ferguson, Niall, *The Cash Nexus: Money and Power in the Modern World, 1700–2000*. London: Penguin, 2001.

Frank, Thomas, *One Market under God: Extreme Capitalism, Market Populism, and the End of Economic Democracy*. New York: Anchor, 2001.

Friedman, Thomas L., *The Lexus and the Olive Tree*. New York: Anchor, 2000.

Fukuyama, Francis, *The Great Disruption: Human Nature and the Reconstitution of Social Order*. New York: Simon & Schuster, 2000.

Galloway, Alexander R., *Protocol: How Control Exists after Decentralization*. Cambridge, Mass.: MIT Press, 2004.

Galtung, Johan, "Violence, Peace and Peace Research," *Journal of Peace Research*, 6, no. 3 (1969): 167–91.

Garnham, Nicholas, *Capitalism and Communication: Global Culture and the Economics of Information*. London: Sage, 1990.

Giddens, Anthony, *The Constitution of Society: Outline of the Theory of Structuration*. Berkeley: University of California Press, 1984.

——*The Nation-State and Violence*, vol. 2 of *A Contemporary Critique of Historical Materialism*. Berkeley: University of California Press, 1985.

——*Modernity and Self-Identity: Self and Society in the Late Modern Age*. Stanford, Calif.: Stanford University Press, 1991.

——"Living in a Post-traditional Society," in Ulrich Beck, Anthony Giddens and Scott Lash (eds), *Reflexive Modernization: Politics, Tradition and Aesthetics in the Modern Social Order*. Cambridge: Polity, 1994.

——*The Third Way: The Renewal of Social Democracy*. Cambridge: Polity, 2000.

Gilder, George, *Microcosm: The Quantum Revolution in Economics and Technology*. New York: Simon & Schuster, 1989.

Glaser, Barney G. and Strauss, Anselm L., *The Discovery of Grounded Theory: Strategies for Qualitative Research*. Chicago: Aldine, 1967.

Graham, Stephen, "Introduction: Cities and Infrastructure Networks," *International Journal of Urban and Regional Research*, 24, no. 1 (2000): 114–19.

Gramsci, Antonio, *Selections from the Prison Notebooks*, trans. Quintin Hoare and Geoffrey Nowell-Smith. London: Lawrence and Wishart, 1971.

Guéhenno, Jean-Marie, *The End of the Nation-State*. Minneapolis: University of Minnesota Press, 1995.

Habermas, Jürgen, *The Structural Transformation of the Public Sphere: An Inquiry into a Category of Bourgeois Society* (1962), trans. Thomas Burger with the assistance of Frederick Lawrence. Cambridge, Mass.: MIT Press, 1989.

——*Lifeworld and Systemworld: A Critique of Functionalist Reason*, vol. 2 of *The Theory of Communicative Action*. Cambridge: Polity, 1987.

——*Die postnationale Konstellation*. Frankfurt am Main: Suhrkamp, 1998.

Hacking, Ian, *The Social Construction of What?* Cambridge, Mass.: Harvard University Press, 1999.

Halcli, Abigail and Webster, Frank, "Inequality and Mobilization in *The Information Age*," *European Journal of Social Theory*, 3, no. 1 (2000): 67–81; reprinted in Webster and Dimitriou, *Manuel Castells* (2004), vol. 2, pp. 237–53.

Hamelink, Cees J., *Finance and Information: A Study of Converging Interests*. Norwood, NJ: Ablex, 1984.

Hardt, Michael and Negri Antonio, *Multitude: War and Democracy in the Age of Empire*. New York: Penguin, 2004.

Harvey, David, *Social Justice and the City*. London: Edward Arnold, 1973.

——*The Condition of Postmodernity: An Inquiry into the Origins of Cultural Change*. Oxford: Blackwell, 1989.

Hawkins, Stephen, *A Brief History of Time*. London: Bantam, 1988.

Heiskala, Risto, "Informational Revolution, the Net and Cultural Identity: A Conceptual Critique of Manuel Castells's *The Information Age*," *European Journal of Cultural Studies*, 6, no. 2 (2003): 233–45.

Hekman, Susan, *Weber, the Ideal Type, and Contemporary Social Theory*. Notre Dame, Ind.: University of Notre Dame, 1983.

Held, David and McGrew, Anthony (eds), *The Global Transformations Reader*, 2nd edn. Cambridge: Polity, 2003.

Herman, Edward S. and Chomsky, Noam, *Manufacturing Consent: The Political Economy of the Mass Media*. New York: Pantheon, 2002.

Herman, Edward S. and McChesney, Robert W., *The Global Media: The New Missionaries of Global Capitalism*. London: Cassell, 1997.

Hirst, Paul and Thompson, Grahame, "Globalization and the Future of the Nation State," *Economy and Society*, 24, no. 4 (Aug. 1995): 408–42.

——*Globalization in Question: The International Economy and the Possibilities of Governance*, 2nd edn. Cambridge: Polity, 1999.

Hobsbawm, Eric J., *Age of Extremes: The Short Twentieth Century, 1914–1991*. London: Michael Joseph, 1994.

Holland, John, *Emergence: From Chaos to Order*. Oxford: Oxford University Press, 1999.

Huntington, Samuel P., *The Clash of Civilizations and the Remaking of World Order*. New York: Simon & Schuster, 1996.

Innis, Harold A., *Empire and Communications*. Oxford: Clarendon Press, 1950.

——*The Bias of Communication* (1951). Toronto: University of Toronto Press, 1995.

Jessop, Bob, "Informational Capitalism and Empire: The Postmarxist Celebration of US Hegemony in a New World Order," *Source Studies in Political Economy*, 71–2 (2003): 39–58.

Johnson, Steven, *Emergence: The Connected Lives of Ants, Brains, Cities, and Software*. New York: Scribner, 2001.

Juris, Jeffrey S., "Networked Social Movements: Global Movements for Global Justice," in Castells, *The Network Society* (2004b), pp. 341–62.

Kalathil, Shanti and Boas, Taylor, *Open Networks, Closed Regimes: The Impact of the Internet on Authoritarian Rule*. Washington: Carnegie Endowment of International Peace, 2003.

Kauffman, Stuart A., *At Home in the Universe: The Search for Laws of Self-Organization and Complexity*. Oxford: Oxford University Press, 1995.

Kelly, Kevin, *Out of Control: The New Biology of Machines, Social Systems and the Economic World*. Reading, Mass.: Addison-Wesley, 1994.

Keohane, Robert, *Power and Governance in a Partially Globalized World*. London: Routledge, 2002.

Keohane, Robert and Nye, Joseph, "Globalization: What's New? What's Not? (And So What?)" *Foreign Policy* (Spring 2000): 104–19.

Klandermans, Bert, "Social Movements: Trends and Turns," in Stella Quah and Arnauld Sales (eds), *The International Handbook of Sociology*. London: Sage, 2000, pp. 236–54.

Kobrin, Stephen J., "Back to the Future: Neomedievalism and the Postmodern Digital World Economy," in Aseem Prakash and Jeffrey Hart (eds), *Globalization and Governance*. London: Routledge, 1999.

Kroker, Arthur, *Technology and the Canadian Mind: Innis, McLuhan, Grant*. Montreal: New World Perspectives, 1984.

Kuhn, Thomas, *The Structures of Scientific Revolutions*. Chicago: Chicago University Press, 1970.

Landes, David, *Revolution in Time: Clocks and the Making of the Modern World* (1983), revised edn. Cambridge, Mass.: Harvard University Press, 2000.

Lash, Scott, *Critique of Information*. Thousand Oaks, Calif.: Sage, 2002.

—— "Reflectivity as Non-linearity," *Theory, Culture & Society*, 20, no. 2 (2003): 49–57.

Lash, Scott and Urry, John, *Economies of Signs and Space*. Thousand Oaks, Calif.: Sage, 1994.

Latour, Bruno, *Science in Action: How to Follow Scientists and Engineers through Society*. Milton Keynes: Open University Press, 1987.

—— *We Have Never Been Modern*, trans. Catherine Porter. New York: Harvester Wheatsheaf, 1993.

—— *Pandora's Hope: Essays on the Reality of Science Studies*. Cambridge, Mass.: Harvard University Press, 1999.

—— "When Things Strike Back: A Possible Contribution of 'Science Studies' to the Social Sciences," *British Journal of Sociology*, 51, no. 1 (Jan.–Mar. 2000): 107–23.

Lefebvre, Henri, *The Production of Space* (1974), trans. Donald Nicholson-Smith. Oxford: Blackwell, 1991.

Lessig, Lawrence, *Code and Other Laws of Cyberspace*. New York: Basic Books, 1999.

—— *The Future of Ideas: The Fate of the Commons in a Connected World*. New York: Random House, 2001.

Levinson, Paul, *The Soft Edge: A Natural History and Future of the Information Revolution*. New York: Routledge, 1997.

Leyshon, Andrew and Thrift, Nigel, *Money/Space: Geographies of Monetary Transformation*. New York: Routledge, 1997.

Lovink, Geert, *My First Recession: Critical Internet Culture in Transition*. Rotterdam: V2_/NAi Publishers, 2003.

Luhmann, Niklas, *Ecological Communication*. Cambridge: Polity, 1989.

Lyon, David, *Surveillance after September 11*. Cambridge: Polity, 2003.

Machlup, Fritz, *The Production and Distribution of Knowledge in the United States*. New York: John Wiley, 1962.

Mansbridge, Jane, "What is the Feminist Movement?" in Myra Ferree and Patricia Y. Martin (eds), *Feminist Organizations: Harvest of the Women's Movement*. Philadelphia: Temple University Press, 1995, pp. 27–4.

Marcuse, Herbert, *One-Dimensional Man: Studies in the Ideology of Advanced Industrial Society*. Boston: Beacon Press, 1966.

Marcuse, Peter, "Depoliticizing Globalization: The Information Age and the Network Society of Manuel Castells," in John Eade and Christopher Mele (eds), *Investigating the City: Contemporary and Future Perspectives*. Oxford: Blackwell, 2002, pp. 131–58.

Margalit, Avishai and Buruma, Ian, "Occidentalism," *New York Review of Books*, 49, no. 1 (Jan. 17, 2002).

Martin, Christopher, *Framed! Labor and the Corporate Media*. Ithaca, N.Y.: Cornell University Press, 2004.

Maturana, Humberto and Varela, Francisco, *The Tree of Knowledge: Biological Roots of Human Understanding*. Boston: Shambala, 1987.

McChesney, Robert, *Rich Media, Poor Democracy: Communication Politics in Dubious Times*. New York: New Press, 2000.

McLuhan, Marshall, *The Gutenberg Galaxy: The Making of Typographic Man*. Toronto: University of Toronto Press, 1962.

——*Understanding Media: The Extensions of Man*. New York: McGraw-Hill, 1964.

Milicevic, Aleksandra Sascha, "Radical Intellectuals: What Happened to the New Urban Sociology?" *International Journal of Urban and Regional Research*, 25, no. 4 (2001): 759–83.

Monge, Peter R. and Contractor, Noshir S., *Theories of Communication Networks*. Oxford: Oxford University Press, 2003.

Mosco, Vincent, *The Political Economy of Communication: Rethinking and Renewal*. London: Sage, 1996.

Mulgan, Geoff, *Communication and Control: Networks and the New Economies of Communication*. London: Guilford Press, 1991.

Mumford, Lewis, *Technics and Civilization*. New York: Harcourt, Brace, 1935.

Musso, Pierre, *Critique des réseaux*. Paris: Presses Universitaires de France, 2003.

Nas, Peter J. M. and Houweling, Antonia J., "The Network Metaphor: An Assessment of Castells' Network Society Paradigm," *Journal of Social Sciences*, 2, no. 4 (1998): 221–32.

Omae, Ken'ichi, *The End of the Nation State: The Rise of Regional Economies*. New York: Free Press, 1995.

Ong, Walter, *Orality and Literacy: The Technologizing of the Word*. London: Methuen, 1982.

Parsons, Talcott, *Societies: Evolutionary and Comparative Perspectives*. Englewood Cliffs, N.J.: Prentice-Hall, 1966.

Patomäki, Hekki, "An Optical Illusion: The Finnish Model for the Information Age," *Theory, Culture & Society*, 20, no. 3 (2003): 139–45.

Perkmann, Markus, "The Two Network Societies," *Economy and Society*, 28, no. 4 (1999): 615–28.

Pickvance, Christopher G., "La Contribution de la sociologie urbaine à la recherche," *Les Annales de la Recherche Urbaine*, no. 64 (Sept. 1994): 54–7.

Piore, Michael and Sabel, Charles, *The Second Industrial Divide*. New York: Basic Books, 1984.

Plant, Sadie, "On the Mobile: The Effects of Mobile Telephones on Social and Individual Life," Motorola Research Report funded by Motorola, Schaumburg, IL, Oct. 21, 2001.

Podolny, Joel M. and Page, Karen L., "Network Forms of Organization," *Annual Review of Sociology*, 24, no. 1 (1998): 57–76.

Porat, Marc Uri, *The Information Economy: Definition and Measurement*. Washington DC: Office of Telecommunication, US Department of Commerce, 1977.

Powell, W. W., "Neither Market nor Hierarchy: Network Forms of Organization," in L. L. Cummings and B. Staw (eds), *Research in Organizational Behaviour*. Greenwich, Conn.: JAI, 1990, pp. 295–336.

Reich, Robert, *The Work of Nations*. New York: Knopf, 1991.

Rheingold, Howard, *Smart Mobs: The Next Social Revolution*. Cambridge, Mass.: Basic Books, 2002.

Rifkin, Jeremy, *The End of Work: The Decline of the Global Labor Force and the Dawn of the Post-market Era*. New York: Putman's Sons, 1995.

Ross, Andrew (ed.), *No Sweat: Fashion, Free Trade, and the Rights of Garment Workers*. London: Verso, 1997.

Said, Edward W., *Orientalism*. New York: Vintage, 1979.

Sandbothe, Mike, *Die Verzeitlichung der Zeit. Grundtendenzen der Modernen Zeitdebatte in Philosophie und Wissenschaft*. Darmstadt: Wissenschaftliche Buchgesellschaft, 1998.

Sassen, Saskia, *The Global City: New York*. Princeton: Princeton University Press, 1991.

——*Cities in a World Economy*. Thousand Oaks, Calif.: Pine Forge Press, 1994.

——*Losing Control? Sovereignty in an Age of Globalization*. New York: Columbia University Press, 1996.

Saunders, Peter, *Social Theory and Urban Questions*, 2nd edn. London: Unwin Hyman, 1986.

Schiller, Dan, *Digital Capitalism*. Cambridge, Mass.: MIT Press, 1999.

Schiller, Herbert I., *Who Knows: Information in the Age of the Fortune 500*. Norwood, N.J.: Ablex, 1982.

——*Information and the Crisis Economy*. Norwood, N.J.: Ablex, 1984.

Schlosser, Eric, "The Prison Industrial Complex," *Atlantic Monthly*, Dec. 1998, pp. 51–77.

Sennett, Richard, *The Hidden Injuries of Class.* New York: Vintage, 1973.

——*The Corrosion of Character: The Personal Consequences of Work in the New Capitalism.* New York: Norton, 1998.

Shapiro, Andrew L., *The Control Revolution: How the Internet is Putting Individuals in Charge and Changing the World.* New York: Public Affairs, 1999.

Sklair, Leslie, *The Transnational Capitalist Class.* Oxford: Blackwell, 2001.

Smart, Barry, "A Political Economy of New Times? Critical Reflections on the Network Society and the Ethos of Informational Capitalism," *European Journal of Social Theory,* 3, no. 1 (2000): 51–65.

Smith, Anthony, *The Age of Behemoths: The Globalization of Mass Media Firms.* New York: Priority Press, 1991.

Snow, David, "Collective Identity and Expressive Forms," in *International Encyclopedia of the Social and Behavioral Sciences.* London: Elsevier, 2001.

Sokal, Alan D. and Bricmont, Jean, *Fashionable Nonsense: Postmodern Intellectuals' Abuse of Science.* New York: Picador, 1999.

Stack, John J. (ed.), *Ethnic Identities in a Transnational World.* Westwood, Conn.: Greenwood Press, 1985.

Stalder, Felix, "The Logic of Networks: Social Landscapes vis-à-vis the Space of Flows," *CTheory* (Feb. 1998).

——"The Network Paradigm: Social Formations in the Age of Information" (review essay), *Information Society,* 14, no. 4 (1998): 301–8.

Stehr, Nico, "Deciphering Information Technologies: Modern Societies as Networks," *European Journal of Social Theory,* 3, no. 1 (2000): 83–94.

Strogatz, Steven, *Sync: The Emerging Science of Spontaneous Order.* London: Penguin, 2003.

Tajbakhsh, Kian, *The Promise of the City: Space, Identity, and Politics in Contemporary Social Thought.* Berkeley: University of California Press, 2001.

Thayer, Millie, "Transnational Feminism: Reading Joan Scott in the Brazilian Sertão," *Ethnography,* no. 4 (June 2001).

Thompson, E. P., *The Making of the English Working Class.* New York: Vintage, 1966.

Touraine, Alain, *Return of the Actor: Social Theory in Postindustrial Society,* trans. Myrna Godzich. Minneapolis: University of Minnesota Press, 1988.

——"Global Thinking for the Information Age," *Prometheus*, 2 (2000): 49–57; reprinted in Webster and Dimitriou, *Manuel Castells* (2004), vol. 2, pp. 127–33.

Turkle, Sherry, *Life on the Screen: Identity in the Age of the Internet.* New York: Simon & Schuster, 1995.

Urry, John, *Sociology beyond Societies: Mobilities for the Twenty First Century.* New York: Routledge, 2000.

——*Global Complexity.* Cambridge: Polity, 2003.

Van Dijk, Jan, "The One-Dimensional Network Society of Manuel Castells," *Chronicle World* (n.d.); at www.chronicleworld.org.

Virilio, Paul, "Speed and Information: Cyberspace Alarm!" *CTheory* (Aug. 27, 1995); at www.ctheory.net.

Waldrop, Mitchell, *Complexity.* New York: Simon & Schuster, 1992.

Walton, John (2000). "Urban Sociology," in Stella Quah and Arnauld Sales (eds), *The International Handbook of Sociology.* London: Sage, 2000, pp. 299–317.

Wasserman, Stanley and Faust, Katherine, *Social Network Analysis: Methods and Applications.* Cambridge: Cambridge University Press, 1994.

Watts, Duncan, *Six Degrees: The Science of a Connected Age.* New York: W. W. Norton, 2003.

Weber, Max, *Max Weber on Law in Economy and Society*, trans. Talcott Parsons. Cambridge, Mass.: Harvard University Press, 1954.

——*Economy and Society* (1921), trans. Günther Roth and Claus Wittich. New York: Bedminster Press, 1968.

Webster, Frank, "Information and Urban Change: Manuel Castells," in Frank Webster, *Theories of the Information Society.* London: Routledge, 1995; reprinted in Webster and Dimitriou, *Manuel Castells* (2004), vol. 2, pp. 15–40.

——*Theories of the Information Society*, 2nd edn. New York: Routledge, 2002.

Webster, Frank and Dimitriou, Basil (eds), *Manuel Castells*, 3 vols. Thousands Oaks, Calif.: Sage, 2004.

Wellman, Barry, "Physical Place and Cyber Place: The Rise of Networked Individualism," *International Journal of Urban and Regional Research*, 25, no. 2 (2001), pp. 227–52.

——"Computer Networks as Social Networks," *Science*, 293 (Sept. 14, 2001): 2031–4.

Wills, John E. Jr, *1688: A Global History.* New York: W. W. Norton, 2001.

Wolf, Harald, "Das Netzwerk als Signatur der Epoche?" *Arbeit*, 9, no. 2 (2000): 95–104.

Wriston, Walter, *The Twilight of Sovereignty: How the Information Revolution is Transforming our World*. New York: Maxwell Macmillan, 1992.

Index